D0918860

Edward Johnston revived the lost craft of calligraphy and exerted an immense influence upon almost every form of lettering, both in England and on the Continent. His own work in type designing and that of his pupil, Eric Gill, changed the face of British printing. His influence extended over the whole of the Western world, ranging from the lettering for the London Underground to the rarest of illuminated manuscripts.

Now, for the first time, his story has been told—that of a man devoid of personal ambition who was inspired by his love of the book hands to rediscover techniques which had been lost with the invention of printing and, by training up students, to make calligraphy a living craft.

Priscilla Johnston's biography is a beautifully written study of her father remarkable for its insight.

Foreword by Sir Sydney Cockerell.

Edward Johnston

Edward Johnston

by

PRISCILLA JOHNSTON

BARRIE & JENKINS

COMMUNICA-EUROPA

Carlyle Campbell Library
Meredith College
Raleigh, N. C.

© Priscilla Roworth 1959, 1976

Second edition published 1976
by Barrie & Jenkins Ltd
24 Highbury Crescent London N5 1RX

All rights reserved. No part of
this publication may be reproduced
in any form or by any means without
the prior permission of Barrie & Jenkins Ltd.

ISBN 0 214 20253 4 (cased edition)
ISBN 0 214 20295 X (paperback)

Printed in Great Britain
by The Anchor Press, Tiptree, Essex

Foreword

Priscilla Johnston is the youngest of the three daughters of Edward Johnston. Because I knew him from the very beginning of his career as a calligrapher she has asked me to bless her book. This I do with all my heart, but as the judgment of a man of ninety cannot be trusted I withhold the superlatives that are at the tip of my pen.

To the unsympathetic observer Johnston could appear an exasperating eccentric but his daughter has shown the lovable quality of this eccentricity and has given what is, in my view, a wholly authentic portrait of the man, while revealing something of his unparalleled genius as a scribe.

Kew, 1958.   SYDNEY COCKERELL

106757

Author's Note to Second Edition

This book was originally published by Messrs Faber and Faber in 1959. The present edition is an exact reproduction of the earlier one except for a few minor corrections and alterations in the text and some new notes. It has also been possible to include more illustrations.

The cover design and end-papers are by Irene Wellington, well-known as a calligrapher and teacher, who figures largely in the last chapter of this book. The device on the back cover is an enlargement of an early form of signature used by my father. It is very immature and lacks the sharpness which he considered an essential feature of good lettering, but it expresses an attitude of mind which characterised his whole life. It reads *In Nomine Dei*, the *ei* of *Dei* having a double purpose as being also the *E.J.* of his signature. The end-papers are an arrangement of the first two lines of the 'perpetual calendar' described on page 285. The motto or heading reads *In manibus tuis tempora nostra:* Our time is in Thy hands. The second line consists in the initial letters of the days of the week, in alternate red and dark brown, the old form, *thorn*, being used for *th*. There is a reproduction of this calendar in *Formal Penmanship* by Edward Johnston, published originally by Lund Humphries and now by Pentalic Corporation, New York.

Acknowledgments

I should like to record my gratitude to Sir Sydney Cockerell for much help and encouragement and an unflagging interest in the progress of this book from its first inception, and to all who have helped me by the loan of letters or in other ways. In particular I am indebted to Mr and Mrs Hubert Wellington, Mrs E. Rinder, Mrs M. Rooke, Mrs Mary Ethel Gill, Miss Margaret Alexander, Mr Alfred Fairbank, Sir Edward Bridges, Mr S. M. Cockerell, Mrs Kenneth Walker, Mr Evan Gill, Sir John Rothenstein, the late Mr James Wardrop and the staffs of the Victoria and Albert Museum and of St Bride's Typographical Library; also to Mr Philip Wayne for kindly making the translation from Goethe on page 186, to Mr Charles L. Pickering for collecting and preserving the *Tributes to Edward Johnston*, to the editors of *Everybody's* and *Punch* for permission to quote passages on pp. 160 and 208 respectively and to Messrs Jonathan Cape for permission to quote from Eric Gill's autobiography; also to my sister Barbara, Mr Alan Roworth, and the unknown photographer of the Dresden blackboard, and to Mr G. T. Friend. The photographs of my parents at Cleves (facing p. 193), which to me evoke them most vividly, were taken by Miss Margaret Alexander and I am indebted to her for allowing me to publish both them and part of a page from her notebook (facing p. 241).

P.J.

Contents

Notes to Second Edition

Page 22, line 8. '. . . the Abolition Act became law'. In fact the Abolition Act became law in 1833 but it did nor come into force until August 1, 1834.

Page 193, line 3. '. . . collaboration with Meynell'. This appears to be incorrect. J. H. Mason wrote in his notebook: 'I have heard that Meynell claimed to have been jointly responsible with me in the production of the *Imprint* type. It is true that it was he who sent me the proofs as they were produced but he had not the technical experience required.' Mason said that it was Jackson who introduced him to Meynell and the three of them frequently dined together at Meynell's house and discussed 'my views on trade printing. As a result of this we decided to launch a printing journal of wider outlook than those existing. Both Cobden-Sanderson and I had attended E. J.'s classes at the Central and I felt that we needed his help. I invited Johnston to join us and he became lettering editor.'

Page 74, line 14. In a report on Art Schools which Lethaby had prepared for the L.C.C. only a few months before his first meeting with Johnston he had written: 'Lettering of all kinds is almost without exception *bad*. Such students as endeavour to apply lettering harmoniously to their designs seem to endeavour to invent new and contorted forms out of their heads. Of all things the form of letters has been shaped by tradition, and in most cases the effort to be original is an effort to be *bad*. The way to "write" lettering is to take some well-recognised example and practise "writing" that until a thorough knowledge of the forms is attained.'

Page 196, line 23. 'E to Sopers . . .', The Peplers' house in Ditchling.

Page 204, line 15. John Dreyfus wrote, in 1947, 'The Johnston Underground "sansserif" was the greatest single practical contribution that has been made to "good printing" in the last thirty years. But this is not all. Its standardisation on the Underground conferred upon it, as lettering, a sanction, civic and commercial, such as had not been accorded to an alphabet since the time of Charlemagne.'

Page 250, line 10. In a description of the Keighley Roll of Honour, the first important MS. in this hand, Johnston wrote: 'The writing may be described as an "Italic hand" which I have evolved directly from a "book hand" in a Winchester MS. of the 10th century and modified in sympathy with the 16th century Italic—evolved, that is to say, by using the pen in a natural manner, tending to produce the characteristics of Italic writing, namely compression and branching.'

Page 281, line 31. Margaret Alexander was not secretary of the Arts and Crafts Exhibition Society but of the Society of Scribes and illuminators. She was a former student of Johnston's and friend of the family.

Page 286, line 4. A carpenter helping to prepare the centenary exhibition of Johnston's work showed particular interest in the frame of this calendar and asked who had made it. When told that Johnston had made it himself he was sceptical at first but, when convinced, turned it this way and that and finally said 'Well, if he made *that* . . . he must have been all right.' Johnston would have asked for no better epitaph.

This is the revised edition of a delightful biography which has not been in print for many years. It is now designed to be available in a cheap attractive form for students, although everyone will be fascinated by this story of a remarkable single-minded man.

Illustrations

Illustrations

It has not been possible to include a fully representative selection of Johnston's work because most of his larger manuscripts are unsuitable for reduction to the size of this book. The illustrations have therefore been chosen principally from small manuscripts and this necessarily limits the range, excluding the bold in favour of the intimate.

Other reproductions of Johnston's work may be found in *Tributes to Edward Johnston* (privately printed by Maidstone College of Art, 1948), also in *Lettering of Today* (The Studio, 1937); *Artwork*, Autumn 1931; *Die zeitgemasse Schrift*, July 1936; *Alphabet and Image*, Spring 1946; and *The Studio*, November 1946.

P.J.

Portrait

The Downs change as much as the sea but, like the sea, are changeless. The weather and the time of day can make them blue or tawny, faint or clear. Even their contours seem to change. The cockle-shell chalk pits, in the early sun, are scooped left-handedly from their rounded flanks; the light of evening shows them in reverse. These are pastoral, domestic hills, grazed for hundreds of years by the flocks that made South Down mutton famous. They stand in a high, unbroken line between the Weald and the sea, their crest running in a series of gentle, familiar curves, from Black Cap in the east to Wolstonbury in the west with Ditchling Beacon between.

From their feet the ground falls gently away as far as the southern outskirts of the village; beyond, it rises sharply and the tight, steep little High Street faces the hills. As you walk up it they, too, climb sharply with each step until they stand like a wall across the end of the street and rise up higher than the chimney-pots.

The house called Cleves looks down the length of an overgrown garden to where, beyond meadows and woodland, rise the Downs. It is a sizeable house, designed by an architect of more taste and imagination than was common at the beginning of this century; a house of character and charm.

It has never exactly been 'furnished', but furniture has come to rest there as sticks come to rest in a pool. In the centre of the dining-room stands a large, immensely strong oak table, a straight-forward carpenter's product having no truck with the niceties of furniture designing. Round it are rush-seated, ladder-back chairs of unstained ash. They have cushions on the seats because, all those years ago, the table was accidentally made a little too high. On these cushions, under the table, cats may be found sometimes and cats' hair always. Under the cushions there are always newspapers. This is a mystery; I have never understood how they get there, but there they always are. It must be connected with the fact that newspapers, in this house, are not lightly to be thrown away and therefore they tend to infiltrate into positions where they can remain undisturbed. Such positions, as it happens, are fairly numerous. A child's chair with a brokendown rush seat is stacked high with them, so is the old box-table next to it. This table has the body of a wooden crate, four removable feet and a removable top which can be folded and made to form a lid. The table then becomes a strong packing case for transporting work in, and the remains of old luggage labels on the sides testify to an active life in its younger days. Besides the piles of newspapers on top of it, other piles accumulate, like the ocean bed, in a series of deposits. Parcels are opened, glanced at and set aside there, still in their wrapping paper. They may contain consignments of stationery from the Army and Navy Stores, or possibly the typescript of a book by some hopeful scribe or typographer who wants an opinion on it. Gradually these are silted up with fresh deposits: receipts, bulb catalogues, circulars, company reports and among them letters enquiring about manuscripts, lectures or classes, or simply enquiring about typescripts of books which, their owner fears, 'may have been overlooked'. He is right: they have.

Beside this table is a massive white cupboard filled with every imaginable object from extinct fishing-tackle to broken teapot lids, but with a preponderance of amateur electrical apparatus and home-made crystal sets. Beside it, in the corner by the gas ring, is a narrow, unpainted door with a home-made handle. It leads into a carpentry workshop impinged upon by a confusing array of steps and platforms, all in unstained deal. A private staircase leads from here to the still more private workroom, above.

On the dining-room mantelpiece stands a carriage clock. It bears a small card, beautifully written, with a date four months old, announcing to all whom it may concern that the clock is—

or, at least, was at that date—three-and-a-half minutes slow. Along the back of the mantelpiece are propped postcards; reproductions of early manuscripts, or Elizabethan embroideries or the drawings of Blake. These remain for months, with corners gradually curling, accumulating a fine layer of dust, until the annual spate of Christmas cards sweeps them away. On the hearth is a clockwork contrivance for blowing the fire and an odd assortment of fire-irons. Beside it are bookshelves of unstained wood where P. G. Wodehouse and Jeffery Farnol rub shoulders with Sir James Jeans, Lancelot Hogben and J. W. Dunne.

To the door is fixed a curious-looking apparatus consisting of a vertical bar and a handle. This was a home-made doorstop. It worked very well before the spring gave way, but is now only used by the cats which have sharpened their claws on it for generations until the upper part of the bar has been eroded to half its original thickness. (All over the house there are blocks of wood screwed to the walls, bearing hooks or loops of soldered wire or perhaps only retaining the time-worn marks of the forgotten purpose which once they served.)

Such is the room, the hour is half-past twelve and the table is laid. It is not clear whether it is prepared for the next meal or left over from the last, but in this house the table is nearly always laid.

The door now opens and Edward Johnston comes in. He is a man in his sixties, of medium height but with a massive head: 'A magnificent head—whichever way you take it', as Sir William Rothenstein remarked when drawing him. The hair has receded from his high forehead but remains at the back and sides so thick and dark—almost untouched by grey—that he looks like a monk with a tonsure. The hair sweeps down to rest on his coat-collar in a sort of Lloyd George curl. This might suggest a pose of the maestro—and, indeed, it has a rather noble and distinguished look—but the real reason is that he puts off going to the barber's from day to day until the days become months. High cheek-bones and deep-set eyes indicate his Scottish origin and must partly account for the frequently noted resemblance to Robert Louis

Portrait

Stevenson. He has a straight nose, slightly hollowed cheeks, a humorous mouth and a firm chin. His full moustache is of a light, almost tobacco brown, in contrast to his hair. His eyes are dark as toffee with the distant, unfocused gaze of one who looks beyond the immediate prospect to some realm of thought. To no one could Hamlet's words be more truly applied: 'I could be bounded in a nutshell and count myself the king of infinite space'.

He is wearing a good but very old suit of grey herring-bone tweed, with bulging pockets, and a grey-blue linen shirt with a collar so many sizes too big that it assumes the shape of a horse-collar. This is to ensure that in no circumstances shall it be tight. His black silk tie is pulled through a gold ring. It is worn thin by now, the little ring with which Christian Deuchar, his great-grandmother, was married in 1809. On his feet are slippers, and round his neck, suspended by the laces, a pair of brown boots. In one hand he carries a cup of cold tea, in the other a pile of books. This contains, unfailingly, the *Concise Oxford Dictionary*, with the back of its binding gone and the covers loose, and probably *The Innocence of Father Brown* and *Orlando the Marmalade Cat*.

He puts down his burden and looks with vague intentness at the preparations on the table. Then he picks up the morning paper, opens it out, and reads, leaning with both hands upon the table, neither willing to sit down nor able to escape. At last he turns to the porridge pot which is keeping warm on the hearth. He lights the gas ring on the wide, tile windowsill, turns it full up and puts the porridge on. Soon it is smoking furiously. Later the pot will go out to the scullery, lined with a thick coating of burnt porridge, and soak for the rest of the day. When the porridge is ready the kettle goes on to heat. The purpose of this is to heat the cup of cold tea, which is balanced on top of it in place of a lid. Meanwhile he sits down to his porridge, eating it with salt and butter, the milk in a separate cup, in the Scottish way. When the tea is heated he brings it to the table. It is now too hot to drink and he sits reading the newspaper until it is cold again. Then back it goes on the kettle to heat once more. He turns to the fire to make his toast, propping the fork in his own particular way. This operation is almost a ritual: techniques are involved and the craftsman is uppermost. Just so must the fire be mended and tended, just so must the toast be made. He has often said that women do not care very much how a necessary job is done so long as it *is* done, but men 'will go to the stake for *method*'. They invent games, he points out, and what are these but essays in technique, devices for the exercise of method?

By his place is his own particular knife. This was an ordinary table knife until he accidentally burnt the handle off. Then he made it a new handle of a piece of cherry wood, sandpapered to perfect smoothness and treated by a process he invented to make it waterproof. Where the handle meets the blade it has been bound with brass wire, soldered over and then rubbed down till solder and wire are one.

Bacon is brought from the kitchen. He whistles and a grey, striped cat appears; Merry, scion of an ancient house, last and most loved of a line that has been a part of the family of Johnston for the best part of thirty years. He strolls up, casual, gentlemanly, affably ready for what may befall. His master bends over him, smiling, holding up some titbit. 'Taxi!' he whispers, 'Taxi!' Obligingly Merry begs, raising one front paw above his head in the gesture described as 'hailing a taxi'. He is rewarded, rubbed, talked to, till he settles himself on the footstool before the fire.

Johnston studies the newspaper through a magnifying glass, wearing rimless spectacles, their gold side-pieces mended with solder and sealing wax. A long piece of pink string hangs down behind his right ear. This is so that when he lays his spectacles down upon the table he will not lose them because somewhere, from beneath the litter of papers, a tail of string will always be projecting.

He once described himself as 'a hurried and careless reader of the paper', but this description is misleading because, as ever, his standard of comparison was not other people's behaviour but a concept of absolute perfection. By this standard he was hurried and careless, although he was probably less so than almost any other of the million and a half readers this paper boasted. He read it from cover to cover, advertisements and household hints and all, and it might well take him as much as a couple of hours. To friends who were surprised by his choice of one of the more 'popular' of the daily journals he used to explain that 'All newspapers are full of lies, but at least if you read *The Daily* —— you're not tempted to believe them.'

He is still sitting over his breakfast when someone comes to try to set the table for lunch. He lays aside the paper and begins to talk, stooping to put on his boots. He speaks slowly and with long pauses but never an actual break, for his thought pursues the subject in undeviating concentration, to the almost complete exclusion of everything else. It says in the paper that miners form two per cent of the population. Doesn't that seem very high? Where are all the shopkeepers, railwaymen, soldiers and factory hands to come from? What percentage of the population are working men, do you suppose, when you've deducted women, children, old people, invalids and so on? At this point he glances up from his boots to see who he is talking to. It may be the maid or it may be one of his daughters, but the discovery will not affect his discourse. What matters is the subject under consideration, not the person addressed. 'Would you', he asks, 'say thirty per cent, or is that putting it a bit too high? Well, say, for the sake of argument . . .'

The table-setter is poised in the open door now, holding a loaded tray and waiting to leave the room. 'Well, then, let's see,' he says, 'that leaves twenty-eight per cent—no, wait a bit . . .'

She waits.

His boots are done up now. He puts on a little round tweed hat and goes out on to the verandah, to the suspended coconuts, the thin sunshine and the timeless view of the Downs. He takes out tobacco and papers and rolls a cigarette. Then he puts it between his lips and tries a burning-glass on the end, but the sun is not strong enough to get a light. Instead he takes out his flint and steel—a file without a handle and a flint from the garden with a length of yellow tinder, neatly accommodated in a home-made case. Two or three sharp taps and he gets a spark, blows on the tinder and lights his cigarette. He puts the case back into his pocket and goes off down the garden to his hens just as lunch is brought in.

Watching him going on his way is like watching an animal bent on some private errand. There is about him that air of essential solitariness. He lives a domestic life here with his family—and he thinks family life important—yet in himself he lives the life of a hermit.

As he walks down the wide, grass path he is not aware that the ancient Shetland cardigan which he has tied round his waist against lumbago has one sleeve dangling from beneath his jacket like an artificial tail. He is not aware of the thoughts and feelings of the people in the house behind him, or of a dozen things that would be obvious to the most casual observer. He is aware that he is on a planet spinning through space, held to the sun by an invisible thread. He is aware that he, miraculously adhering to the surface of this globe, is held there only by the force of gravity—and, he would add, by the grace of God.

I

Ancestry

'Tomorrow there will not be a slave left in any British possession and I am to be married to Mr Johnston.' So Priscilla Buxton is said to have written on July 31, 1834. Thomas Fowell Buxton's ten-year fight for the abolition of slavery was over. Two of his staunchest supporters, his daughter and the member for St Andrew's, drawn together by their mutual devotion to the cause, would not marry until the slaves were freed. On August 1, 1834, the Abolition Act became law and Edward Johnston's grandparents were married.

The bridegroom was the fourth successive Andrew Johnston of Rennyhill in Fife. The family had originally come from Annandale in Galloway.

> In the vale of Annandale
> The gentle Johnstons ride.
> They have been there a thousand years,
> A thousand years they'll bide.

So says the old rhyme, though the term 'gentle' is sometimes held to have been ironically bestowed upon a family probably as lawless as the rest of the Border clans whose stories survive in the Ballads.

Some time in the seventeenth century the son of a certain Sir James Johnston was shipwrecked off the coast of Aberdeen. He was befriended by fishermen and remained among them, marrying a fisherman's daughter. This marriage caused his family to disown

[22]

him and he found himself penniless, obliged to work for a living and to bring up his son to hawk mussels through the streets. The boy was known as Mussel Andrew to those who bought his wares but he is said to have worn a velvet cap to show that he was of noble blood. Grimy, it must have been, and with fish-scales adhering to it, but real velvet, perhaps made from some garment of his father's that had survived the wreck.

Mussel Andrew's son, a successful merchant, restored the family fortunes and bought the house and estate of Rennyhill. For the next hundred years or so the house was handed down from father to son through four generations of Andrew Johnstons until Mussel Andrew's great-great-grandson married Priscilla Buxton and removed to Norfolk.

The Buxtons were Suffolk squires. Priscilla's father, Thomas Fowell, was the son of the High Sheriff of the County and a Quaker mother, a Hanbury, who had imbued him with an intense hatred of slavery. As a boy he was 'of a daring, violent, domineering temper', but apparently neither particularly clever nor remarkably devout. The whole course of his life was changed by a visit he paid to Earlham at the age of sixteen. This was the home of the Quaker family of Gurney and they exerted an immediate and most powerful influence upon him. It was as though he fell in love with the whole family.

John Gurney was a widower with seven of the gayest Quaker daughters imaginable. 'A set of dashing young people, dressing in gay riding habits and scarlet boots, riding about the country to balls and gaieties of all sorts'—so a contemporary described them, adding 'accomplished and charming young ladies they were . . .' Their 'romps' included locking young men into the pantry and they smuggled Prince William Frederick upstairs to a private session at which Rachel, who was 'so droll' and such a good mimic, gave a lively imitation of their local preacher at the Quaker meeting house in Norwich. In summer they lay on the haycocks on the lawn of lovely Earlham and sang together or read poetry aloud to spell-bound young men. One such young man was Thomas Fowell Buxton.

Ancestry

All the Gurneys adored each other and used up all possible superlatives in describing not only their brothers and sisters but all their innumerable relatives and connections. Fowell joined in wholeheartedly. He, too, adored the whole family, saying of one sister, Louisa, that 'she came as near perfection as any human being I ever knew', and of another, Priscilla, that she was 'a saint of God'. It was Hannah, however, whom he married, having fallen in love with her at first sight when they were both sixteen. While he was at Earlham she arrived home from a visit to her married sister Betsy, later known to the world as Mrs Elizabeth Fry, the pioneer of prison reform. Hannah stepped out of the carriage with Betsy's baby in her arms and Fowell recognized his future wife. Thirty years later he wrote that he loved and admired her ten times more then than he had at the beginning and that 'her spiritual instruction has been invaluable to me, constant, invariable, steady and indefatigable, she sought and found the truth and taught it to me'. The Gurneys, by their example and their powers of fascination, transformed him from a boy whose chief interests were shooting and fishing into a young man who studied like a demon and, by sheer determination, outstripped his fellows at college. He also became, partly through their influence, profoundly devout. The faith of the Gurneys was not of the simple kind inculcated in childhood and cherished till death. Their minds were too active and enquiring for that. As children they seem not to have been particularly pious, although when a friend spoke to them of his own religious experiences Louisa, who was twelve, remarked in her journal that 'he spoke so charmingly and became so animated about it, it was enough to make one religious'. They found their beliefs for themselves, not without travail, some, like Elizabeth Fry, becoming 'plain' Quakers of the more austere sort, some joining the Church of England.

Fowell Buxton's Hanbury uncles got him a position in the brewery of Truman and Hanbury, and he threw himself into the work with such dynamic energy that very soon the firm became Truman, Hanbury and Buxton, under which name it continues to this day. The brewery was in Spitalfields, surrounded by some of the worst slums in London. Fowell made great efforts to improve conditions there and one of his first speeches was made at a public meeting organized for this purpose. He must have been a born orator (later his speeches in the House of Commons appear to have been extremely telling) for, according to a friend, his descriptions of the sufferings of the poor 'set a whole benchful of turtle-fed aldermen whimpering'. He also studied conditions in prisons and discovered there 'a system of folly and wickedness which surpassed all belief' which led to his publishing *An Inquiry Whether Crime be Produced or Prevented by our Present System of Prison Discipline*. In the same year, 1818, he entered Parliament as member for Weymouth and, soon after, Wilberforce, who was growing old, asked him to support and take over his campaign for the abolition of slavery. Wilberforce had already got through a Bill to make the slave *trade* illegal but this, though it prevented more slaves being shipped from Africa, did nothing for those already in captivity or for their descendants. For more than ten years Buxton fought to set them free.

To modern ears the whole thing sounds so natural and easy. It is obvious to us that the abolition of slavery was one of those many reforms which the nineteenth century was bound to bring forth. One man or another would have brought in the Bill—it was only a matter of time. At this distance we forget the vested interests and the hornets' nest of hatred and fury, the fantastically fabricated calumnies and slanders of those whose pockets were threatened. 'The degree of—*opposition* I will not call it, but *virulence* against me is quite surprising,' wrote Fowell Buxton mildly. 'I much question whether there is a more unpopular individual than myself in the House at the moment.' An anxious supporter, less coolly courageous than his leader, once asked him 'What shall I say when I hear people abusing you?' 'Say?' he answered, 'Say *that!*' and he snapped his fingers. 'You good folk think too much of your good name. Do right and right will be done to you.'

When things went against him, when even his own friends were doubtful and divided, he repeated to himself '*Be not afraid*

[25]

nor dismayed by reason of this great multitude, for the battle is not yours
but God's.' In commending this text to his daughter, Priscilla, he
wrote 'If you want to see the passage, open my Bible. It will turn
of itself to the place.'

Priscilla was the eldest of his eleven children, of whom six
died in childhood, four of them within a few weeks of each other.
To a man devoted to children as he was this must have been an
unthinkably awful blow, but to him and Hannah his wife, all
things came from God. His affection for his children was such
that, however urgent the work upon which he was engaged, he
could hardly bring himself to turn them out of his study and only
did so with great reluctance and with presents of sweets and cakes
which he used to 'hoard up' for them. His views on education
were wise and progressive and he particularly stressed the importance of teaching children 'habitually to seek for *the truth*,
whether for or against our previous opinions or interests.'

Priscilla was a delicate child and for years suffered from some
trouble with her hip which made her unable to walk. When she
was fourteen they travelled from Cromer to London by sea and
she described her terror as she, being unable to walk, was carried
down the cliff on a mattress in the dark and then out in a small
boat to the steamer. As the sea was rough there was considerable
difficulty in transferring her from one to the other, but now her
fear left her. 'I felt the only thing was to be still and let them do
what they would or could with me,' she said, 'and through it all
there was an indescribable peace granted to me.'

They all seem to have possessed this fortitude and mental discipline; it was bred in them by the certainty of their faith. It was
that which gave Fowell Buxton and Elizabeth Fry the courage of
lions and that which enabled Priscilla's cousin Caroline Fox,
when prostrate at the feet of an angry bull, to experience 'a rest in
the dear will of God, which I love to remember'. Of such stuff
martyrs are made.

In London, Priscilla met 'Mr Wilberforce' and thought that
nothing could exceed his kindness. 'He is so extremely affectionate to me—it is quite delightful.' She seems to have been just that

kind of angelic invalid child who plays so large a part in nineteenth century fiction. She lay there planning how to improve herself and be a greater comfort to her parents, worrying about 'the poor slaves' and, in the true family tradition, recording in her journal the superlative virtues of everyone who came to the house.

One little entry is of particular interest in regard to the subject of this book. 'I think,' she wrote, 'the three things I most wish for now are, first, to draw beautifully . . . second, to write beautifully, and the third is only a help to writing well but is the greatest convenience in life, and that is to mend pens charmingly. I am determined to accomplish this by my fifteenth birthday.'

She could not teach her grandson to write beautifully, or even to mend pens charmingly, for she died many years before he was born, but it is pleasant to imagine that the inclination to do these things was hereditary and that she would have applauded the charm with which he did them.

As she grew older Priscilla's health improved so that she was able to throw herself wholeheartedly into the business of helping her adored father in his campaign. The extent of her success may be judged from the letter he wrote her the day after her wedding:

My dearest, sweetest Pris—Ten thousand thousand blessings on you and a good lot for your husband. I—though not given to regrets—have been mourning all day that I did not value you one half a half enough. Never shall I have such another companion, friend, counseller, comforter, helper.

So she married 'Mr Johnston' and, in her own words, 'Never enjoyed a wedding day half so much', in spite of the fact that her white shoes pinched her toes. 'My father is wonderfully struck with his costume for the day,' she wrote, '—his splendid blue coat, bright buttons, white silk waistcoat and new white hat!' Her own clothes were even more lyrically described: 'The snow is not so white and the light not so shining as my white satin.' As for the service—' "I will", said Mr Johnston in so sturdy a manner and with so broad an accent that I (inwardly) laughed. My voice and power were astonishing to myself; but I should leave others to tell of my superior behaviour.'

The happy couple went off on a tour of the Highlands for their honeymoon and their joy was completed when they were joined there by Elizabeth Fry. 'I think I never was happier or so happy,' wrote Priscilla. 'Being with dearest Aunt Fry is a great pleasure.' One is relieved to learn that being with Mr Johnston was a pleasure, too. He was 'such a support to her' and 'just what she needed', remarked her eagerly observant relatives.

'Mr Johnston' returned with his bride to the home of his fore-fathers, Rennyhill. She professed to find the tall old Queen Anne house delightful with its gardens full of fruit trees and roses and its dairy, stables, ducks and 'doocot', but it was strangely quiet after the life she had been used to, hurrying from urgent conferences to the House of Commons and back again. She missed all her friends and, above all, her father and 'the stream of excitement I always drank from him'.

Scotland was almost a foreign country. 'I shall make my husband be mistress,' she said, 'for I am sure I can't undertake to regulate this Scotch household with all its plans of porridge, oat-cake, broth, etc.' But she did the 'redding up' and sorted the linen that had been spun by her husband's great-grandmother and her maids. She wrote home nostalgically of having 'heard of the success of the waistcoat of the M.P. for Weymouth'—her father —'Elizabeth Wilkinson says it was of lilac satin with purple flowers edged with gold.' Here, in Scotland, it was wintry weather and 'I trudge along well clothed with my bearskins and with Indian rubber shoes, more curious than beautiful, certainly'. True to type, she tried to start a Sunday-school and Dorcas meet-ings, but these wild Scots were independent people and un-familiar with the proper mode of life for the peasantry, as recog-nized in Norfolk.

When she visited London with her husband she got an intoxi-cating whiff of the old life, full of action and urgency. Writing from her father's house in Devonshire Street she gave a wonder-fully vivid glimpse of a typical breakfast scene there. 'Here we sit,

Ancestry

Mr Bannister's long arms stretched out across the table, my father but just down, but the Report supersedes his egg and a strange mixture we present of tea and ink, plates and papers . . . enter Mr Christie. My father holds out a hand to him without looking up from his book. A. and Mr B. give him a nod. I venture a whisper of gossip and on we go again. They are planning to get it [the Aborigines report] received before Easter. "I can't have the proofs too quick," says my father, "tomorrow we'll meet." My mother puts in, "Now, darling, I will have thee eat breakfast; thy tea is entirely spoiled." My father—"Now, Andrew, how do you mean to vote tonight"?'

She could not stay at Rennyhill while such things were going on. In the end they moved to East Anglia and Andrew went into the Gurneys' bank at Halesworth, which was later merged into that of their cousins, the Barclays.

Here they reared their two sons and four daughters. Of these the eldest, Andrew, was in especial a delight to his grandfather who, reluctantly obliged to return to London and 'the House', wrote of 'a poor night in the mail' and 'How much I should prefer hearing little Andrew speak, to Peel'.

Sir Fowell did not see his beloved little Andrew as more than a small boy, but would probably have continued to regard him with the same pride and satisfaction if he had. Andrew seems to have come as near to being a model son as any parents could hope for, little as his father's continual letters of admonition would lead one to suppose so. The younger son, Fowell Buxton (known as Buxton or Buck) was an altogether different proposition, and gave more reasonable cause for anxiety. Andrew was always being adjured to exert a good influence over him and to persuade him to wash his neck. His mother wrote of his being too masterful and per-emptory with his young brother and impressed on him that 'Every child, to respect himself, must be respected by others'. The source of the words is unmistakable: either it was an edict of her father's or it was he who taught her to think along such lines. Her views, so much in advance of their period, must sometimes have come into conflict with those of her husband, a more orthodox

Victorian parent. He loved and admired her, however, and no doubt her ideas did much, at first, to mitigate the austerity of his own. But then, when the young Buxton was thirteen, he and Andrew were rushed home from Rugby to be present at their mother's deathbed. This was an incalculable loss to the children, as their father frequently pointed out to them. Moreover, the idea that he was now solely responsible for their moral welfare seems to have weighed heavily upon him.

Even their leaving school and coming of age did not relieve this burden. Andrew was twenty-two when his father wrote: 'I doubt not a time will come when you will appreciate my warnings and fault findings. You forget that I am the only person who has the right and the will to find fault with you. There have always been serious defects in your character, in my view, and these I have endeavoured faithfully to bring before you. That you have not been grateful to me for this I cannot help. I have a heavy responsibility as a sole parent and I must try to do my duty. . . . Your brother is a heavy care to me and I do not know that you have done all you could by advice and example for him. . . . If you marry prematurely misery in the present and ruin in the future would probably be your portion. Don't let an idea of a home for B. [his brother] influence you. Two to one he is so odd he would not avail himself of it.'

The two sons grew up as different as two brothers could well be. Andrew was tall, athletic and strikingly handsome with the straight nose and high cheekbones of the Johnstons to which he added a wealth of beard in the Victorian manner. He was wise and upright in business, affectionate and kind at home, public-spirited, philanthropic and, like his sisters, much given to good works. He was an M.P., J.P., Clerk of Quarter Sessions, High Sheriff of Essex, verderer of Epping Forest and, above all, Chairman and so-called 'father' of Essex County Council, as well as a director of several companies.

In appearance Buxton was a modified version of his brother, though lacking his noble beard. In character he was opposite in almost every way. He was decidedly not wise in business, nor was

[30]

he affectionate at home. He held no public offices and took no interest in good causes. Worst of all, he read Darwin's *Origin of Species* and became an agnostic. He was, in fact, the black sheep of what may well have seemed to him an almost oppressively snowy flock.

His father may, perhaps, have derived some melancholy satisfaction from finding how right his forebodings had been, at least in regard to his second son. He wrote to Andrew more in sorrow than in anger, 'Oh, had it been given that he could have read his brother as a "living epistle" of the Lord Jesus!' Had not Andrew set the whole family by the ears by going to a theatre, a form of entertainment known to be frequented by 'women of a certain sort'? They had almost decided then that he was lost and what more natural than that his brother should become an agnostic?

Actually they were inclined to dismiss Buxton's agnosticism as a passing phase. They did not perceive the magnitude of Darwin's influence, foreshadowed in what seemed to them the contrariness of a single individual. By the time they realized their mistake they had probably ceased to hope for any sign of grace from this least satisfactory member of the family.

Buxton is an enigma, an erratically brilliant ne'er-do-well, contrary, original and highly eccentric. How he came to be what he was remains a mystery, but one to which certain contributory causes may perhaps be traced. Many have found it a mixed blessing to have a handsome, successful elder brother. His position in the family, too, may have been somewhat isolated; on the one hand were Andrew and his sister, Effie, devoted friends, on the other the three 'little girls', a group on their own. He seems to have started with a grudge against life, firstly because his father took him away from Rugby prematurely, as he thought, and secondly because he was thwarted in his plans for a career. He wanted to become a naturalist and to travel and explore. The best preparation for this, he thought, was to qualify as a doctor, but here his father intervened, telling him roundly that medicine was 'not a profession for a gentleman' and putting him into a solicitor's office. There he kicked his heels, unhappy, bored and resentful, and when a friend enlisted in the army he impulsively did the same. Again a ripple of horror and distress spread through the family, but he could disregard it now. He had got away.

He bought a commission in the III Dragoon Guards and went out to India but his military career was abruptly cut short by an illness so severe that he was not expected to survive. He made a complete recovery, however, and in 1866, at the age of twenty-seven, he emigrated to South America and bought a ranch. This seems to have been the fashionable thing to do at the time among young men who failed to make good at home or wanted a more adventurous life. By them South America was held to be the land of promise.

The ranch, which was called The Arazaty, was in the province of San José in Uruguay. The place was remote; the nearest town was Monte Video but it took several days to get there. Buxton is said to have had a scheme for making soap from wild horses. Whatever he actually did it seems probable that he lost a good deal of money over it. The house he built resembles a fortress in its yellowed photograph. He designed it himself, no doubt incorporating many interesting features—for he was inventive and original—but leaving out the stairs. These were added on outside when the omission was noticed.

Three years after his arrival Buxton married Alice Douglas, the daughter of another Scottish rancher. Like the Johnstons, the Douglases were a border family and this branch had lived for some generations at Coldstream in Berwickshire, where they were bankers. Adam Douglas, a widower, had gone out to the Argentine with his grown-up family and bought a ranch in Cordoba.

Alice, with her large dark eyes, must have been something of a beauty. Captain Johnston, or Don Federigo as the peons called him, was certainly not without charm where women were concerned, and was said to have been a dandy when in the Dragoons. A photograph shows him at The Arazaty in an open-necked shirt with high boots and a sash round his waist, a decidedly romantic costume.

Buxton and Alice were married at Buenos Aires. The bride's

Ancestry

father had no money to buy a present—there had been trouble at the ranch, first with Indians, then with locusts—so he gave her the most precious thing he had: her mother's tea-set. This, with its elegant little cups adorned with exquisite bouquets of flowers and a wealth of gilding, must have been in strange contrast with the uncompromising architecture of her new home.

So Alice came to The Arazaty and with her came the tea-set and with her also, and perhaps less happily, came her sister Maggie.

It is hard to know what to say of anyone as unselfishly devoted as Maggie. She was almost a saint according to her lights, but one may question whether her partisan and unforgettable presence was calculated to assist the difficult early stages of a marriage—or, indeed, the even more difficult later ones.

Of Alice's character little is known, but the other two of that trio had neither of them the temperament to make things run smoothly. Buxton was capricious and wilful, liable at any moment to pronounce some extraordinary decree and insist that his household should adhere to it. Maggie was as restless as a little bird, always in a twitter of anxiety, full of old wives' tales on subjects like health and hygiene and ready to give her life for her beliefs. Moreover the two sisters were every bit as pious as Buxton's own sisters at home. He had escaped from one such family only to find himself inextricably involved with another, his agnosticism evoking just such pained silences as it had, no doubt, in the drawing-room at Halesworth.

It was into this strange household that Edward Johnston was born.

If one looks, in this ancestry, for a key to his character, it is there unmistakably. It is there in the father's refusal to be swayed by convention or to adopt ready-made opinions as his own. It is there in the whole Quaker tradition of integrity, conscientiousness and service. It is there in the dictum of his great-grandfather, Thomas Fowell Buxton, that, above all, children should be taught 'habitually to seek for *the truth*, whether for or against our previous opinions and interests', and in the character of Hannah Gurney who, in her husband's words, 'sought and found

c   [33]

the truth and taught it to me.' 'To search out and live the truth,' echoed their great-grandson, 'the one thing I care most about.'

Edward Johnston has been called a great man. If he was so then the root of his greatness was that—that to him the truth was, always, 'the one thing I care most about.'

II

Childhood, 1872-1891

Fowell Buxton Johnston and Alice Douglas were married in 1869. The following year, a son, Miles, was born to them and, on February 11, 1872, a second son, Edward.

Exactly three weeks later and half the world away, the wife of the bank manager in a little Scottish town presented him with a daughter. Although Edward was in Scotland eleven months later it took nearly thirty years for their paths to converge, but when they did so it was with the swift certainty of destiny fulfilling itself.

If tradition is to be trusted Edward must have been near death on that journey home, for it is said that his father, in a mood of more than usual intransigence, refused to allow the baby food to be brought on the voyage, or alternatively, that he threw it overboard, with the result that the baby made the long journey in a state of semi-starvation.

Edward was christened in Edinburgh in January but it was mid-June before they returned to South America. An interesting account of their departure is given in a letter to Andrew Johnston from Miles MacInnes, the husband of his sister, Effie. 'Buxton was sorely tried at leaving in such a rush yesterday that he never even shook your hand, and he had a good cry as the train started. It is delightful to hear his admiration of you.' They arrived at Falmouth to find that their ship, the *Leopold*, was due sooner than expected and instead of having a good night's sleep they must be prepared to leave in a few hours. 'Buxton and I set to work at

[35]

once on the chaos of luggage and after about an hour got nearly all of it on board a small steamer, where we left it for the night. Meanwhile, the others had all come here' [the Falmouth Hotel] 'and we found them at 11—over a cold meat supper—Sidney[1] soon went to bed but Effie was faithful to the last and read and prayed with Buxton and Alice in their room, when it must have been past midnight. They seemed much calmed afterwards. She and I did not attempt any sleep but I think most of the others went to bed. Nob Fox[2] joined us in the coffee room for tea and biscuits at 1.30. All were beautifully punctual. We drove down in a bus to the pier and it was just light enough to see as we steamed out of the harbour at 2.40. There was a very slight swell outside the harbour but we could scarcely have had a better start, the waves just breaking with a gentle ripple and all looking beautiful in the early dawn. We steamed to meet the *Leopold* and were nearly six miles out before we sighted her. She looked very well as our little steamer ran alongside, and was steady as a rock for the hour we were on board. We had brought out fresh meat and vegetables and two tons of ice which took some time hoisting on board, so we could see all about the cabins, etc. There is only one other passenger at present. . . . B. was exceedingly upset by the early start, and certainly it was forlorn enough. We left them at 5.30 and my last sight of the party was Buxton's sad, earnest face gazing at us over the bulwarks with a boy in his arms, the others all about him.'

About a year and a half later they sold the ranch and came home for good, with a third child, Ada, who had been born since. It may be that Alice's health was already beginning to fail under the strain of the hard life and the local methods of midwifery. Equally it may be that the ranch did not prosper or that they were too homesick to continue there. At any rate, some months before Edward's third birthday they left what was really the only home they ever had and returned to England. He had been dragged three times across the Atlantic before he was as many years of age: what

[1]Sidney Buxton, later Lord Buxton.
[2]The Foxes of Falmouth were cousins of the Gurneys.

wonder that in later life he showed such intense reluctance ever to go further afield than the letter-box at the cross-roads?

There then began a strange nomadic life spent in furnished houses and lodgings. Maggie continued to live with them and indeed grew more and more indispensable as her sister's health declined. This ménage, with the addition of a cockatoo, a jackdaw, rabbits, dormice, pigeons, a canary, an aquarium, generations of cats and, eventually, even a baby sister, trailed endlessly from place to place accompanied by 'bullock trunks', bags, boxes, holdalls, bundles of screens and sixteen packing cases.

It is understandable that, for a man, a furnished house with an ailing wife, a fussy sister-in-law and children who spent half their time in bed with colds, might lack something of the charms of home life. Buxton was frequently away from home and is reputed to have found more congenial companionship elsewhere. It is, of course, not possible to determine whether his frequent absences were the consequence or the cause of his wife's illness. She may have seen that she could no longer hold him and, in that atmosphere, heavy with forebodings about everyone's health, succumbed to the most natural expression of her unhappiness and become an invalid.

Maggie alone might have driven him to leave them altogether. Her ceaseless activity and ubiquitous presence must have been impossible to forget or ignore. Edward's diary mysteriously records that, on an April evening when he was just fifteen, 'Father was displeased so he went outside twice with nothing on but his ordinary clothes'. One longs to know the rest of the story, what else he should have worn and how this demonstration was supposed to relieve his feelings. The answer may well be connected with Maggie's profound distrust of fresh air and belief in the necessity for always 'wrapping up well'. Perhaps Buxton was driven to demonstrate, twice in one evening, that he could leave the house without an overcoat and not be instantly struck down with pneumonia. In the field of intellect Maggie thought there was no one like him but she could not forgive him for his treatment of her sister, and there must have been continual tension between them, which occasionally flared up, as on this April evening. Another bitter grievance she had against him was that he *'would not be careful'* about colds. The children were removed from the dining-room and shepherded upstairs, to eat their meal in their bedroom, because he had been heard to cough or sneeze.

Colds and draughts were, together, Maggie's constant bugbear. Her world was fraught with dangers; the children were never safe. In winter the rain was the enemy, in summer the heat, and all the year round draughts lurked, colds threatened, noses ran and then there were thunderstorms. They had a book of instructions on how to deal with this particular hazard. Following its advice she raced round the house at the first distant rumble drawing all the curtains and covering looking-glasses, knives and all polished metal. Even the author himself, however, seems to have had little confidence in the ultimate efficacy of his methods for his final piece of advice was to draw your bed into the middle of the room, lie down upon it and 'commend your soul to your Maker'. This performance naturally made an indelible impression upon the children, the desperate urgency of the ritual and then the darkened rooms, the swathed objects, and themselves huddled together awaiting annihilation. To the end of Edward's life a thunderstorm could ruin a day's work for him.

Most of their childhood was spent in or near London, but at first, on their return from South America, they settled near Torquay. It was there that Edward was photographed in a velvet dress trimmed with fur, thick woollen stockings and button boots, gazing intently at the camera from under a short fringe like a French boy's. There was little enough of the country or the open air for them and it is good to know that he had at least one memory of rural freedom. 'I don't know when my heart has been so glad,' he wrote of a time of miraculous happiness twenty years later, 'since the days when I ran or toddled, brain free and joyous, when I rolled in the green grass and thought red and white clover lovely flowers and so filled my hands with sweet bundles of them. When I caught "hopper-grasses" and, witless of cruelty, put them in my pockets with hard little green apples, small potatoes and carrots and string.'

Afterwards, inhabiting some dim London suburb, he stood gazing down the length of a grey street, having been informed by some vague, grown-up gesture, that Devonshire lay 'that way'. In his serious, six-year-old mind he was considering the possibility of getting back to his lost paradise. If he walked along that road, he wondered, as far as he could possibly go, would he—*would* he —reach the farm in Devonshire?

There seem to be two kinds of children, those who are born with their characters unformed, who change and develop sometimes almost out of recognition and look back upon their early selves as strangers, and those who, from their earliest years, are definitely and recognizably themselves as they will always be, lacking only experience. Edward was one of the latter kind. As he gazes at the camera in his velvet frock and his button boots his intense scrutiny is something more than idle curiosity. He is wondering what this strange contrivance is and how it works and, very likely, whether he could make one. He wanted to get at the facts, at the truth behind everything, and he was often exasperated by the way the grown-ups brushed his questions aside or answered with vague and careless inaccuracy.

Once, when he was perched on a chair with 'Aunty', as they called her, kneeling before him, buttoning his boots, he was wrestling with a problem and trying, as he always tried, to put his speculations into words. His aunt, hurried and anxious, continually cut into his slow and earnest attempts to state his problem with a stream of doubts and warnings. Edward's brain was like the mills of the gods, it ground slowly but it ground exceeding small. At no time in his life could he be deflected from pursuing his mental quarry to the limits of his power. So now, with the mounting pressure of a problem that demanded to be expressed, he made attempt after dogged attempt, but to no avail. Suddenly he could bear it no more, his foot wrenched itself free from his aunt's ministrations with the buttonhook and expressed the pent-up frustration in an unprecedented kick, while, with all the force of his bitterness and desperation, he almost shouted, '*No let me 'peak at all!*'

No one who knew him as a man could doubt that it was the same person.

As a child, Edward was subject to strange, recurrent dreams. There were at least four of these and they returned at intervals for a number of years but ceased as he grew older. In one he was marching across a limitless plain with a band of men at whose head walked one who carried a great disc on a pole. At intervals there was a noise like the striking of a gong and they all fell on their faces. In later years he came to believe that this had been an atavistic dream of sun-worshipping.

In another dream he was surrounded by beautiful Japanese ladies in gay silk kimonos and sashes who smilingly embraced him and took him in a boat across a lake to an island of cherry-blossom. They greeted him afresh with delight whenever the dream recurred until there came a night when they were sad and he realised that it was because they were saying goodbye. After that the dream never came again.

The most remarkable of these dreams was one that he came to connect with the lifelong fascination exerted upon him by the mysterious recurrences in mathematical series. He dreamed that he climbed a great brass chain till he found himself in a scale pan. There he saw the Trinity throned in glory, surrounded by the Apostles. Their robes were of the most intense and brilliant colours, reds and blues and greens. The whole scene was one of the greatest splendour and yet, as he gazed at it, he had the feeling that, wonderful as it was, this was not quite *it*, not the ultimate and final vision. With this thought he looked up and there was another great brass chain. Again he climbed and reached another scale pan and again there was the vision but even more brilliant than before. The colours filled him with delight yet still he knew that this was not quite what he sought. So he continued to climb up and up and each time the vision increased in brilliance until at last he reached a scale pan where the colours almost vanished in pure light and he knew that he had reached his goal.

Childhood, 1872-1891

Afterwards, when he began to be fascinated by the illuminations in early manuscripts he found again what seemed the very colours that he had seen in his dream, and recognized them with a thrill of joy.

Edward's earliest surviving diary was begun at Balham when he was fifteen. Like all his early diaries it is more concerned to explain exactly how he fixed a bracket or drilled a hole than to pander to his biographer with information of a more personal character. He appears to have been attached to his mother, perhaps deeply; he was certainly dutiful to his father, but when one seeks to penetrate further into these relationships the boy says only 'I have got my bar-magnets. Father went about a Wimshurst machine to Dale', and tells how they had rhubarb for dinner and the maid got drunk and they shot with bows and arrows on the common. 'Ada went to the Bishop's on sunday and had a sick-atack on monday she has not been sick since 12.15 p.m. on the 3rd'. Illness, of course, is always documented. He tells us, always, who came down for the first time, or out for the first time, after how long, and who was suspected of starting a fresh cold.

Ada seems to have been a robust, unsentimental little girl. At the age of eleven she wrote to Edward of one of their many kittens: 'Miss Bayle got it but she found it was a lady cat and she sent it back to be drowned or kept as we like. If it is clean we are going to keep it and if not kill it it is very sweet and weighs 2 lbs. 13 oz. Your affect sister, Ada Johnston.' To this her mother has added, 'Hitherto hath the Lord helped us', not, presumably, intending any reference to the disposal of the kittens, though this must have been a very real problem. She has further added a note, 'So thankful you are all well and all here nicely, thank dear Jesus . . . Tell Aunty I half wonder if Olof has a little cold, but not sure.' Periods when they were wholly free from such speculations must have been rare indeed.

Olof was the little sister, eleven years younger than Edward. It is said that when she was born her father announced that she was to be called either Olof or Kettelred or he would not come to the christening.

Childhood, 1872-1891

Maggie and the older children spent several winters in Ventnor, leaving Olof and the parents at Balham. Their mother sometimes visited them and Edward wrote asking her to bring some books as he wanted to do lessons: 'Douglas grammar, Colliers English History, the red geography and a small green atlas—I think they are all in the tool-room.' They had no regular education at any time and never went to school, probably because they were considered to be too delicate. Sometimes they had governesses for brief periods and once, to Edward's joy, a tutor—a man who really *understood* about mathematics. In general however, they picked up their education for themselves. As their father's conversation was full of interesting information and ideas and they themselves were lively-minded and intelligent children and keen readers this system worked pretty well. Learning was not forced on them, it was sought and enjoyed.

They were permitted more freedom of speech than was usual at that time. 'We were allowed to argue as children,' Edward wrote, years later, to his wife. 'We had a somewhat narrow upbringing and we inherited a good deal of wilfulness. I told you how I used to talk to Aunty and how sorry I had been.' 'Aunty' had this unfortunate effect upon people. Her fussing goaded them to irritable replies and then the knowledge of her truly loving and selfless devotion filled them with remorse.

Like most children of the period they were made to learn poetry and on one occasion their father promised Edward ten shillings if he would learn the whole of *The Chronicle of the Drum* before the year was out, but 'I only learnt the first 21 verses—we left where they had a copy of Thackeray's poems before I had any more copied out.' He was more successful with *The Destruction of Sennacherib*, *Cophetua and the Beggar-maid*, Calverley's *Fly-leaves* and, of course, Kipling's *Recessional*. Various notes are written against the verses he copied into his book. One, *Freddie and the Cherrytree*, is marked 'taught me by Miss Pope, who was nice, though she was a governess, but didn't know any better'. And another, 'This is about the most horrible thing I have had to learn yet'. A third has a note obviously added later, 'taught us by

F.B.J. [their father], who promised each of us 6d. if we could say it to him without laughing while he sat and made faces at us. We tried many times but never got the 6d. as far as I remember.' Later he graduated to Kipling's tough-sentimental *Mary Pity Women*. Afterwards, inevitably, sordid realism was forgotten and along came *The Blessèd Damosel*, fairly intoxicating him with her pre-Raphaelite stars and lilies.

He had already made the acquaintance of Ruskin and been impressed by his instructions on drawing but the impact of the pre-Raphaelite movement had probably not yet reached him. He knew no one in the world of art. His mother, who may first have aroused his interest in drawing, had been to Edinburgh School of Art for a time before her family emigrated to South America, but none of the august and numerous relatives had any particular interest in the subject, and friends he had none. As they neither went to school nor stayed for long in one place there was little opportunity of making any. Shut in between the four walls of the house of the moment, with windows tightly closed in case of draughts, they seem to have had almost no contact with the world outside. Only relatives, doctors and servants, with the occasional governess, could penetrate that barrier.

The boys pored over all the books in each successive house and, when short of literature, read the newspapers that lined the drawers. They delighted in that marvel of the period *The Boys' Own Paper*, with its Jules Verne and Conan Doyle stories and *The Adventures of a Three Guinea Watch* by Talbot Baines Reed. The author's name meant nothing to the boys; it was the story that mattered, but the distinguished young typographer who wrote it was already an inhabitant of that world towards which, in an infinitely leisurely and devious way, Edward's path was leading. But for the early death of Reed their paths would certainly have crossed, for he was then associated with William Morris, for whom he cast the famous Golden type for the Kelmscott Press.

Edward's own summing-up of his education, in a note written in 1938, was: 'Without a classical education, have a fair know-

[43]

ledge of the Bible and L.C.'s[1] two *Alices* besides a good grounding
in folk tales. Possibly a real affection for Bks. 1, 3 and 4 of *Euclid*
and for the simple demonstrative virtues of algebra.' Their devotion to mathematics, in fact, was such that on one occasion, when
Miles was seriously ill, the doctor thought it necessary to forbid
him to do algebra and lent him some story-books instead. They
both kept up their mathematics all their lives as a pure diversion,
loving them for their truth and accuracy. Edward would soothe
himself to sleep by going through the theorems of Euclid, plunge
into algebra as a refuge from unhappiness or anxiety and respond
to every chance reference to statistics with mental calculations
that were made as much for pleasure as for the sake of the solution.

They were both keenly interested in electricity and were constantly getting or making apparatus and doing experiments—
sometimes, apparently, much more dangerous ones than their
elders had any idea of. Their interest in science was pretty general
and included, in particular, physics, chemistry and astronomy. At
the age of fourteen Edward copied out page after page from a
book called *The Aerial World* (perhaps they had to leave it behind
in one of the houses they were forever quitting). These dealt with
sound, light, wind and so on; subjects in which he retained an
intense, life-long interest. In the same year his diary notes two
other important events: 'Began wearing stick-up collars' and 'Had
window open with us in the room'. In February of the following
year appears the entry 'Had our window (dining-room) open for
about five minutes' and, triumphantly, on July 2, 'Window open
all day'. This does not, however, seem to have indicated any real
progress, except in the weather, for in August, when both boys
were in bed with 'slight bronchitis' and the doctor prescribed an
open window, his advice was evidently not well received. Next
day the diary announces significantly that Aunty did not care for
that doctor so they got another one. They frequently changed
their doctors, indeed it seems to have been almost a hobby of
their mother's. As her condition failed to improve, her husband

[1]Lewis Carroll.

[44]

stayed away longer and life dragged on in a monotonous series of other people's houses, she must have felt at times that if only she were ever really well it would be different, and surely there must be someone who could do something. The changing of houses may well have been due to the same cause, a recurrent fancy that she would be better somewhere else. Her husband, too, may have shrunk from anything which, by its permanence, might seem to bind him to them more firmly.

Doctors were always there and, like the houses, always much the same but with different names. They were easily disposed of. 'Dr Young came and father explained to him about mother giving him up. He took it very nicely.' A week later comes the entry 'Dr Burd was rather cross with mother the other day and mother wishes to change back to Dr Young. Father and Aunty spoke to Dr Y. about it.' Every possible variation was tried, including the retention of a cast-off doctor for the children while a new one attended their mother.

It was the same Dr Young who 'came again this morning and mother wanted him to see M. and I. M. had a slight cough but there is nothing the matter with *me* and I told Aunty, "I would not see him" as Aunty seemed to think I was to and as I knew she would call me up (like I was called up to see that Aldous) I just (telling Aunty first) put on my boots (they turned out to be M.'s) and went out.'

Edward was eighteen when he put on his boots (which turned out to be Miles's) and walked out. Behind him lay years and years of doctoring, of being cooped up indoors sometimes from October to April without a breath of fresh air. His little sister Olof was kept indoors for nearly two years without ever going out, except when they moved house. From this incarceration she emerged just after her sixth birthday, hardly remembering what the outside world was like. It is difficult to determine whether their poor health was really the cause or the consequence of the extreme precautions employed to protect it. Probably it was a mixture of both and set up a sort of vicious circle. Edward's health may actually have been fairly good. It is true that he spent a

Childhood, 1872-1891

considerable part of every winter in bed, reading and 'sniffing the hartshorn bottle', a mysterious remedy which does not inspire confidence, but he seems not to have suffered from anything more serious than colds or slight bronchitis. He never had a serious illness until near the end of his life; on the other hand he never had the energy and vigour of a normally healthy person. 'I was born tired', he used to say, and this seems to have been as near as possible to the literal truth, for the whole family appears to have suffered from a hereditary lack of thyroid. This may have been aggravated by malnutrition in infancy: unsuitable diet at the ranch and the voyage without proper food. At any rate he was 'born tired' and tired he remained all his life. This tiredness, manifesting itself as slowness, became an essential part of all that he did. He was slow and he could not be otherwise and because he was slow he possessed in a high degree the especial virtues that go with slowness: patience and thoroughness. Nothing would satisfy him that was not as nearly perfect as he could reasonably hope to make it. If genius lies in an infinite capacity for taking pains then he came about as near to having it as is humanly possible.

By the time Edward was sixteen he had lived in Uruguay, Torquay, South Norwood, Hastings, Ventnor, Turnham Green, Upper Norwood and Balham. In October 1888 they moved into London, to 25 Regent's Park Road. The following August, with a suddenness that must have left them absolutely shattered, Ada died. She had seemed the least delicate of the four. It is ironical, in view of the doctor-ridden life they led, that she was killed by a complication attendant upon puberty that could have been dealt with quite simply had it been diagnosed.

Edward's diary for August 9th, eleven days before her death, describes a shopping expedition to the Army and Navy Stores at which she was present, and gives details of the handsome lunch they had there. The next day the diary says only that 'The jasmin is all coming into flower. Aunty and Miles went to Gt. Portland Street, to Collins. . . .' There it breaks off and is not continued until the following Christmas. Ada, who died on August 20th, her fourteenth birthday, is never mentioned again.

Childhood, 1872-1891

Their childhood had not been altogether happy but nothing had prepared them for tragedy on this scale. Ada had been most dearly loved, particularly by Edward who was nearest to her in age. To him her loss was an overwhelming blow. She had also been the only one of the family for whom their father had felt any deep affection. When she was dying he forgot his agnosticism and knelt by her bed praying for her life. This deeply impressed the others to whom it seemed a sign of the truth of religion, that even he must return to it at a crisis of his life.

After Ada's death his chief link with his family was broken. He had a sort of affection for Edward but probably very little for the other two. Miles is reputed to have said once 'I wish father would sometimes speak kindly to me as he does to Edward'. Olof was a nervous, timid child and probably wished only to avoid his notice. Desolation came upon the house and from that grey world Edward escaped into desperate bouts of algebra.

Then they moved house once more and life settled down in something like the old way. The boys had their toolroom with a lathe and spent much of their time working there. At the age of ten Edward had examined a carriage clock that had stopped, deduced that there should be a pin in a certain hole, cut one to the right length, fitted it, and, behold! the clock went. (It still does.) After this encouraging experience he never looked back. Like his brother, he was for ever winding armatures, fixing electric bells, trying to make telephones. They also made toys for Olof. Edward made her a toy stove with tiny saucepans, beautifully soldered, and wooden soldiers and endless pictures of cats. When he discovered that she was terrified of hens because a nursemaid had threatened to 'throw her to the chickens' he made her a toy hen-run with toy chickens, hoping thus to overcome her fear. She could not but love such a brother.

Her father frightened her, her mother was always ill, her aunt's continual fussing got on her nerves, Miles, though truly good and kind, could appear aloof and sardonic, but Edward, with his infinite patience and gentleness, his skill in drawing and making toys and his readiness to play with her, must have been an almost per-

[47]

fect brother. As she grew older he taught her carpentry and later helped and advised her with her drawing when she took it up seriously. During the whole of her rather sad and solitary life he must have been the person who mattered most to her.

Besides their carpentry and electrical experiments each of the boys had his own line. Miles, the scientist, had his microscope and aquarium and his experiments with chemistry. Edward, though he shared in all these interests, was recognized as the artist of the family. Even before he began to draw, the idea of lettering had captured his imagination. When they were small children they used to write out texts on Sundays. For this they used hard sticks of paint that had to be rubbed down on a slab and one of his earliest memories was of being taught to do this, with Aunty firmly grasping the hand in which his paint was clenched. Each word was painted in a different colour and the colours seemed glorious, luscious crimsons and blues and greens, and so the lettering came to seem glorious too. In a lifetime spent in the service of lettering, one of the things that he was doing was to repay the glory of smacking a crimson paint-brush down on a capital G and writing GOD IS LOVE. As he grew older the texts became more ambitious and were decorated with realistic bunches of flowers—one fallen along the bottom, the others grouped casually on the left, behind them a wash of blue faded off at the edges, in the approved manner of the day. These he gave as Christmas and birthday cards to his relations. The lettering was typical of the period—'just like *real* texts', in fact. For Olof he produced a continuous stream of cats, all most carefully drawn and coloured. There were cat butchers with striped aprons, cat bakers with white hats, cat fishermen, cat nurses and cat postmen. For her birthday he made a sumptuous book containing a sequence called *Aunt Balls' Dinner Party*, after a cat of theirs named Airballs. Here cats are shown dressing for dinner and seated at a Beetonian feast in a Victorian dining-room with rich wall-paper, appropriate pictures and heavy crimson curtains.

At about the same time he began to do what he called 'parchments'.

[48]

Edward Johnston
by *Sir William Rothenstein, 1922*

By courtesy of the Artist's Executors

Fowell Buxton Johnston

Alice Johnston

Edward, aged 3

Edward, aged 9

Andrew Johnston

Greta Greig, aged 20

Childhood, 1872-1891

When he was seventeen his parents gave him an 'illuminating book', probably Loftus's *Lessons in the Art of Illuminating*, from which he copied illuminations by tracing them on to parchment. He did cards for everyone that Christmas and had great fun putting them into old envelopes and making them appear to have come by post. The joke succeeded perfectly; it was not until a family catch-word was recognized that their authorship was discovered. Cards could be either pious or comic. A couplet he composed for Miles in the latter vein is typical:

> *May fortune smile on you and send you vittels*
> *And strew your path through life with beer and skittles.*

The following January and February he was doing what was perhaps his first really ambitious 'parchment'. He wrote out and illuminated the *Magnificat* for 'Aunt Buxton'. The illumination, which was extremely lush and heavy, was traced from his book and then drawn and coloured with infinite labour. The writing, done with a crow quill, was subsidiary, hardly more than an excuse for the illumination. The words, probably, were hardly more than an excuse for the writing.

During the next fifty years he worked his way slowly but steadily to the extreme opposite view. His last manuscripts were plain pieces of writing with no illumination, no gold, no colour; writing which had one clear and definite purpose—to say something which required to be said.

This *Magnificat* caused something of a sensation. Buxton took it to show to his brother, Andrew: 'Uncle Johnston'. 'Uncle' took it home to show to 'Aunt'. Next day, on his brother's advice and with his introduction, Buxton took it to a Mr Whittingham who seems to have dealt in something of the sort. 'Mr W. said it was very good work and very careful work. Father took some bits of drawings and he admired them slightly and said to the effect that he could take any amount of comic cards. He sent a clerk to take down my address.' This is followed by a row of exclamation marks in an attempt to express what was entirely beyond him to put into words, the astonishment, excitement and triumph of the whole incident, but above all of a clerk being summoned to take his name and address when he was hardly aware of possessing such grown-up attributes. There, surely, was fame and glory!

Mr Whittingham had made the pronouncement that the manu-script was 'worth 10s.' and Edward, recalling the incident long afterwards, remarked with a twinkle that he had been rather im-pressed at his knowing *exactly* what it was worth. He did actually do a number of 'comic cards' for Mr Whittingham, including such eminently 'period' subjects as men in nightshirts blandly unaware of situations threatening immediate disaster. One almost sees the six-line caption in *Punch*, beginning '*Briggs, who is under the impression that . . .*'

These comic cards presumably brought Edward his first earn-ings, and it was time that someone thought about earning money. What Buxton did at any time after returning from South America is not known. He seems to have had a job sometimes—and some-times not. He had probably got through most of his patrimony that was not tied up in trusts—a family habit—but his brother and sisters were endlessly good and kind and whatever they may have thought of him personally they had a strong family feeling and sense of responsibility. They must often have said among themselves how unfortunate it was about the boys, how they should have gone to Rugby with their cousins and how odd they were said to be. They did not meet the rising generation of the Buxtons, Gurneys or Barclays or any of that great network of wealthy relatives spanning East Anglia, the people who would have been 'useful to know'. Over and over again Uncle Johnston would drop the tactful hint, utter a word to the wise. Cousin So-and-so had been decorated, a letter of congratulation, now . . . Cousin Such-and-such had been made a director, it would be proper to call and pay one's respects. Did they ever, ever call, ever write? He never lost hope but there was no doubt about it, the boys *were* odd. What else, after all, was to be expected? They were at least not as regrettable as their father: 'my wretched brother', as he once described him, in a burst of more than ordinary frankness.

Childhood, 1872-1891

Meanwhile he did his best to see that his brother at least kept up an appearance of respectability and did not disgrace him publicly. A man in his position could not have such a brother being seen about in the City. 'Uncle pushed Father into a hatters and made him get a stiff felt hat' (a bowler, to judge from the accompanying drawing), 'while he took Father's old hat (giving him 1/- for it) for the Salvation Army.' A few days later 'Father was away in the City and saw Uncle Johnston who gave him a frock coat and nice pair of trousers that had originally been Cousin Edward's. Father has had to give Uncle in exchange his ordinary coat and trousers for the S.A.' (To ensure that he should not appear in them again, no doubt.)

By this time Alice was completely bedridden. Perhaps Ada's death had made it seem that it was not worth trying any more. At any rate she now lay on her back being waited upon by Maggie. A new doctor diagnosed chronic enteritis and prescribed asses' milk. He also made the revolutionary suggestion that she might feel better *if she sat up.* He simply said the word and up she sat and took her beef-tea from a bowl instead of a feeding-cup and the children were summoned to see this remarkable sight.

In July 1890 they left London and moved to Plymouth, perhaps for her health. Buxton seems to have been out of a job and to have borrowed money from his sister for the move.

Edward's diary describes the journey in detail. Alice was taken by ambulance to the station and lay on a mattress in the 'saloon carriage' supported by two bullock trunks. For the rest, the luggage consisted of:

'Aunty's "dingy" box, uniform case, portmanteau, yellow tin box, black trunk, horse, toolbox, M's and my box, yellow tin box (Father's), scuttle, black bag, wicker basket, bundle of blankets, bundle of screens, Florence's box, Annie's box, wine box, Olof's mattress, Imperial, big yellow box, little box, mogny box, box of crockery, bath full of pots, bundle of sticks, string bag' and sixteen sugar boxes.

During the latter part of the journey, when Olof was becoming tired and fretful, Edward brought out the book with the cats'

[51]

Carlyle Campbell Library
Meredith College
Raleigh, N. C.

dinner party, to which more pictures had been secretly added. Just so, when he had children of his own, did he beguile the annual journey to Scotland.

Olof was pacified but now the journey took on a fantastic and dreamlike quality. The train went faster and faster and began to rock violently. 'Miles was standing up when suddenly a great jerk threw him with his elbow bang up against the plate-glass window which cracked in all directions with a loud crash. As the train went tearing on the lemonade bottles went rolling and clinking about the floor, Olof was crying, Flint began to mew and bits of broken window dropped in at intervals.'

At the end of the journey Buxton lifted Alice out and carried her to the waiting cab. They found their new house all ready with supper laid and flowers from the garden on the table. Alice lay on a sofa and the cats were released and began 'taking the inventory' and had to have their stomachs tickled to make them settle down.

They had not been there much more than a month, however, when 'Mother fancied that Okehampton might be a nice place to go to' so to Okehampton they went. There, on their arrival, 'the station master, who is a funny old man, said that he noticed that Mother looked sharp and lively', and, indeed, she began to show marked signs of recovery and even managed to come downstairs, leaning on her husband's arm.

Meanwhile the boys were delighting in the country round. They had discovered two rivers and were all agog to fish. Their uncle, Miles MacInnes, sent them £5 to buy rods, and 'Cousin Edward', original owner of their father's frock coat and 'nice trousers', sent grouse from Scotland. The boys picked quantities of blackberries and optimistically sent them off by post to all their aunts. They went for long tramps on Dartmoor and loved it. Edward used to stumble home dog-tired, looking forward gloatingly to a change of clothes, a warm fire, tea, and then—'a real orgy of algebra'.

They rented more land to enlarge the garden and decided to keep hens, whereupon the boys set about building a henhouse. It really looked as though they meant to settle down at last.

Childhood, 1872-1891

Christmas came and, as a present for his mother, Edward fitted up an electric bell, working desperately to get it done in time. (Never in his life could he finish his Christmas presents without staying up most of the night.) The boys gave Olof a box of carpentry tools and their father brought home the Christmas number of *The Graphic*. All this, and a sumptuous turkey sent by Aunt Effie, and their father at home and their mother so much better; everything seemed to be going splendidly. After Christmas came hard frosts and skating, when they found 'a curate, young lady and clergyman' on the ice, just as they would have been in *Punch*. There was even a comic policeman, sliding, to complete the picture.

In February, 1891, the diary breaks off. There is no clue to what happened between February and June. And so we can never now know whether the blow was gradual or sudden, whether they had already moved to Hampstead or whether there was a crisis and a last minute dash to London. Time has covered their tracks. Every person mentioned in this chapter is now dead and there is no way to know. A newspaper cutting tersely gives the information that at Hampstead, on June 7, 1891, Alice, the wife of F. B. Johnston, died.

III

Interlude, 1891-1898

U p to now the children had seemed to exist in a static world beyond the reach of time and change. Now, suddenly and completely, that life came to an end.

Their upbringing, deplorable as it had been, had had one peculiar advantage. They never had had the corners rubbed off or found their own level or gone through any of those processes which are supposed to be so beneficial. In consequence their individual traits, including certain gifts and aptitudes, were never levelled out or watered down. They grew up in a forcing-house of Johnstonianism. For better or worse, they were what they were to the utmost.

For years their lives had gone on just the same until it began to seem as if nothing would ever happen to alter them. No one left school because no one was at school. No one ever talked of leaving home. The boys had grown into men without anyone appearing to have noticed. Edward was now nineteen and Miles twenty-one but no one, apparently, had mentioned the word career.

Their financial position would seem to have made it essential that they should earn their livings, but probably any decisive move was postponed indefinitely until they should be 'stronger'. Meanwhile life continued in an atmosphere of perpetual school holidays. Time was of no account; one day was the same as another. They had plenty of interests and were always occupied. Reading the diaries, one feels that they might have gone on like that indefinitely. Fifty years later there might still have been two eccentric old gentlemen shut away in an old house, watched over by a wizened but indestructible aunt. They would have gone on making more and more minute observations through their microscopes, inventing more and more perfect apparatus for their experiments, perhaps even achieving posthumous fame, if anyone discovered their discoveries.

Their mother's death broke the spell. The charmed circle was breached and life came pouring in. Uncle Johnston appeared, condoled, assisted, and suddenly whisked Edward away to be a clerk in his office. He did not intend this as a career but simply as a means by which the boy could be earning a little money and seeing something of the world while they decided what to do with him. At about the same time it was decided that Miles was to study medicine, and off he went to Edinburgh University.

For exactly a year after his wife's death Buxton lived with Maggie, Edward and Olof in New Cross. At the end of that time he suddenly married again and departed. The news of his prospective second marriage must have filled his relatives with the gravest apprehensions. Uncle Johnston, in particular, was no doubt prepared for any folly, misalliance or open scandal from 'my wretched brother'. In fact the second wife turned out to be unexceptionable and possessed of a private income into the bargain.

Edward, as an office boy, was earning ten shillings a week. He brought to the work all his usual thought and care. Among his duties was that of preparing the room for committee meetings and he used to amuse himself by observing the mannerisms of the members and laying ready for each such objects as he was seen to like to toy with—a ruler for one, a piece of string for another.

Just six weeks after his mother's death Edward wrote to Aunty 'Today I began work in Mr Cole's office', Mr Cole being Uncle Johnston's clerk. This letter is exuberantly stamped all over, back and front, with a rubber stamp bearing the words: *Chairman's Office, Essex County Council, 35 New Broad Street, London, E.C.4.* Another letter, soon afterwards, is entirely given up to a long and meticulously detailed explanation—with illustrations and diagrams—of the method of copying letters in a copying press. If

Aunty had been contemplating earning her living by such work he could not have given her more, or clearer, instructions. With him the faculty of being a teacher was not acquired, it was inborn. He ends triumphantly by saying that he has copied letters which 'Mr Cole confesses were better done than his'.

They were living now in Woodford, where they had rented a house. Aunty and Edward worked out the housekeeping accounts together—he had discovered that the books were always in arrears if left to her—and sent Olof to a little school for the sum of 9*d.* a week.

The choice of Woodford was no doubt determined by the fact that Uncle Johnston lived there. Edward, who had perhaps always been his favourite, was now definitely established as his protégé. It was his greatest grief that his own three children had all died in infancy. Like his grandfather, Fowell Buxton, he was a great lover of children. He also possessed strong family feeling and had wanted to continue the line of Andrew Johnstons that had come down to him unbroken from father to son for six generations. This being so he would probably have taken the two Johnston nephews under his wing but for the intransigence of their father. To stand aside and watch them growing up with no education must have been very painful and very difficult for a man who was accustomed to have his opinion deferred to. He was an enthusiast for education and paid for the schooling of many of his young relatives—including myself and my sisters—so that it seems safe to assume that he would have made offers in regard to his brother's children and that they were refused.

He lived at Forest Lodge, a large house where he received all his many relations. As head of the family he tried to bring all the young cousins together and to introduce them to all their East Anglian connections. His annual 'Forest picnic', held in winter, was a great event for the younger members of the family. They used to set off for the Forest with a pony loaded with provisions and cook sausages over a camp fire.

Forest Lodge became a second home to Edward after his father's departure. There, probably, he got to know his cousins, notably the MacInneses. There, too, he must have come to feel what it meant to belong to a family; to occupy, from birth, a ready-made place in an existing social structure, to have large groups of relations dotted about from Essex to Cumberland and Edinburgh, and—however 'odd' they might think him—unquestionably to be someone, to 'belong'. It was a mixed blessing, the family, at once a support and a threat. They hung together, they had a great interest in all their relations and a great sense of responsibility. They would never let each other down: on the other hand it meant being continually exposed to a kind of condensed and intensified public opinion. Letters were sent the rounds, reports were circulated and one and all came to the conclusion that poor, dear Buxton had made a sad mess of his affairs and that the poor, dear boys were really most odd.

Forest Lodge, though a home to Edward, was not an altogether congenial one. His uncle, though extremely good to him, gave little outward sign of affection. There remained that formidable figure, Aunt Johnston.

Long afterwards, his cousin, Hilda Walker, uncle's favourite niece, wrote of 'his pride in and love for you, never fully expressed I think because of Aunt'. She also recalled how once she had been angry with Edward for not answering a letter and had told Uncle that she meant to write and tell him so. He had answered at once 'Don't, Pippin, he's so sensitive'.

Aunt Johnston was an autocrat. What was more, she was a woman who had lost all her own children and could never, perhaps, quite forgive other people's children for having survived. This must certainly have been the meaning of the ban on the name of Andrew. *Her* son should have been Andrew and no one else's son was to bear his name. Such was her influence that although three boys in the family were christened Andrew each was obliged to be known by some other name. Thus Buxton's son by his second marriage, though christened Andrew, was known as Tod. When he was once accidentally referred to as Andrew in her presence she burst out 'Let them call him Tod or Clod or whatever they like—Andrew he shall *not* be!'

[57]

She was kind in her own way and as charitable as her husband, to whom she was a devoted wife, but she was strict, and only too keenly aware that Edward, with his unfortunate upbringing, required improvement. To this task she addressed herself whenever occasion offered and Edward confessed that he never went to Forest Lodge, even after he was grown-up and established, without expecting to be sent away from the table to wash his hands. As he wrote to his wife long afterwards, 'You said Aunt Johnston had shown you what *I* had minded so much—anyhow we were bad-marked from babyhood and have been treated intermittently as bad babies ever since. Our relations have grown old in this view and they cannot help themselves—they *expect* us to do the wrong thing and to be extraordinary: I do not say they are wrong! But it's no easier to live in that intermittent fear.'

It was not only at Forest Lodge that Edward met his relatives. He also paid frequent visits to Rickerby. This was the home of his cousins the MacInneses, in those days in its glory with all its adjuncts of liveried coachman and butler and an army of maids in starched aprons, family prayers and hip-baths and brass hot-water cans and all the solid splendour of Victorian country house life. It was near Carlisle with a terrace overlooking the river Eden and wide lawns sloping down to the water's edge.

This house was presided over by Aunt Effie, sister of Edward's father, who had married Miles MacInnes, a former school friend of her brother Andrew, 'Uncle Johnston'. Andrew, in turn, had married a school friend of hers and so the two couples were closely united. On their honeymoon, Andrew's wife, writing to the MacInneses, pinned in a scrap of the material of her dress and wrote against it 'Effie may like to fancy what I am wearing'. Thereupon her husband snipped a fragment from a seam of his suit, pinned that in also and added 'Miles may like to fancy what *I* am wearing'.

In appearance Aunt Effie was immensely aristocratic, with a noble bearing, an aquiline nose and the high cheek-bones of the Johnstons. She also had her full share of their eccentricity and would, on occasion, override convention with royal unconcern.

Interlude, 1891-1898

At Rickerby, even more than at Forest Lodge, the family met together, for the house was larger and had a constant population of visitors coming and going. In the background there would always be one or two elderly ladies given to good works and perhaps a missionary or two. Superimposed upon this would be parties of young cousins or their friends. While the elder members of the party went off in the carriage to hear dear Miss So-and-so speak on the wonderful work the dear So-and-so's were doing in Nigeria, the younger ones would go off shooting, fishing or skating, according to the season.

It may have been at Rickerby that some rowdy boy cousins, no doubt regarding Edward as a 'sissy', threw him into a cold bath. From this he emerged gasping and, between chattering teeth, exclaimed '*How glorious!*' and thereafter had a cold sponge-down every day for the rest of his life.

During this time the question of a career for Edward was under consideration, both by himself and, no doubt, by all the family. He had been promoted from office boy to clerk at a salary of one pound a week, but this was never regarded as a permanent solution. All sorts of possible careers were discussed. Uncle even said he had heard that stretching the pleated silk panels on pianos was a well-paid line. 'I'm glad I *didn't* go in for it,' Edward said, many years later, in his thoughtful, serious way, 'I don't like the way those things are *done*.' Material has to be eased and coaxed into position; his passion for precision would have been outraged.

In the end it was somehow decided that he should go in for medicine. Miles was doing it, so why not Edward? There is no evidence that he ever felt any enthusiasm for this career. It seems probable that he accepted the suggestion, perhaps with some misgiving, from a sense of duty, feeling that thus at least he would be some use in the world. One looks for some connection between the father's frustrated wish to study medicine and the sons' both doing so, but he had little interest in them now. Moreover, sentiments of his, though they might have carried some weight with Edward, would hardly have done so with Miles who, at some point, had thrown an inkstand at his father's head, thereby

[59]

probably severing relations between them. Edward's keen interest in science, coupled with a lifetime spent in the observation of ill-health, no doubt contributed to his choice. 'We had such training in taking care of people's healths—we fancy ourselves as good caretakers and nurses to the distrust of most others,' he wrote once, with unconscious irony.

Had he been more robust he would surely have reacted against the prevailing attitude to illness and perhaps gone to the opposite extreme, as happened in the case of boiling kettles. Because Aunty would drop whatever she was doing and make a desperate dash for the kettle the instant it boiled, Edward would let it steam and splutter at his elbow without reaching out a hand to turn off the gas. Unfortunately in the matter of illness he did not react against her attitude but adopted a modified version of it. The gallant stand he had made at Okehampton at the age of eighteen when he walked out and refused to see the doctor, seems to have come to nothing after all. Perhaps Ada's death, followed so soon by his mother's, had impressed him too deeply with the ever-present danger of illness. Moreover his own lack of vigour coupled with a nervous, sensitive temperament and a streak of that Scottish pessimism that is a kind of insurance against disappointment, inclined him to take a sombre view. To give the impression that he was in any way a hypochondriac would be entirely false, but he was inclined to be over-anxious about the risk of infection and the necessity for extreme precautions in this as in other hazards, such as fire and road accidents. (He strongly deprecated his infant daughter being taken for a drive '*in a motor*' in 1904.)

In May, 1895, Aunty, Edward, Olof and the cats left Woodford and established themselves in a flat at 3 Merchiston Crescent, Edinburgh, where Miles joined them. Edward was twenty-three and had had no regular education of any kind. He had picked up all sorts of information, much of it quite abstruse, and often found himself better informed than the conventionally educated upon subjects which seemed to him no more out of the way than any others. At the same time he found that he was ignorant of things that everyone else seemed to know. All his life he regretted not having had a classical education, not only because he revered and loved Latin, but because he felt it would have provided a common meeting ground with other men, which he lacked. Something of this early difficulty remained with him always. Once when a grown-up daughter cut short his lengthy exposition of some simple fact by saying that she knew it, he answered, in an injured tone, 'Well, *I* never know what you *do* know. *Do* you know that a red-hot poker is larger than a cold one?'

Before he could enter Edinburgh University it was necessary for Edward to acquire the rudiments of a more conventional education and for about a year he studied at the University Preparatory Institute. With him, there, was his cousin, Mary Douglas, who later became Miles's wife. When asked, once, what he was like at that age she replied, 'Oh, very much the same, you know. He'd sit there putting on one boot and talking.' Yes, he would sit there putting on one boot, with that remote, intent look in his eyes, talking of inter-stellar space and forgetting what he was doing. Just so he would sit, years later, slowly raising a soup spoon to his lips, then hesitating, as a new thought struck him, half lowering it while he spoke, then beginning to raise it again and again being interrupted by a thought that demanded utterance. Sometimes in the end he would even lay the spoon down altogether, producing a sense of frustration and anticlimax in his hypnotized audience.

Edward entered the University in the autumn of 1896 and in the following June Miles married Mary Douglas, in the thick of the Diamond Jubilee celebrations. Uncle and Aunt Johnston came to Edinburgh for the wedding and stayed with connections of the family, the Pearsons. I quote his account of the visit at some length as it is of considerable interest. Indeed this visit of his uncle's may well have had far-reaching results for Edward.

'We came down, as you know, by the 2.20, and were warmly received by David Pearson. Mrs Pearson was gone up to the

Interlude, 1891-1898

Jubilee—profuse regrets on both sides—but it is not the first time that we have borne with a good deal of resignation the absence of the Lady of the House, which leaves one so free to do as one pleases. . . . David accompanied us to the wedding, making, with us two, the only representatives of the Johnston side. It was funny to hear Douglas [Miles] endowing Mary with all his worldly goods—consisting of a fly hook and a dissecting knife. Funny, too, to see mousy little Olof in a smart hat with high, yellow roses, and funny to go off to Mary's house, a nice little villa standing in its own grounds.

'On Monday I was away early to the 9 o'c Jubilee service at the Cathedral. . . . Sir Charles[1] came to early dinner, as did Edward. He and I started at 3 to go up Arthur's Seat. We took it easily and did not come back till 6. I did not think that what I could easily do would be too much for him, but, poor little beggar, he was quite pumped. I can't imagine that he can go through that hard medical course but meanwhile he is full of interest about it—off to botany classes at 7.15 every morning, and I would not for the world discourage him.'

Edward himself, recalling those days long afterwards, said that he had been 'lazy and tired' and only really enjoyed the lectures of Professor Tait. Indeed his memories of the University were chiefly of Tait, whose eyes, according to Barrie, could 'flash round the room like a rapier or twinkle like a schoolboy's'. It is no wonder that Edward was fascinated, if one may judge from Tait's own description of the experiments at his lectures: 'I reserved to the last the beautiful one of balls and egg-shells suspended on a vertical jet of water as they cannot be shown without some risk of a wetting to the performer and to the nearest of the audience. Tomorrow I bring into play the large American induction coil and show the rotation of a stream of violet light in vacuo round a straight electro-magnet.' What boy could resist such lectures? Not Edward, certainly. Clearly Tait impressed him both as a teacher and as a man. Afterwards, when he had a class of his own, he used to make a point of greeting his students with

[1]Sir Charles Pearson.

[62]

particular courtesy and would sometimes tell them of the great Professor Tait and how he used to bow on entering and the students used to say among themselves that he did this because there might be a future great man among them.

That August Edward went camping on the Fells with the Mac-Innes boys and, later, spent a week-end at Inverallan with his Aunt Isa and her daughter, Hilda. Of this visit Aunt Isa wrote to her brother, Uncle Johnston, 'We have had Edward since Saturday, he goes this evening. We have enjoyed his company much. He draws so nicely and is so sweet and good and thoughtful and full of intelligence, as you know.'

It was on this journey to Inverallan that Edward bought and read the current number of *The Artist*. In it he found an article on Illumination with reproductions of the work of Harry Cowlishaw which he studied with intense interest and admiration. Perhaps the article stirred some longings and discontents in the back of his mind and vague dreams of 'going in for Art' took shape only to be put aside with a sigh as he said to himself '*Life is real, life is earnest . . .*' It was no use thinking about illumination: that sort of thing was a hobby, not a profession. Mr Cowlishaw was an architect who merely beguiled his leisure with such glorious pastimes. Going in for Art meant something much more serious than illumination.

Edward returned to his studies and put from him thoughts of 'Art'. Physics and chemistry he had found interesting but now he was dissecting human bodies and he could no longer disguise from himself that he hated it. Now, however, changes were on the way. Perhaps it was a combination of Uncle Johnston's visit and Edward's week-end with Aunt Isa that set in motion, very gradually, events that led to what was to be the turning point in his life. As occasionally happens, when the time is ripe, the idea seemed to be in the air so that everything conspired to bring it about.

To begin with, Uncle Johnston was worried about Edward. Perhaps in reply to his sister's letter he confided his fears to her and asked her to keep an eye on him as she was in Edinburgh.

This she did, and came to the same conclusion as her brother, that Edward's health was a matter for some concern and that he would never be strong enough to complete the course. Finally she persuaded him to consent to see a doctor at her house. The doctor's opinion apparently confirmed her own and her brother's. Within a week she wrote to Edward: 'Uncle Johnston said he had put it before you—the giving up of your medical course. I feel there is *much* to say in *favour* of your giving it up. The strain is severe and will become more so and unless you become very much more robust I can't believe that you would endure the rush and responsibility of medical practice. There are a number of things which you want to examine into and do, which you would have time to do under Uncle Johnston's plan and which would probably develop into great use to yourself and others. All of us love you and you would never be anything but a great help all round. This side of it is worth much consideration. . . .'

Uncle Johnston might very well have thought that Edward had had all the time for 'examining into' things that any boy could possibly expect. For nearly four years he had had him in his own office chiefly for the purpose of letting him look round and make up his mind. At the end of that time Edward had decided to study medicine and someone, probably Uncle himself, had found the fees. He was, however, a patient man and a wise one. He saw that Edward was developing late and that, at the age of twenty-five, he was still extremely young in some ways, though old in others. It was finally arranged that he should leave the University at Easter, though what he was to do then seems still to have been uncertain.

At the same time there was a general awakening of interest in his writing. Aunt Isa's daughter, Hilda Walker, had asked him to write out two things for her, the words *A passage perillus makyth a port pleasant* and the first verse of *And does the road wind uphill all the way?* which were perhaps his first commissions. 'I have wondered you did not try to make some money by doing them before,' she said. 'Send me one to put in some shop windows in London.'

Johnston's room at Vernon Place

Pen and ink sketch in a letter, 1898. Reduced

Johnston at Lincoln's Inn, 1902

These manuscripts were received with enthusiasm and the assurance that they had really 'helped one small bark on its way'. To this Edward answered: 'I, to whom as yet my life has seemed to be of little use—and much abuse! Can you not think what it is to me to be told that I have, however slightly, helped someone heavenward? I do declare, if the other parchments should be half as welcome, I could die happy on Boxing Day!'

He wrote out texts and verses that Christmas for all the aunts and cousins and the enthusiasm with which they were received should certainly have made him happy.

He had another reason to be happy, too. He must have heard the bells ring in the New Year with a very special thrill, for the sense of change was in the air and he must have hoped that 1898 would be *his* year—the year in which, somehow, at last, he would find his true vocation. Whatever wishes he may have made that midnight, we may take it that they were fulfilled, for he could hardly have asked for more than the year was waiting to give.

Hardly had it begun than it gave him a foretaste of what was in store, for, after spending Christmas at Woodford, and going to see his father and new baby brother at Kenley, the night before returning to Edinburgh he dined with the MacRaes at Vernon Place.

IV

The Beginning, 1898

That part of Hart Street which lies between Bloomsbury Square and Southampton Row is known as Vernon Place. Here, in 1898, there lived a family of sisters called Mac-Rae. Their grandfather had walked from Scotland to London to seek his fortune and had found it in leather. Their father, whose chief interest was in painting, had neglected the leather business and spent all his money in helping young artists. The girls were left to manage as best they could and as they combined their grandfather's initiative with their father's tastes their best was decidedly good. One, Georgie, had been known to Edward for years because she had acted as companion to his cousin, Mary Douglas. Later she had run a *pension* in Paris so that her adored young sister, Mollie, could study art there: now she was running a boarding-house in London.

These girls were unlike anyone else Edward had ever known. They were almost his first introduction to the world of the arts and he found himself feeling not only charmed and stimulated by their society but strangely at home and happy in a world that was new to him. They opened windows for him through which he glimpsed untold riches—all the glamour of the pre-Raphaelites, the early romances of William Morris, the paintings of Rossetti and Burne-Jones. It was all splendid and glorious and quite astonishingly different from 3 Merchiston Crescent, Edinburgh. Moreover Mollie MacRae and her friends used sometimes to amuse themselves by wearing what they called 'Rossetti clothes',

[66]

loose garments of soft purples and greens caught in with embroidered girdles and hanging in heavy folds. To them this was great fun and to Edward, no doubt, a revelation of beauty and good sense in female attire. These girls were not like the conventional, chaperoned girls that he had known; they were sensible, lively and free, gay when they tried to teach him to dance, eager and knowledgeable when they discussed the arts. Edward wrote of them, in his youthfully pompous way, 'They are to my mind much more companionable than the very proper "ordinary persons" and, knowing the opposite sex better, they are less likely to make foolish or unhappy mistakes'. Mollie told him of Paris and the art students' life there. She must have seemed to him a fabulous creature, no older than himself and already such a woman of the world, possessed of such freedom and poise.

Edward went back to Edinburgh with his head full of the MacRaes. The prospect of another term at the University held little charm for him. His one thought now was to escape to London, to the new and so much more vital life that he had discovered there. Moreover he now had at least a tentative idea of what he wanted to do—daring and unpractical as it must have seemed to him. He wanted to 'go in for Art' and that meant going to an art school and 'learning to draw'. As to what this would lead to, he probably had no very clear idea. While in Devonshire he had written, beneath a tiny drawing of a fungus in his sketch book, 'Note (for use of my Biographer). The above sketch was made by him when but a child of some 19 summers and is not to be confounded with the elegant series of Highland and Fancy pictures, the outcome of his maturer years.'

Exactly what 'Highland and Fancy pictures' are his biographer is unable to say, and it is doubtful if he knew himself, but if there is any serious meaning behind this piece of exuberance it seems to suggest that he had long cherished some vague dream of becoming a painter.

The only artist he knew in Edinburgh was his friend James Cadenhead. He consulted him about his plans for the future and he consulted Mollie. All through that term he kept up a correspondence with her and awaited her letters with more eagerness than he felt for anything at Merchiston Crescent or the University. Moreover he had discovered that the MacRaes actually knew that same Harry Cowlishaw whose illuminations he had so much admired in *The Artist*. Not only that, but Mollie actually promised to show him specimens of Edward's work.

She was as good as her word and, later, wrote him a very full and careful report of what Cowlishaw had said. 'He was very interested in your work and thinks that you certainly have a great talent for it—but he said the letters were not well enough proportioned and not strong enough—he thought you had made them more picturesque than beautiful and advised you to study the real lettering of the 13th and 14th centuries. He also said your colours were not rich enough or bright enough compared with the old illuminations and that the gold ought to have some sort of raised foundation. Morris and Burne-Jones tried all sorts of experiments using honey, white of egg and all sorts of things. Harry will write you out all the M. and B.J. receipts he has. He was very pleased with your work and said he knew so few who were really doing it well now. He said you ought to study a great deal and do some big things for exhibition. The Arts and Crafts Exhibition will be held next year again, that is the best to send to. Mr Cowlishaw uses goose quills. He said the difficulty at first is cutting them but really it is a matter of a very sharp knife. He cuts his slanting. [*diagram*] He said he would introduce you to Somebody Walker,[1] the man who is carrying on Morrise's Press. He likes No. 10 but thought you must have done the letters with a brush as they are rather undecided. He said he hoped you would go in for it thoroughly. In fact we all think it is your duty. What is one given talent for?'

Edward read and re-read this letter and hurried round with it to James Cadenhead. Cadenhead read it, remarking at intervals, 'What a nice letter. . . . What a very nice letter!' Edward warmly agreed with him.

He wrote to Mollie: 'The letter is most encouraging and the

[1]Emery Walker.

extracts from it that I will send to my "patrons" will certainly be impressive and may make a good deal for a favourable decision. Cadenhead's opinion is that I have 1. Some talent of *style* 2. *Invention* (which would be my stock in trade) 3. Some literary and decorative tastes. (I understand him to mean by the first an ability to reproduce the *style* of a thing—not imitation but a power of grasping a thing's spirit). He *thinks* these things worth cultivating in me. That there is a future for artistic Bookwork of all kinds (Title paging, Binding, picturing and, generally, decorating). That I should go to some master of such work:— (R. Anning Bell, Liverpool—Slade School, late Legros, Lond.— Birmingham School of Art.) and go through an eliminating course of drawing for at least a year before I begin to do things. That this connection with Book-Art (while offering openings for such out of the way things as "parchments") will best develop any good there is in me. AMEN.

'You have my true thanks, the matter in hand is my Life—not very great, you will say, but all I have. I am thy grateful friend, Edward Johnston.

'A third sheet is unconscionable but, with my brain in such a buzz, I can't compose what I have to say on a postcard.'

A week later he wrote again '. . . Mr Cowlishaw's remarks have evidently impressed my people—Uncle Johnston writes:— "I knew nothing till the other day of this gift of illuminating beyond that he had *drawn kittens* &c. to amuse Olof. I think he had certainly better try it." The italics are mine but, though quaintly put, it exactly expresses my own state of mind.'

Aunt Johnston had written already, early in January, 'I am glad you sent my scriggle to the artist provided he is careful with it and returns it intact! Mr C's letter is very flattering, thank you for sending it. He will be sure to give you good advice about pursuing scriggles and such things. . . . Be a good boy and don't scriggle when you ought to be out.'

'Mr C' is probably Cadenhead, as this was written before Mollie's letter about Cowlishaw. Her tone suggests that she regards his writing as being much on a level with drawing kittens for Olof. This was probably the accepted view before Cowlishaw's comments were known and was evidently even partly accepted by Edward himself, who seems to have been surprised to be taken so seriously. 'Scriggle' seems to have been his own word and was quite a descriptive one for some of his more tortured productions. Much of his work was quite straightforward but his more ambitious attempts suffered from an excess of ingenuity and tended to develop into almost indecipherable birds'-nest entanglements. He had nothing to guide him, but some grace—perhaps his native honesty, perhaps sheer lack of sophistication—had prevented him from wallowing in *art nouveau*, then in its heyday. It was an easy and tempting style to copy but though his 'scriggles' did suffer all manner of distortion he never succumbed to the facile ribbons and water-lilies that writhed on the title-pages of half the books being produced.

Edward had not considered calligraphy as a profession probably because, as such, it did not exist. When he did take it up seriously some of his friends, at a loss to understand what he was about, referred to it as 'engrossing'. One relative, on hearing what he was doing, remarked incredulously, 'But that's dead, isn't it?' It was dead. Calligraphy was truly a lost art. William Morris had experimented with it, trying to rediscover the secrets of its lost technique. Cowlishaw had done the same. Both had studied medieval manuscripts, but Morris had a dozen other irons in the fire and Cowlishaw had a full time job as an architect. There were a few other amateurs producing rather 'precious' illuminations for the Arts and Crafts exhibitions, but a plain page of writing would hardly have seemed to them to be worth doing. Some years later when Professor Lethaby's students at the Royal College of Art were told to do designs for an inscription they spent a happy hour or so trying to devise the most original kind of fancy lettering. When he told them this was not what was required and that it was to be plain Roman lettering but well proportioned and spaced, they were quite resentful. An inscription like that was not a subject for design students, they considered; it was too easy. *Anyone* could do a bit of plain writing but *they* could write 'artistically'.

It was a revelation to them to discover their mistake.

Ruskin had taught, long before, in his *Lectures on Art* that 'to make the writing *itself* beautiful—to make the sweep of the pen lovely—is the true art of illumination', but he was ahead of his time and the words had not borne fruit. They did not do so until they fell upon the ready ears of Edward Johnston.

The only professional calligraphy being done at this time was the hack work purveyed by commercial firms and was on a par with such things as the imitation Gothic pulpits turned out for Victorian churches. In 1902 Edward went to see an exhibition of five hundred and fifty addresses presented to 'the poor Duke and Duchess of Cornwall' and was 'depressed by the almost universal and lamentable bad taste shown'.

In the end of March 1898, Edward passed his first professional examination and left the University. Meanwhile a number of other things were happening—indeed it must have seemed to him that everything was happening at once. Firstly there was the problem of Olof.

Olof was fourteen and, in Edward's words, 'a faithful, though perhaps exaggerated, mirror of my own bad habits, which can be briefly summed up as want of discipline'. The fact that he was about to leave Edinburgh no doubt brought things to a head; for him Olof would do anything, but Aunty's alarms and lamentations fell on deaf ears. Like her brother, she would not get up in the morning and was vague, dilatory and chaotically untidy. She was also in a very nervous state and the doctor agreed with Edward that she might benefit from 'an atmosphere where less notice was taken of minor ailments'. Edward decided that she must go to boarding school, in the belief—as he informed their father—that it would 'help her to turn out a decent, God-fearing English woman (to my mind the highest type of creation).' Were his aunts responsible for this exalted impression, one wonders, or was the highest type of creation personified in the form of Mollie MacRae? He went on to explain that he intended to send her to 'a large and good public school' ('a "potty" little school would be no good') and, finally, that two or three years at St Leonard's would be the making of her. The matter was arranged—in spite of some difficulty in finding the fees—and he set about writing to the school authorities, instructing them on the treatment Olof was to have, the importance of her not being overworked, the care necessary for her health, and demanding answers to a whole questionnaire about conditions at the school. 'Ten old maids in one are less niggling than this silly young bachelor!' was the reply he got from the school—from a friend on the staff.

He hoped, of course, for a panacea to erase the impression of all the unhappy years and unsatisfactory influences that Olof had known. For that, however, it was already many years too late. Olof was just as 'odd' as her brothers and remained to her dying day as vague, careless and untidy as ever.

Another important decision was made during this eventful Lent term. Neil MacInnes was going on a trip to America and Canada and Edward was invited to go with him. This was a dazzling offer yet even so he may have been in half a mind to refuse it, with his head so full of hopes and plans for the future. It is probable, however, that his relations were anxious that he should go for the sake of his health, and Neil equally so for the sake of his company. Fortunately he decided to accept and, as soon as term was over, he went off to London to make preparations for his journey.

He left Edinburgh on a Sunday night—with Aunty running after him, no doubt, to thrust 'cookies' and cough drops into his hand—and reached Vernon Place, where he was to stay, on the morning of Monday, April 4.

It is easy to imagine with what excitement he must have looked forward to this moment, to seeing Mollie again after all the letters they had exchanged, to returning to the stimulating atmosphere of Vernon Place, and even perhaps meeting the great Mr Cowlishaw. Being young, with his brain 'in a buzz' and feeling himself on the threshold of adventure, he may well have beguiled his long journey with daydreams about the wonders in store for him. There are times, however, when the splendours of real life put all daydreams in the shade. This was such a time, for on that fourth of April there occurred what Edward afterwards looked back upon as 'the miracle of my life'.

He had not been in London above a few hours when Harry Cowlishaw appeared. They met and talked, Edward asked for advice, and straight away, there and then, Cowlishaw took him round to Gray's Inn Square and introduced him to W. R. Lethaby. This may not sound like a miracle and probably did not appear so to him at the time. It was many years later when he had been able to assess the effects of this meeting and judge of the possible alternatives that he wrote 'indeed, I think it nothing less than a Divine providence'. What he saw, looking back, was that on the very day of his arrival he had been taken straight to the one, the *only* man who could have helped him. 'I should most like have gone to the bad,' he said, 'or to the *New Art* of that day, without his help.'

Lethaby, a distinguished architect, was the principal of the newly formed Central School of Arts and Crafts in Upper Regent Street. He had been the friend of William Morris and had almost as large a part in initiating the Arts and Crafts Movement as its illustrious founder. Morris was the prophet but it was Lethaby who, after his death, carried on what he had begun and bred up a generation of craftsmen in that tradition. Of him Eric Gill wrote, some forty years later, 'Who shall measure the greatness of this man—one of the few men of the nineteenth century whose minds were enlightened directly by the Holy Spirit?'

What is particularly interesting about him in relation to Edward Johnston is the similarity of the two men. They were, by their nature, fundamentally in agreement. Both were *whole* men whose attitude to their work was an inseparable part of their attitude to everything else, their philosophy of life. They were both idealists and they were both utterly sincere, with a sincerity which took account neither of fame nor profit. Lethaby was simple and unpretentious, possessed of a sense of humour and a great love of life. In regard to the crafts he had perhaps a clearer, truer vision than anyone else at that time and a unique ability to pass that vision on. He was engaged in a battle against *New Art* and against all the 'artiness' and superficial cleverness that seduced so many students, a battle for sound workmanship and rational design arising from it. 'If you draw a straight line with a heart at the top and a bunch of worms at the bottom and call it a tree, I've done with you!' he warned Johnston at the start.

'It was not,' in the words of George Clausen, 'that Lethaby taught you how to do anything. He just taught you how to think about the thing' and, in the words of Edward Johnston, 'He made me feel that Arts and Crafts were True and Natural Things, not put on but part of good workmanship.'

As principal of a school Lethaby realized that comparatively few of his students would ever be able to make their livings by painting pictures and he urged them to specialize in particular lines of their own and to decide in advance what they wanted to do. 'That a student should wish to learn "Art", in general,' he said, 'is much as if a seedling putting its nose out of the earth wanted to be a *tree* in general, when no such thing as a "tree" other than the varieties, oak, beech, palm etc. exists.'

When, therefore, on this fourth of April, he was confronted with yet one more hopeful young man who told him, stumblingly, that he thought of 'going in for Art', no doubt he groaned inwardly. 'What particular branch of art, Mr Johnston?' he must have asked, and the young man said that he understood he ought to 'learn to draw'. Lethaby leaned back in his chair and closed his eyes and he uttered what were to prove some of the most memorable words that his listener ever heard. 'Learning to draw!' he murmured, intoning it almost in a chant, 'Learning to draw! Thousands of young men and women—*learning to draw!*'

He urged Johnston to give up these vague ideas and specialize in a line of his own, a craft, for instance—he suggested bookbinding or silversmithing. Perhaps this led Johnston to speak of having played about with some 'parchments' and to ask if he might bring them round, for next day he called upon Lethaby again and shyly showed him his work.

He was very diffident, and not without cause. He had never studied the subject seriously and his work was weak and amateur-ish. 'If a young man came to *me* with work like that,' said Sir Sydney Cockerell long afterwards, examining some early John-stons, 'I should tell him there was no hope for him!'

Lethaby looked at those amateur efforts and uttered a pro-phecy: 'You will do very beautiful work, if you stick to it.' Without the slightest doubt, he said, this was the work for him. He praised the manuscripts warmly and, to show his confidence, commissioned one for himself.

Edward must have left Gray's Inn feeling that he walked on air. He did the only possible thing—went straight to Mollie and poured it all out to her. She gave him tea in her studio—'the nicest tea of my life'.

Not only were the doors to his longed-for career springing open as though at the utterance of a magic word—Lethaby had 'made the most encouraging criticisms of my work that (even) you can imagine;' he wrote to Aunty—but he had the nicest tea of his life as well. When fortune favours her chosen she knows how to do it in style!

Edward at once bought materials and, after some experi-menting with different alphabets, set to work on Lethaby's commission, *Over the sea our galleys went* from Browning's *Paracelsus*.

From the very start there seemed a charm upon it so that nothing could go wrong. As though the contact of pen and parchment transmitted a current to his hand and brain, some intimation of his power began to come to him. Perhaps he began to understand that this tool in his hand, the broad-nibbed pen, was his guide, his familiar; it would *see him through*. It was the key to all, to instruct, discipline, inspire—'A most potent and magically-seeming tool', as he described it, thirty or more years later. With no one to tell him he had come to understand 'that the forms of written letters would somehow properly depend upon the pen which wrote them'. This may sound like a truism now but it was a discovery in 1898.

The wonder of it all seemed almost too much, so that he feared some disaster. After four hours spent upon the manuscript he confessed that 'I am more pleased than I can say with the result, for which I thanked God and prayed—childishly, perhaps—that my hand and eye might not be damaged in Canada. I think this is the first time that I have ever "made" a Thing and felt *quite* satisfied with the result. When I look at the parchment I get quite excited and restive—is it not a prophecy?'

He longed to get Mollie to himself to show it to her but the 'Jingly Joneses'—the MacRaes' name for some boarders they found rather a trial—refused to retire to bed. Next day he finished the manuscript and managed to show it to her 'without giving the J.J.s a chance of poking in'. (He so rarely allowed himself to be uncharitable about anyone that this reference to the 'Jingly Joneses' is particularly engaging, though I am sorry to say that he afterwards expressed regret for having laughed at them.) Alone with Mollie he poured out all that he had been longing to say and she 'listened and sympathised like a saint', and pointed out that the margin was crooked.

He must have returned to that manuscript again and again in those few days, each time with a shock of delight. He wrote to James Cadenhead in Edinburgh that it was 'the substance of things hoped for'.

'I can't tell you how keen I have been about it,' he said, 'or what odd feelings I have experienced in seeing such a thing, that *I know is beautiful*, growing under my hand, which faithfully interpreted my imagination; each idea, almost without exception, taking its right shape and place and in its concrete form excelling my expectation. I believe it is prophetic. I will tell you more about this another time. It is only three small pages of black-letter with some curly red and blue borders and little enough extrinsically, but for me it has a meaning that, I feel, cannot be mistaken.'

It was as though Lethaby had not only told him what to do but had inspired him to do it. Johnston came to believe that appreciation was an essential part of any art and to find a special significance in the passage in Genesis which states that, after each phase of the creation, 'God saw that it was good'. This he believed to be the final act of creation and he even extended the idea to include the appreciation of other people besides the artist himself as being actively creative. Perhaps Lethaby's enthusiasm and the new vision and confidence it had given him set him free to excel himself and to tap a source of power not previously available to him.

A fit climax to all this was provided by his final visit to Lethaby when he handed over the work. All he had felt and hoped was now confirmed. Lethaby, studying the manuscript, exclaimed that it was 'As pretty as it could be!' and, again, 'As pretty as it could stick!' He was 'glad and proud' to possess it. Was it signed, he asked? That was important; and Johnston, almost blushing, showed him that it was. When asked the price he said that he had thought perhaps twenty-five or thirty shillings, but that might be too much? To show that he did not think so, Lethaby said, he would make it thirty.

Before they parted Lethaby remarked that he was thinking of starting an 'illuminating class' at the Central School the following winter. Johnston no doubt received this news with enthusiasm and at once decided to be one of the first students. He must have been entirely unprepared for what followed. 'If all's well,' said Lethaby, 'I shall put you in charge of it.'

Johnston, gasping, tried to explain that he knew nothing of the subject. It must have been a little like one of those dreams where one finds oneself about to go on to the stage to perform the leading part in a play which one has not even read. He was most grateful for such a mark of confidence, he said, and much appreciated Lethaby's suggestion that it would bring in a little money while helping to make him known, but he could not teach such a class—he was not competent to do so.

Lethaby smiled. 'That,' he said, 'is for the hirer to judge.'

'Is not this overwhelming?' Edward wrote in his diary.

It certainly was. Such a thing could only have happened as a result of the meeting of two extraordinary men. Had Johnston not possessed extraordinary promise no one would have made him such an offer; had Lethaby not possessed extraordinary insight no one would have recognized that promise. That he did possess such insight seems to have been an accepted fact among those who knew him best. 'He seemed to look right *through* people' was how one close friend of his put it. In archaeological matters it was said that he seemed to know, in a manner incomprehensible to his colleagues, what certain fragments must be. The same flair enabled him to assess the potentialities of a young student.

When he looked at these first, uncertain essays of the young Johnston, what did he see? Perhaps, though lacking in technical ability, that writing showed—to his penetrating vision—the spirit of life. It was not just a painstaking copy, it was a *thing* in its own right. This may have been part of what he saw in the work. As to what he saw in the man, Johnston was, in his own words, 'incredibly innocent and ignorant' but it must have been obvious that, for better or worse, he was quite outside the ordinary run of students. His large, intellectual head and deliberate speech, his utter sincerity and his air of existing in another world—of having his whole attention concentrated on some mental sphere to the exclusion of his immediate surroundings—all must have marked him out as someone unusual. Perhaps it was because Lethaby recognized him as one of his own kind, a man for whom religion, work and life were all one and the same thing, that he was able to appraise him with particular certainty.

Life was 'best thought of as service', Lethaby said, and art as 'fine and sound ordinary work'—service, also. With the first of these maxims Johnston was already in full agreement. He was ready to embrace the second also and to renounce his dreams of 'Art', with a capital A. 'Only daily-work art is worth a button,' Lethaby said, 'all the High variety is disease. All that art-teaching is like learning to swim in a thousand lessons without water.'

The Beginning, 1898

He should not go to any art school to study, he told Johnston, but to the fountain-head: the British Museum.

Twenty years later, in the colophon of an address to Lethaby which he was commissioned to write, Johnston apologized for his delay in finishing the work with the words 'Alas! He who showed the scribe a better way than "Art" did not show him a longer way than "Life".' Later experience had by then confirmed his adherence to Lethaby's views and strengthened the devotion to the man himself conceived at those first meetings.

This miraculous week made such an impression on Edward that he was moved to record the events in a special diary under the heading *Red Letter Days*. This he inscribed in the bulgy, Lombardic capitals which he favoured at the time, but on which his book[1] makes the wise pronouncement that they are 'rather doubtful models for us to follow.'

'He says there are only two or three men at present who can illuminate and he seemed to think I could make an opening for myself, possibly,' he wrote to Cadenhead. 'Such a plan has this, of course, greatly in its favour, that I should work—though in a small field—with plenty of elbow-room: possibly being a pioneer, whose course, whether "failure" or "success" in the public eye, is always useful and heart-stirring and whose end must be glorious'.

Up till now he had probably thought of himself as something of a failure, unable to find his vocation or to stick to any course, but that April there must have come to him one of those rare moments when, perhaps only for once in a lifetime, youth really is all it is said to be. The whole week must have seemed like a dream, a fairytale, to which the enchantment of Mollie lent the final touch of intoxication. Even among all the other aspects of this high tide of fortune Mollie stands out, for she was as sensible as she was charming. Edward had it in him to love very deeply and, with a little encouragement from her, would probably have done so now. She saved him untold suffering by allowing him no illusions about her attitude. The previous

[1] *Writing and Illuminating and Lettering.*

February he had sent her a Valentine with an elaborately inscribed verse, in the course of which he spoke of 'a barbèd dart' being implanted in his heart. In reply she had advised him to 'take it out as soon as possible'. She gave him a new and delightful experience of feminine companionship which must have been highly educational and was also, through her capable management, almost painless.

On April 25, gloriously equipped with a new travelling rug, 'grey check Cheviot suit', 'brown Harris Norfolk jacket and knicker breeches' also a 'shooting coat, breeches, gaiters and *Sportsman* hat' from Burberry's, Edward set sail for New York. A blue letter-card to Aunty, written in pencil, contains a sketch of the 'very roomy' cabin he was sharing with Neil. He tells her that he has managed to get practically everything done, that his luggage is all stowed in the cabin and that '*nothing* need be a cause for anxiety or sorrow if we believe that God is good'. This assertion is wrung from him by the last of innumerable cautions and entreaties in regard to taking care of himself. 'It is very sweet of you to beg me so,' he says, with a touch of exasperation born of the conflict between gratitude and irritation, 'but I take what I consider conscientious care of myself and I can't do more, whatever you may think.'

This voyage, he used to say afterwards, was the one time in his life when he had been conscious of real, positive health and energy. He was filled, as never before or after, with the eager energy of a boy who looks for feats on which to expend himself. It led him to climb a steel hawser that slanted upwards from the deck and, being more occupied with the climbing than with where he was getting to, presently to find himself clinging dizzily above an open hold where, far below, cattle lurched and lowed. The picture of himself high up, looking out over the sea and down upon the cattle remained in his mind as a sort of symbol of the one time in his life when he had experienced a sense of vigorous vitality.

Their trip lasted more than three months and took them right across the continent from New York to Vancouver Island. In their journeying they found something of the old America that boys' stories must have built up for them and 'just the Rocky Mountains that I have always imagined'. At Pulman they were shown where two men had been lynched only the year before while awaiting trial for murder; at Salt Lake City the roads were so deep in mud as to be uncrossable in wet weather and the trams pitched like ships at sea.

It was the time of the Klondyke gold rush and when they reached Seattle they suddenly found themselves in the thick of it. 'The word KLONDYKE met your eye at every turn, in the shop windows, over the shops, painted on strips of canvas hung across the street and occupying every possible position. The shops were full of warm clothing of every conceivable kind, sleeping bags, tents, stoves, camp requisites, leggings, boots, mining tools, magnifying glasses (for ore), revolvers, knives and thousands of other things, useful and useless.'

Here they left the United States and crossed to Victoria on Vancouver Island. 'On the 8th June we ran into Victoria at 6 o'c—a lovely summer morning and a beautiful harbour. We both were glad to be under the British flag again . . . we wonder *when* that hoped-for alliance will come about between nations seemingly so much akin, in reality so radically and hopelessly different.'

They camped by Cusheon Lake on Salt Spring Island, after staying for a time at the remote little post office at Vesuvius Bay. The postmaster was 'a young man, very kind and happy-go-lucky' and while they were there he went away leaving them in control of the telephone exchange. No happier accident could have befallen Edward and, though his and Neil's ministrations were more enthusiastic than successful, the subscribers seem to have been 'kind and happy-go-lucky' like their postmaster, for no one appears to have complained.

It comes as a shock, after this, to read that on Sunday the Rural Dean preached and his wife 'knew a good deal about Cromer and had met one or two Buxtons'.

F

The Beginning, 1898

When they left the post office it was to camp deep in the forest by the lake. He described driving for four hours through the huge pine trees with 'towering column-like stems creative of mysterious dusky distances' and underbush 'lit up by the glowing colours of the wildflowers. Pale purple loosestrife, a plant with bright crimson-tipped leaves, the scarlet leaves of the Oregon grape, patches of ruddy gold, almost red, moss—here and there small, orange tiger-lilies and occasionally, almost within reach of our hands, glowing red salmon berries (a kind of wild raspberry).'

Every day they walked half a mile to the nearest farm for supplies and used to see the eleven cats mustering, aware that it was milking time. It was here that the farmer's wife promised them two cockerels and, with a hurried apology for using such a word, explained that she meant 'gentlemen pullets'.

They bought nails and rope, cut wood in the 'primeval forest' and made themselves improvised furniture. Edward also did some sketching. The post office dog adopted them and they were presented with a kitten, 'to keep down the mice'. 'I brought her home in my pocket,' Edward wrote, 'she was very wild— quite a little wild cat—and till she was hidden in my pocket, that seemed to her a refuge, howled with fear. I rowed back with her thus and then, having to cook and work before bedtime, I hung up my coat with her still there, lest she should get lost in the dark. She spent about three hours that way and then slept with me hidden under the thick Klondyke blanket. Now she is tame but unsubduable, roaming round the camp working her wicked will, purring like an angel but repaying our kindness with teeth and claws.'

His letters are lavishly decorated with pen-and-ink sketches of the lake, the camp, the inside of the cookery tent with its 'Klondyke' stove, diagrams of how to lash posts for various purposes and a lovingly illustrated list of all their pots, pans and enamel-ware in pen-and-ink with a wash of colour. This last almost manages to convey the unique importance and personality that each object must have attained in camp, where possessions are precious and few.

[82]

The Beginning, 1898

There is a sad little passage, at the end of the last letter, of farewell to the 'Klondyke' stove. 'It may be considered weak to dwell so fondly on a mere cooking stove, but I cannot help being fond of fires and hearths and grates and even stoves when they are pretty and good, and when I think of this stove and remember that it has been as good as it is pretty I have quite a warm feeling for it and write these in sadness as a memoir, knowing that this warm-hearted, biddable and gentle thing must be left behind to pine and rust away in chilly Canada.'

There never was a man who so much hated ever throwing anything away.

They stayed in camp for about a month and then packed and set out for home. At Montreal they parted. Neil stayed on to hunt reindeer and caribou but Edward had work ahead and London was calling. He had a career to begin and, having wasted so many years, he could not afford to be late.

V

The First Class, 1898-1901

Edward reached England towards the end of August and went to Edinburgh where he saw his family and collected his possessions. In the beginning of September he moved to London.

It was to a different Vernon Place that he returned, for Mollie had gone. She was about to be married. Georgie had feared that he would refuse to come there and go somewhere else where he would be underfed and overcharged, but he was not heartbroken, only a little sad. He had a bed-sittingroom at the top of the house, with a north light, overlooking Bloomsbury Square. Here he was in the very heart of London with cabs and horse buses rattling by under his open window. He was only ten minutes from Lethaby's chambers, five from Cowlishaw's and with the British Museum just across the way there, waiting for him. All this for a pound a week.

He scribbled a pen-and-ink sketch of his room on one page of a letter to Aunty.[1] This was ambitiously labelled 'Studio' and had only a corner of an iron bedstead showing to indicate that it had other functions. He got a desk made to suit his needs, with a sloping top to work on, space inside for papers and a shelf on the right-hand side. It was made of unstained deal, rough but solid. It went all through life with him and almost all his work was done on it.

On the windowsill, beside him as he worked, was a little kettle on a spirit lamp so that he could make himself tea at any

[1]Plate facing page 49.

time he liked, even far into the night, when the house was asleep, when his light must often still have been shining out towards the darkened mass of the British Museum. Between the two windows hung bundles of cane for making baskets and a waste-paper basket of a curious shape, his own make, hung from a hook on his desk. That, too, went with him all through life. He was intensely conservative about his possessions and would never willingly exchange an old one for a new, nor allow his things to be used by other people, nor to be spoken of by his family with the prefix *the*, suggesting communal ownership, for which he would substitute an emphatic *my*.

In his enthusiasm Edward had arrived too soon, while the dusty holiday season still shrouded London. Lethaby was in France, he learnt, and Cowlishaw also away. He occupied himself with getting a reader's ticket for the British Museum, setting his room to rights and going on fruitless errands to enquire for Lethaby, for Cowlishaw.

Cowlishaw returned first, welcomed him warmly and carried him off to spend a week-end with himself and his wife at their farmhouse in Kent. Edward found everything entirely delightful. Kiln Farm was a place where, from the first, he felt instinctively at home. It was with a sense of wonder and triumph, now, that he recalled how, a year ago almost to the day, he had bought a copy of *The Artist* in which he had first seen the name of Harry Cowlishaw. Now here he was, actually spending the week-end with that very man.

Soon Lethaby himself returned. He had not forgotten the young man who had aroused such hopes in him six months before. He saw his latest work and pronounced it 'Just right'. Johnston was developing as he had hoped and foreseen. The class, he feared, was impossible just yet but he would do his best. 'A committee blocked that hope,' Edward wrote to Aunty with elaborate discretion, as was his way where any subject could possibly be regarded as confidential, 'but he is going to try to "pull wires", he says, and IF (I'm afraid it's a big IF!)—then I'm his man *without a doubt!*'

The First Class, 1898-1901

In another letter he said 'Uncle and Aunt now seem in favour of my trying this plan for the winter, at any rate. *Do not things fit in!* I think the number of artistic people I meet here has impressed them.'

Things did indeed 'fit in'. His entrance was timed almost to perfection. The scene was set and everything was ready. The Arts and Crafts Movement was in the first flush of enthusiasm and filled with a real hope of transforming the world such as is hard for us to imagine now. Morris's socialism and the revival of the crafts were to bring about a new order. All was young, enthusiastic, eager; all was possible.

The Central School of Arts and Crafts, where Johnston was to teach, had only come into existence two years before. The ground was prepared and the field was clear: no one was doing his work. 'Fortunately for me, there was nobody to teach me,' he said, 'for nobody knew anything about my subject.' The great revival of interest in printing, and therefore in lettering, had begun ten years before. In 1888 a lecture delivered by Emery Walker at the first exhibition of the Arts and Crafts Society had inspired Morris to start the Kelmscott Press. But, so far, no one was working seriously on calligraphy.

The one thing that made it regrettable that Johnston had not appeared a little sooner was the death of William Morris two years before. To Johnston, Morris was the very greatest of contemporary names. To meet him would have been glory indeed and he would certainly have done so, for he was now meeting all the Arts and Crafts set, including men like Sydney Cockerell and Emery Walker who had been among Morris's closest friends.

Morris's energy and inspiration had brought the movement into being and given it such impetus that even when he died it did not falter but went on growing, finding other, younger men through whom to express itself. One of these men was Edward Johnston.

One man, even a man as dynamic as Morris, could hardly have achieved such a thing but for the fact that the time was ripe for it. Like the aesthetic movement, but on a more practical level,

[86]

the Arts and Crafts Movement was a revolt against industrialism. The Victorian faith in the triumph of progress was no longer enough for the discerning, who had awoken to the ugliness, shoddiness and human degradation produced by the Industrial Revolution.

One of the first things Lethaby did in that autumn of '98 was to introduce Johnston to Sydney Cockerell. Cockerell, though only a few years older than Johnston himself, was already an acknowledged authority on ancient manuscripts. Lethaby went so far as to say that he was *the* authority. He had been Morris's secretary and had had charge of the many manuscripts in his possession. He met Johnston, by arrangement, in the manuscript room of the British Museum and showed him round, pointing out the finest specimens and telling him of Morris's researches in calligraphy. A few days later Johnston dined with him at Richmond and spent the evening delightedly poring over Morris's manuscripts. 'Was impressed more than ever by the sweetness and naturalness of his work,' Johnston noted, 'the absence of strain and the beauty of it. His writing became *v. beautiful.*' When he returned home he felt that he himself wrote the better for having seen it.

Johnston recalled those early days long afterwards in a letter to Sir Sydney Cockerell—as he had by then become. Cockerell had written to congratulate him upon being made a C.B.E. and had spoken of his 'adherence to a high ideal'. Johnston answered: 'My high ideal owed very much to you and dear Mr Lethaby. I can hardly claim beginning with any ideal but with three fixed *ideas* that had somehow become my own. These were (1) That there was something fascinating about lettering. (2) That letters were primarily intended to be read, and (3) that the forms of written letters would somehow properly depend upon the pen which wrote them. Lethaby told me to stick to lettering and illuminating and to work at the British Museum and to show him what I did. He praised anything of the least worth. Dr R. Bridges gave me Maunde Thompson's Handbook and told me to study half-uncials. Then you drew my attention to specific MSS,

[87]

particularly the 10th century Winchester Psalter, and so the Ideal came—to make *living letters* with a formal pen.'

Living letters—that was the key. It was the greatest single secret of his supremacy—which, to this day, remains un-challenged by any of his thousands of pupils—that he had a unique power to make a manuscript come to life under his hand. It is a paradox that vitality, of which he had, himself, so little to spare, should have been the outstanding feature of his work. It can hardly have been a coincidence; it was too marked. Moreover, as his strength waned, in his latter years, the vitality of his work became even more emphatic. What freedom means to the prisoner or sight to the blind, that, perhaps, 'life' meant to him. Speaking on lettering, once, he said: 'Life is the thing we all want and it is the desire for life that is behind all religion and all art. . . . Our aim should be, I think, to make letters live . . . that men themselves may have more life.'

All that autumn Johnston worked hard at the British Museum, developing a 'new, plainish script', among more colourful essays in Celtic strapwork and heads of strange beasts swallowing their tails. He wrote out Yeats's *Stolen Child* in this 'new, plainish script' with 'blue and red Lombardic capitals, outlined red. Border: blue wire wriggles lined red and filled in red lines.' Lethaby received this with reservations. The script he found 'affected and needing simplification' and the blue 'swimming with red'. '(I saw this but really rather liked it, gave L. pain in stomach—I begin to see it too.)'

Next day Johnston embarked upon a 'reformed script' and later experimented with cutting his nib squarer, which seemed to give satisfactory results. With this new nib angle he wrote some pages of *The Sunken Bell* 'which seem to give promise of great things'. He also wrote the Lord's Prayer 'with notes on significance of each sentence and appropriate lettering for it— bits in italics, words large, etc.' Already he saw clearly that the duty of the scribe was to express the meaning of the words, and this remained for him the supremely important consideration before which all others must give way. He learned, however, partly from such early experiments as this, that interruptions and distractions defeat their own ends: the words must be allowed to speak for themselves. In later years he used to impress this point upon his students. He would instance what he considered perhaps the most splendid words of all, the opening of St John's Gospel, '*In the beginning was the Word . . .*' and ask, supposing they had written that with a lot of intrusive decoration of their own, '*Would you be prepared to meet St John?*' Once when he was ill and unable to attend his class he was asked to send a message to his students. He wrote on a postcard, simply, 'Tell them to think of the words'.

The new year began well. Almost at once, on his return from spending Christmas in Edinburgh, Johnston received an important commission. This came to him through Cockerell and was for an address to Miss Judith Blunt on her marriage to the Hon. Neville Lytton. 'This is my first really "outside" commission' he wrote to Aunty, '(i.e. done for strangers) and I am, of course, elate, as every little in this way is a practical, present help and makes more work more probable.' This was a great event; when the work was done and submitted to Cockerell he received for the first time almost unqualified praise from that most stringent of critics. To him, Lethaby and Cockerell were something like an equivalent of Mrs Do-As-You-Would-Be-Done-By and Mrs Be-Done-By-As-You-Did: Lethaby, always kind and encouraging, gave him all the praise he possibly could; Cockerell, jealously cherishing the highest standards, would pass nothing that fell short of them. Together, said Johnston, they gave him exactly what he needed: the essential encouragement to go on and, at the same time, the relentless scrutiny that let no fault slip by unnoticed.

Once, when he was showing some work to Cockerell at his chambers in Clifford's Inn, they were joined by Emery Walker who, surprised at the drastic criticism he overheard, asked if the work was not good. Cockerell answered 'Not bad, but I always tear Johnston in pieces and I must say he stands it very well.' Recalling this incident, years afterwards, Edward inscribed a copy of his book[1] 'To S. C. Cockerell who (very kindly) "always tore Johnston in pieces".' 'Your criticism was invaluable to me,' he wrote, 'you cannot imagine how really bracing it was. Generally not at all fault-finding but "you didn't say it was *bad*, but you didn't like it—that green was a sour green, but look at this," and you would produce, from your trouser pocket apparently, a marvellous work of an earlier century that completely disconceited me, for the time, and presently spurred me on enthusiastically.'

In February there was an exhibition of the work of Burne-Jones, a revelation to Johnston who had apparently never been to an exhibition of paintings in his life. He got a season ticket with the intention of going two or three times a week. 'The colours are wonderful,' he wrote, 'and Cockerell told me to "soak" myself in them, which is what I have made up my mind to do.' This exhibition, he said, contained '150-200 pictures and a great many drawings.' A more adaptable young man would already have picked up the *language* of the world into which he had entered—the easiest thing to pick up, as a rule: he would have acquired a smattering of semi-technical expressions with which to impress his family at Christmas. Not so Johnston. It was an essential part of his character that he was always utterly himself and utterly unable to be otherwise. This lack of adaptability was at once his strength and his limitation. So, after six months in London 'meeting so many artistic people', he still spoke of 'pictures' rather than paintings.

Surprisingly, in spite of Lethaby, he was still clinging to the idea that he ought to 'learn to draw'. The previous October he had attended a few classes at the Westminster School of Art where he had made drawings of plaster casts. Perhaps this damped his enthusiasm, for, after writing importantly in a letter 'It is a great event for me to begin learning to draw' he gave it up after only three attendances, for the curious reason that 'it was too far'.

In January 1899 he went to the Slade, which was nearer.

[1] *Writing and Illuminating and Lettering.*

The First Class, 1898-1901

'Saw Prof. Brown and paid for 1 term, 4 gns, 1 gn more than last year. I thought he was a secretary and mused "I suppose it is worth it," and the Prof. was almost embarrassed and said "Well, you see, there is such a demand." '

This was, of course, when the Slade was at the very zenith of its fame, but probably Johnston did not know that. He was never quite *in* this world and used to make us think that he should have been a judge, with such observations as 'What is a spiv?' and 'I don't think I *realize* Gary Cooper.'

Two days later he attended his first class. 'Large room, abt. 80 students, mostly young women: Tonks, taking and promising, 6 foot 3 abt. Told him I cdn't draw a bit and he said he didn't suppose I'd have come if I had been able to draw. Till 12.40 drawing Laughing Boy's head, no instructions, Tonks said draw as you would in your own room.

'*Russell* said "Too fat and not appreciated. Had I had any teaching?" '

Johnston said he had had three lessons at the Westminster, to which Russell replied, 'Oh, you've been *there*, have you!' Johnston hurriedly assured him that he had only been three times and had had very little actual teaching, ' "So I haven't picked up any *bad ways*—if you pick up bad ways at the Westminster." After this he was more amiable and said that a certain line had "character".'

Some weeks later Edward wrote to Aunty that 'I get on very slowly with drawing but mean to stick it.' After this the Slade is never mentioned again and seems to have gone the same way as the Westminster. He gave up the idea of learning to draw, once and for all. In his Post Office savings book 'Ed. Johnston, medical student' had been triumphantly changed to 'Edward Johnston, artist', but perhaps he now began to realize that all his old ideas of 'learning to draw' and becoming an 'artist' were beside the point. He was a craftsman. For the rest of his life—after that glorious moment with the savings book—he maintained that he was not an artist and that he could not draw.

Early in 1899 he wrote out his favourite ballad, *The Nut-Browne*

[91]

Maide, in the form of a small book—his first. 'I think of having it bound by some artist binders,' he wrote, 'and it will form an excellent specimen of my writing—being the best I have done hitherto and, as I am somewhat fitted to judge now, I may say that is *pretty good* and, as writing goes now, exceptionally so. This is not conceit, merely a plain statement of what I think.' He had at this time the immense pleasure and encouragement of thinking—with justification—that nearly everything he wrote was 'the best he had done yet'. Both Lethaby and Cowlishaw remarked how rapidly his writing was improving.

There is a P.S. to this letter, after a rather florid E.J.—'Do you notice the 2nd half of this letter is much better written than the 1st—the result of just writing three pages of N. Browne Maide!' At this time his ordinary handwriting was still very round, only beginning to emerge from the hand originally taught him and still bearing traces of its bourgeois origin, so to speak. He still used the old, copper-plate *r* and his capital *I* still had a loop at the top, but since he had begun to think more about writing it had acquired a certain dash. It changed surprisingly slowly, evolving during the next few years into a very good round hand written with a rather wide nib in Indian ink, usually on 'O.W. Paper'—paper such as no money could buy now, smooth, fine and very strong (his fiancée complained that his letters refused to be torn up). This writing had a strong calligraphic flavour and a touch of self-consciousness. Later on it gradually changed again, losing its round character and finally becoming angular, compressed and immensely vigorous and confident. These changes followed a parallel course to the changes in his formal writing where the round, open hand eventually gave place to a condensed and even more vigorous one. In his ordinary handwriting, however, the change occurred a good deal earlier and was a gradual maturing of the round hand over a period of years. In his formal penmanship it came late and was a definite break.

In the end of February Lethaby made another attempt to get the class started but 'the Board' thought it too late in the season and he had to leave it over until the autumn. Meanwhile Johnston had done a small job for Fisher Unwin, the publisher, and was greatly encouraged by this because 'It makes *all* the difference in drawing or (book) writing if you have had anything printed'. He would have been astonished indeed could he have foreseen how many people in the future would try to persuade him to work for reproduction, and with how little success!

Surprisingly, this small job had come to him through his father, who had introduced him to Fisher Unwin at the National Liberal Club. Edward used to meet his father there every Wednesday evening and woe betide him if he tried to put this engagement off. On one occasion when he did so his father wrote: 'I wd. ask you in future not to put *me* off for any dam' loafer who may wish to consult you about his affairs. . . . If a man is going to give you an order and can *only* come between 6 and 7 on a Wednesday by all means throw me over . . . though why it should suit him better than the remaining 167 [hours] in the week I can't quite make out.'

Edward's attitude to his father was probably dutiful rather than affectionate, but he continued to see him regularly in London and to spend occasional week-ends with him at Kenley. Here his little half-brother, Andrew ('An'loo') or 'Tod' became his very dear friend. His devotion to the child no doubt endeared him to the mother too, and he appears to have been on good terms with her. He described his father as having been once 'rather a "dandy", a "swell" young officer in the Dragoons, and now, with all filial respect, the reverse of that to a degree that passes ordinary eccentricity. Father gives the impression that he has a wash and brush up about once a quarter—when he is at home, that is. . . . He goes every day to The National Liberal Club wearing a collar and looking fairly respectable. But he does the marketing in a large sack which he buckles round him with a great strap. He wears a pith helmet when it is hot and goes home in the evening in a cloth cap with the helmet attached by a hook to his coat! You may imagine what a curious couple Father (with a folding camp-stool hooked to his waistcoat) and my dear, serious little small brother (made *so* neat by his mother) are, when they take their walks hand in hand. . . . Curiouser and curiouser when I form a third in my oldest clothes (which you know so well)—and such a contrast to Woodford, where I am trying all the time to be respectable.'

The 'little small brother' showed a precocious brilliance, particularly in mechanical invention. He sometimes disconcerted his elders by the extent of his knowledge, as when a kindly visitor enquired 'Do you know what a saw is, my little man?' and, turning his limpid gaze upon the speaker, he asked 'Vot sort of a saw? Do 'oo mean . . .' and there followed a list of half-a-dozen different kinds of saw, fret-, hack-, cross-cut-, and so on. Edward used to predict a brilliant future for this child and say that he would 'make the name of Johnston famous' but he was killed as a fighter pilot in the first world war.

Kenley had its disadvantages, as had Woodford, but Edward longed for the country. The MacRaes had a cottage in Kent at Winkhurst Green, near to the Cowlishaws at Kiln Farm. In the summer of 1899 the cottage next door to them was empty and Edward took it for June and July, at a rent of half a crown a week. There he lived alone among the wild roses, did his own cooking and catering and set up his desk in a little empty room looking out upon a world of green.

When Uncle Johnston learned of this arrangement he at once sent Edward letters of introduction to related families in the district and told him whom it would be 'as well' to visit and something about them, including the information that 'the Barclays have got a motor carriage. They had a jolly spill with it, too!' He found some difficulty in indicating Edward's profession to his relatives. In one letter he described him as 'a mediaeval writer and illuminator', in another 'an illuminatory artist and mediaeval writer.' With a touch of pride he added 'from what the knowing ones say he has a real gift'.

The letters were never delivered. They were preserved, unopened, for fifty years but that was as far as the relationship ever got between Edward and the Barclays and the Hoares.

The First Class, 1898-1901

'This was before the country had been 'discovered', when people thought it extraordinary that Cowlishaw should live in Kent when his work was in London. Edward, however, was delighted with his little empty house with the bits of camp furniture and the washstand he made himself, the big parcels of provisions from Shoolbreds, the ducks and roses and the last, late notes of cuckoo and nightingale.

It is a nostalgic world upon which to look back, a world where anyone who liked could have a cottage for half a crown a week, where milk was twopence a pint and a fowl cost one and six-pence, and, rarest and sweetest of antiquities, where a spill from a motor carriage could be 'jolly'!

It was during this summer, on one of his visits to London, that Johnston first met Dr and Mrs Robert Bridges. He was given an introduction to them by one of the MacInneses, no doubt because of their interest in handwriting. Mrs Bridges had already written a manual on this subject, which was much in advance of its time. Johnston formed a very warm friendship with them, particularly with Robert Bridges, for whom he retained a great affection and esteem all his life, although they met rarely in later years. Both the Bridges took a keen interest in his work and, soon after this first meeting, Bridges gave him Maunde Thompson's *Greek and Latin Palaeography* and advised him to study half uncials. He did so and became so much fascinated that, for the next six or seven years, he used a hand based upon them. In July of this year—a few weeks after his first meeting with Bridges—he noted in his diary that he was experimenting with cutting pens and 'Studying Kells writing with a view to further assimilation with half uncials'. All his life he regarded the Book of Kells and the Durham Book as the greatest glories of calligraphy, even long after he had abandoned the use of his early round hand that derived from them.

During this summer Edward was commissioned by his much-loved uncle, Miles MacInnes, to write out the wedding service in the form of a small book for the marriage of Neil's brother, John. (He later made a similar book for Neil's marriage, also.)

[95]

He seems to have written it at the cottage and it was received with enthusiasm by the MacInnes family. At the Arts and Crafts Exhibition that year he showed this and another marriage service, also his *Nut-Browne Maide* and a *Pater Noster*. This was the first time his work had been publicly shown, an occasion which he must have found the more inspiring because it included a memorial exhibition of the work of William Morris. Apart from this there was little calligraphy. Cowlishaw exhibited some pages of his richly illuminated *Aucassin and Nicolette*[1] and there were a few other illuminations in which writing was of secondary importance.

Johnston must have made remarkable progress with his writing, for in July of this year, only ten months after he began to study at the British Museum, even the stern Sydney Cockerell pronounced him qualified. 'I am happy to congratulate you on having passed beyond the experimental stage,' he wrote, 'and reached a degree of accomplishment that would not discredit a first rate mediaeval scribe.'

Lethaby had at last succeeded in putting through his project for a lettering class at the Central School and on September 21, 1899, with seven students, Johnston held his first class.

Although he had made such rapid progress in the past year he still felt that 'it was rather cheek of me to be teaching instead of learning' and he did so with 'some fear and trepidation'. This was probably the first class of its kind ever to be held, the parent of all those classes in lettering which appear in the curriculum of so many art schools today. Although on the Continent Rudolf von Larisch and Rudolf Koch both subsequently appear to have started independent schools of calligraphy, almost all such classes in England and many abroad are taught by Johnston's students or their students.

Johnston's notes for his first class read: '*Writing and Illuminating*—A practically lost art worth reviving—MSS the matter for illumination, therefore writing the main point—The qualities of good writing—Readableness, Beauty, Character—Materials,

[1]Plate XXIII in *Writing and Illuminating and Lettering*.

[96]

Blackboard at Dresden after Johnston's lecture (p. 186) 1912. Actual size 11′2″ × 4′8″

Toy shop made by Johnston for one of his children, *c.* 1914
(Actual size $6'' \times 5\frac{3}{4}'' \times 4\frac{1}{2}''$)

The First Class, 1898-1901

Parchment (skins), Pens (quills), Inks (Indian). *Preparation.* Estimating, cutting, cleaning, "pouncing"—cutting pen, form and manner. Ink (soln.) Practice for copies (rough) Ditto (careful).' The words 'rough' and 'careful' are crossed out and 'written pages' is written in, in pencil. Later he discouraged 'practice' altogether and even at this early date he seems to have been moving towards that position, preferring 'written pages' to odd scribbling. 'Handling pen—feel the point, free strokes (no pressure, no drawing or "filling in").'

An undated sheet, written about the same time, seems to be the beginning of fuller notes for the same occasion. It reads: 'In this class an attempt to revive, practically, the almost forgotten crafts of Writer and Illuminator. . . . To justify the bringing to life of a sleeping craft it is only necessary to show that, when awakened, it will be beautiful and useful. Morris, who was a writer and illuminator before he was a painter, has shown us how beautiful modern illuminated writing may be and how in every case the *method* is to be sought in the old work and inspiration is to be found in nature.

'The ordinary illuminated address is impossible chiefly because the writing in it has for long been suppressed and distorted, because it is, in fact, "Illumination" *with some lettering*, not, as it ought to be, a page of writing decorated. The poverty of modern type is mainly due to its having wandered far from its foundation—writing.'

The class was held at the old Central School in Upper Regent Street. This building was a kind of improvisation consisting of two houses joined together by a dilapidated conservatory, full of odd corners, creaking wooden staircases and small rooms packed as full as they could hold with eager students. Over it all presided Lethaby who had brought it into being and who must have filled it with an extraordinary sense of unity, for all, staff and students alike, were united in their love for him. His staff, it was said, never felt that they were working *under* him, but *with* him. Even the students felt themselves to be pioneers taking part in an exciting experiment.

G
[97]

The First Class, 1898-1901

Recalling that old building many years later, after the school had· removed to new premises, Johnston jotted down in a note-book: 'More is necessary to man than the bare necessaries (of life). . . . Perhaps the first of these (under God) is Accident. Thinking of loss of interest in new L.C.C. Central School *although* specially built—apart from Lethaby's leaving—and decided the New aimed at little more than necessary cubic air space and strength—all controlled by expenditure of time and money definitely limited. The old school was comparatively accidentally built. The New was built "without interest". The old had it by accident. Difference between early and late buildings that early builders built so that they had happy accidents or they allowed (or in some way encouraged) them in detail.'

Johnston's students had every reason to regard themselves as pioneers. There was no question of his playing the expert; he told them how little he knew and how much there was to dis-cover and enlisted their help. 'I can claim only to have given, at that early date, a working basis for my students,' he wrote, 'and to have suggested some ways in which they might experiment for themselves.' Together they were a little band of explorers in unknown country. He was the leader of the expedition but as much of an explorer as the rest.

Johnston's goal at this time—even more, perhaps, than to establish himself—was to establish *the craft*. He envisaged a sort of guild of calligraphers, all studying, experimenting and making discoveries which they would then all share. His students were thus somewhat in the position of apprentices being trained up to become the guild of his dreams. The attitude of the staff to the principal was echoed in the attitude of these students to their master: they were working *with* him, not *under* him. They, too, were inspired by devotion.

Noel Rooke, then hardly more than a boy, was in that first class and has left a vivid account of it. 'At the first sight of him,' he says of Johnston, 'although his hands could be seen to be capable, sensitive and strong, the general impression was one of lassitude, of physical strength drained right out. Then he spoke. The clearness and vigour of his mind came as a shock, a delight.'

He speaks of his 'exceptional courtesy' and of the humour that was never far away, then continues: 'When he settled down to work with one student one could no longer hear him but had all the more leisure to look at him, or at any rate at his back. He wore a brown tweed jacket, cloth and cut superb, of quality suppressed by the first world war and not revived. Out of the side pockets would emerge, as required, scissors, knives, pliers, strips of tin, magnifying-glasses, slabs of ivory, sometimes a neatly wiped and scrupulously clean little oil-stone; memory struggles with even a small plane about twice the size of a violin-maker's thumb plane. It was a great pleasure, years later, to see the same jacket on duty in the garden at Ditchling, carrying the additional equipment—screwdrivers and so on—needed to adjust a water-clock he constructed to open the door of his hen-house automatically and punctually at dawn.

'As he worked his way round the class to the student next door, the apparent impassivity of manner revealed itself to be an aloofness from immediate surroundings, a concentration on the subject already in possession of his mind. *That* had to be considered from every point of view attainable. During the first stage of analysis his mind showed scrupulous severity of examination, with no intervals for breathing. I have become aware of a similar concentrated unrelaxed intensity of attention on the bridge of a ship at night, when a group of officers had been peering into the darkness for what seemed a long time watching for the first distant gleam of a lighthouse which was to be their landfall and a deflecting point for the ship's course. When teaching he, as they, felt a responsibility for life and fortune; he, too, once the course to be laid was clear, showed a slight change of demeanour. His discussion became full of zest and humour and wit. . . . Although the students of his later years had the great advantage of learning from his mature experience, they also missed an advantage which was probably even greater; for by then he was moving along courses which he already knew,

[99]

and about which he had made up his mind; so they did not have the advantage of watching the first stage, and of seeing the change come over him.

'One soon learnt that whatever subject was once started it would not be relinquished for any other. . . . He was a man it was impossible to distract, so if there were several points one wished to raise it was important to choose the most important and get it started, as a second or third might never be reached in the time available.

'Another lesson one had learned early was the supreme value of his high and wide preliminary surveys, which related the subject to its position in heaven and earth. . . .

'At the beginning of perhaps his third term of teaching he announced that on each of the three next meetings of his weekly class he would give a half-hour talk on the characteristics of the individual letters of the Roman alphabet on the Trajan Column. In practice each talk prolonged itself to an hour or more and by the twelfth talk, at the end of term, he was beginning on the letter *C*. Those twelve evenings on the letters *A* and *B*, after more than forty-five years, are still an active ingredient in the life of the present speaker.'

The class was at seven in the evening. Johnston would arrive anything up to twenty minutes late and continue sometimes long after the official time for the class to end. His concentration was such that time ceased to exist for him and he would be shocked, on coming to the surface, to find how much of it had passed while he was away. There was a hush of expectancy, Rooke says, when the students were awaiting his entrance: 'The respect and affection felt for him in that small class was indescribable.' Rooke succumbed to the spell which Johnston was so supremely unaware of casting. So, also, did a twenty-year-old architectural student, a callow, eager boy from the provinces whose name was Gill.

'The first time I saw him writing,' Eric Gill recorded long afterwards, 'and saw the writing that came as he wrote, I had that thrill and tremble of the heart which otherwise I can only remember having had. . . .' There follows a list of occasions of outstanding enlightenment or bliss, a view of the North Transept at Chartres, hearing the plain-chant at Louvain or first seeing his beloved with her hair down. '. . . On these occasions I was caught unprepared, I did not know such beauties could exist. I was struck as by lightning, as by a sort of enlightenment. There are many other things as good . . . but these more sudden enlightenments are rare events, never forgotten, never overlaid. On that evening I was thus rapt. It was no mere dexterity that thus transported me; it was as though a secret of heaven were being revealed.'

Every week more students came. 'How the class grows!' wrote Aunty, and Cadenhead, delighted at his friend's success, told him 'You begin to have a past, a fair guarantee of a future. You are seen to be one of a few. You will not have to go to people, they will come to you. And now, with a class, you will have direct personal influence, and few will make better use of that than you. *Formez vos bataillons!'*

The class at the Central School was such a success that a few months later Johnston found himself with a second, at Camberwell School of Art. Among his students at the Central School in the early years, as well as Noel Rooke and Eric Gill, were Florence Kingsford (afterwards Lady Cockerell and famed for her illuminations), Emery Walker's daughter, Laurence Christie and Graily Hewitt. Hewitt was a solicitor with chambers in Lincoln's Inn who found no satisfaction in his profession and longed for some more congenial work. Cockerell had advised him to join the class and he showed such an aptitude for the work that he rapidly became Johnston's best pupil.

During the second term a very unexpected student appeared, a considerably older man with an established reputation in the world of the arts and crafts. This was T. J. Cobden-Sanderson of the Doves Bindery, in Hammersmith, who had bound the Kelmscott books for Morris. He brought his young son and daughter with him to the class. Johnston recalled one evening when 'he sat beside me watching me write, with his son beside him. He said, in a characteristically whimsical way: "It is like watching some strange bird" (to the embarrassment of his son, who said in a loud whisper, "Don't, Daddy, don't!"). . . . He probably always regarded me as "*some strange bird*", with a kind of affectionate and amused appreciation: a feeling which I paid him back, under reverence.'

At this time Cobden-Sanderson was full of his plans for starting the Doves Press, in partnership with Emery Walker, and had ideas of 'an associated scriptorium' and of finding work for Johnston that might link him with their new venture. Cobden-Sanderson was an idealist and dreamer, linking everything with a mystical cosmology with which Johnston must have been greatly in sympathy, up to a point. (Johnston, however unorthodox, was profoundly Christian, which Cobden-Sanderson was not.) It must, at any rate, have provided an inexhaustible fund of material for those nocturnal discussions which so often caused Johnston's friends to miss their last buses home.

By way of starting the 'scriptorium' Cobden-Sanderson commissioned Johnston to write out his tract, *The Book Beautiful*, and sent him a copy. Johnston started to read it when he was going to bed and became so enthralled that he stood where he was, half undressed, and read right on to the end. He then sat down and poured out his enthusiasm in a letter to the author. In this letter there occurs the first reference to his idea of writing a book on lettering. If he should do so, 'some day', he says, he would like to use the tract as an introduction. This was no passing enthusiasm, for many years later he said 'I suppose no one has ever written with such insight, or so eloquently, of *The Book Beautiful* and this brief, comprehensive vision might well be taken to heart by all honest printers'.

Under Cobden-Sanderson's influence, with the Doves Press just starting and the air vibrating with the excitement of his idealistic schemes and Emery Walker's more sober ones, Johnston too became fired with enthusiasm for printing. In the back of his mind there was an uneasy feeling that calligraphy was not a sufficiently 'practical' craft and that 'its natural and practical development must take shape in printing'. As he watched the setting up of the Doves Press at 1, Hammersmith Terrace he could not resist toying with the thought of having a press of his own. With his immensely thorough attitude to everything he did he decided that the way to go about printing would be to learn first to cut punches and then to set up type. He consulted Cobden-Sanderson who eagerly entered into the idea and promised to ask Emery Walker. Walker was the expert and he brought these flights of fancy sharply down to earth. 'I have spoken to Mr Walker about the punch cutting,' wrote Cobden-Sanderson, in his cryptic hand, 'and also about "compositing" at No 1, and am sorry to find he does not take an encouraging view of our hopes in either respect.' Walker had said firmly that punch cutting was hard work and a full time job and also that a part-time compositor would be no use to them at the press. 'Walker, however, admits that though it may not be desirable for the calligraphist to be a student or *practitioner* in punch cutting, it *is* desirable the other way, viz. that the punch cutter should be a student of calligraphy.' The letter is signed with the four parallel lines a little off the vertical, which, to the initiated, stood for the letters T.J.C.S. (Lessons in calligraphy seem not to have influenced his ordinary handwriting.)

In September of that year (1900) Edward went to North Berwick with his family and from there to Rickerby one fateful week-end, to visit Neil MacInnes. He once described in a letter a typical arrival at Rickerby: 'Hansom dashes up with a hollow sound on the stones under the portico. Uncle Miles hurries up fingering his waistcoat pockets and extends a cordial hand to the arrival—E.J. Neil marches up and says "Bravo!" and the hall fills with pleasant folk. Dora sails forward . . . Dora—in Dora's own most singular, nice voice—"Oh, there is Edward" and shakes hands. . . . Then Aunt Effie with uplifted hand, giving benediction to the air, glides majestically, swathed in filmy shawls, and pats E.J. on the shoulder and says "*Dear* boy!" '

On this particular occasion, however, his arrival was more informal. He was bicycling and very dusty and arrived to find the house quiet and most of the party out. Aunt Effie, however, was there to receive him and there was one other guest, a friend of her daughter Dora's, to whom she introduced him.

This guest was Greta[1] Greig, a Scottish girl who had been at school with Dora in Paris and had afterwards studied music at Leipzig, read history at Oxford and was now a schoolmistress. She was vivacious and entertaining and welcomed everyone she met with sincere friendliness and interest. This and her warm, beautiful voice gave her a charm which won her devoted friends wherever she went. She had heard of the cousin who did such interesting work and of the beautiful book he had made for John's wedding. Her researches in mediaeval history had taught her something about early manuscripts and she was eager to hear about his work. They talked uninterruptedly all evening. From his work they passed on to other things: Chaucer, the ballads, *Pelleas and Melisande*.

That night Greta said to Dora 'I like Mr Johnston so much'. 'I am so glad,' Dora answered, but she must have been rather startled when Greta added 'I like him more than any man I ever met'. She was not a young girl, to be swept away by sudden fancies. Dora knew her to be capable, independent, level-headed. Yet her next remark was even more surprising: 'If I had to marry someone tomorrow—like women in books—and could choose, I would choose him.'

But the week-end came to an end and Mr Johnston went back to North Berwick and thence to London to resume his classes in the autumn session. There seemed no reason why they should ever meet again. When Greta returned to work she was near London and spending every week-end there with her sister. There she was in London and there was he, but they did not meet. His image 'kept alive in her heart and strengthened her faith in humanity'. Just to know that he existed made her overwhelmingly glad, but something more was needed to bring them together. She could not, for the moment, think what to do.

The following spring Edward rented half of the MacRaes'

[1]Pronounced 'Gretta'.

double cottage and spent the Easter vacation working there. He
had a lot on hand and foresaw too many interruptions in Edinburgh. He wrote to Aunty: 'A number of things which ought to
be finished as soon as possible make it better that I should not go
North this time. These I could not attend to at 3 M.C.[1] and it is
a worry to have them dragging on'—a worry from which, alas,
he was never to be free—'One is my *Studio* article and specimens
of writing, the other (quite new but to be seen to at once), is
experimental work in connection with lettering in colour some
of Mr Cobden-Sanderson's printed Books. I think of going to my
cott. probably tomorrow and there I shall be able to work
quietly while getting a change. The MRs will be at their cott.
next door.' There follows a sketch of the cottage.

On March 21 Cobden-Sanderson had written: 'Last Monday
night Edward Johnston supped with me and we discussed initials
for the 12 Books of *Paradise Lost*.' This was the first of many jobs
for the Doves Press. Johnston designed initials and headings to
be cut in wood by Eric Gill and Noel Rooke and also rubricated
books by hand, writing in coloured initials and flourishes. Later
he objected on principle to designing for other craftsmen and
refused to do so, holding that only an engraver could properly
design an engraving, but at this time he had not thought such
things out as thoroughly as he did afterwards.

This work for the Doves Press does not seem to have got
beyond the experimental stage for another year, for in June 1902,
a year later, Cobden-Sanderson wrote: 'Last night I received
from Edward Johnston the completion of my design for the first
page of the Bible and am delighted. "In the beginning" with a
long *I*. And on Tuesday he came to the Bindery and made a lovely
drawing of the letters for *Paradise Lost*, First Book, so now we are
really on the way.' The title and author were to be given at the
head of the first page of *Paradise Lost* and the original idea seems
to have been that Johnston should write them by hand in each
copy. Perhaps experiment revealed what a formidable undertaking this would be, for the plan was changed. A wood-block

[1] 3 Merchiston Crescent, Edinburgh.

[105]

was made from Johnston's design and the heading printed from it in red.

The year 1901 was immensely eventful for Johnston. In May two important things happened. He started his classes at the Royal College of Art in South Kensington, where he was to teach for the rest of his life, and he received a truly magnificent commission.

G. B. Gabb, a surgeon living in Hastings, had married a cousin of Edward's. She had died young and Mr Gabb wanted to present something to their church, Holy Trinity, as a memorial to her. He accordingly commissioned Johnston to write out the Communion Service. The terms of the agreement were that he was to 'make the most gorgeous book within his power' and ask for money whenever he wanted it. A young calligrapher's most high-flown dreams could hardly have bettered such a commission.

Mrs Gabb's family were the cousins whom Edward saw least. One reason for this may be conjectured from the following note, written by Mr Gabb, many years later: 'My mother-in-law, Mrs Wilson, was Edward Johnston's aunt so I early knew much of the *very clever* (but on the eccentric side) young nephew. . . . I know well that E.J.'s father was voted quite unusual and odd (she had no use for anything out of the common) by his sister, my mother-in-law.'

The inauguration of a lettering class at the Royal College of Art was no doubt due to the influence of Lethaby who had become professor of design there shortly before. Conditions were very different from those at the Central School. 'I have a very big room,' wrote Johnston, 'with a great blackboard worked by pulleys, and a platform with a railing, where I stand or sit and look down on the 17 embryo scribes below.' This letter contains a sketch showing him writing the *Pater Noster* on the blackboard. Below his dais are backs of heads marked 'admiring students'.

The following term he wrote: 'Yesterday I had a rather surprising and elating experience at S.K. I did a large piece of writing and decoration on the board, explaining the work step by step, and then summed up my remarks and laid down (expounding) one of the chief principles. The students *applauded* me as I came down from my "pulpit"! A thing that has not happened to me before: I imagine it is rather "out of order". Of course what made it so refreshing was its being entirely spontaneous . . . and a proof of the class's appreciation of what I had been (and *have* been for long) trying to explain to them.'

In another letter soon afterwards he says 'I had to swallow an egg and rush to S. Kensington. Applause is beginning to pall—they made it on Monday and again yesterday—besides, I think the real reason may be that they are glad I have finished. As the famous Scotchman shouted at the end of a song "Ongcore, ongcore, we'll hae no more o' that!"'

'I found 17 totally new students on Monday evening, to my horror, so I told them that I only accepted them provisionally, as both the classes were reduced and they might all have to go. Then I tore up "Butter paper" into a pile of fragments and told them to help themselves to "notebooks" and then I took them through the development of letters in *two* hours! For me, I spoke fairly fluently but I was not feeling very happy and I found myself saying heaps of semi-cynical things—which fortunately they didn't seem to notice—and then when it was over they rejoiced with their hands.'

These classes were, from the start, a great strain on him and made Monday a day to dread. There were two sessions with a break between and by the time they were over he was completely exhausted, so much so that it took him most of the next day to recover and he was accustomed to count Tuesday out as well as Monday in estimating the working hours in a week. Another factor which increased the strain was that, despite his efforts to keep the classes to a manageable size, the numbers were continually increasing. His habit of procrastination and his inability to judge times made matters worse. He would leave everything till the last minute and then 'swallow an egg and rush'. This rushing tired and harassed him more than anything else because it was so foreign to his nature. Again, he would leave the jellygraphing of his class-sheets until late on the previous day and stay up half the night doing them. These were sheets of sample alphabets which, for the first eight or nine years, formed a regular part of his teaching. He reproduced them himself—perhaps profiting by what he had learnt in Uncle Johnston's office—and he describes in one letter how he worked on them the night before a class, standing for hour after hour taking prints until he was so exhausted that he fell onto his bed and was asleep before he could get undressed. Later he published a portfolio of sample alphabets based upon these class-sheets, which relieved him of the arduous task of reproducing them by hand.

At the Royal College Johnston was no longer the leader of a band of explorers but the lecturer set apart, above them. The larger classes also made the contact less personal and this was intensified by the fact that the students were nearly all working for diplomas and giving a strictly limited amount of time to the subject as a routine part of their curriculum. There could be no question of spending twelve classes on the letters *A* and *B* when the students were scheduled to reach *Z* by a given date. In the early years, however, conditions may have been more elastic and one account of the early classes at the College does give a delightful impression of improvisation and unconventionality.

This account was given by Anna Simons, a remarkable young Prussian woman who came to England to study because women students were not admitted in Prussian art schools of the period. She was one of the best students Johnston ever had and certainly one of those who exercised the greatest influence afterwards, for she disseminated his teaching throughout Germany where it was perhaps more fruitful, even, than in England.

She says of these early classes at the College that 'To his uncials and half uncials he very soon added—much to the chagrin of his first pupils who thought they had learnt all there was to learn—slanted pen-forms adapted from a 10th Century Winchester MS'. (This was an early appearance of the 'Foundational' hand, which later became the principal hand he taught and used.) 'These were joined in time by built-up Versals and Roman

High dwelleth not in houses made
with hands; as saith the prophet,

The heaven is my
    throne,
And the earth the foot-
    stool of my feet:
What manner of house
    will ye build me?
    saith the Lord:
Or what is the place of
    my rest?
Did not my hand make
    all these things?

Acts, vij, 44-50.

Uncials from *A Book of Sample Scripts*. Black. 1914. Reduced capitals . . . and, later still, by Roman small letters and simple written capitals and italics based on Renaissance forms.'

She also tells us that they used reed pens and that 'a strip of cane such as used for cane chairs was inserted to hold the ink. Later on, when the college chairs gave out and were replaced by all-wood ones, thin strips of metal cut from tin cigarette boxes were substituted.' Was it just a coincidence that the cane chairs 'gave out' at this time, or are we to suppose that they were torn to pieces by an over-enthusiastic lettering class? Probably the explanation is that the chairs were already so dilapidated that strips of cane were hanging from them, waiting to be reincarnated as the springs of pens. If so then this certainly was a 'happy accident' worthy of the old Central School!

VI

Greta, 1901

Edward's situation in the spring of 1901 was one that any young man might have envied. He had come a long way in the three years since his introduction to Lethaby. Indeed he had been spectacularly successful. Already he had gone far towards achieving his aim of reviving the craft. He had keen and crowded classes at the Central School, Camberwell and the Royal College and now provincial art schools were becoming interested. The first of these was Birmingham, soon followed by Leicester. To Johnston's great satisfaction the first of his students had graduated to the position of teacher and a second weekly class was started at the Central School under Graily Hewitt. Above all, orders were coming in. The Hastings book alone bid fair to keep him so busy that other orders must be passed on to Hewitt.

Yet it was of this time that he said 'I was almost in despair about myself.'

Despair is the last word one would associate with this world of beginnings, of earnest hopes and eager aspirations, but for him it was there. It was partly his very success that was to blame. The more classes there were, the more orders, the more business to deal with and letters to write, the more tired he became. His physique and his character together constituted a burden that at times was almost insupportable. He was the hardest task-master that any man could have had, temperamentally incapable of skimping a job or making do with something less than the best.

Greta, 1901

Things had to be done perfectly or not at all and so more and more things were put on one side to be dealt with 'when he felt up to it'. If someone wrote to him with some technical question he could either spend a couple of days on an answer as lengthy, detailed and painstaking as though it had been an article for publication, or he could leave the letter unanswered. He knew of no middle way. The burden of things to be done, and to be done with such minute accuracy, such infinite pains, really weighed him down.

He would feel 'slack', spend half the morning in bed, get up intending to attempt some work, become involved with the newspaper and lose all contact with time. The bell for lunch would arouse him. Afterwards he would have a smoke and a read and it would be nearly tea-time when he resolved to make a start on a certain job. (Starting was always a nerve-racking business and one, therefore, that he was especially tempted to postpone. Long after he was established he confessed that he always suffered from 'a sort of panic' when beginning a manuscript.) First he would look for the letter giving details of the commission. He would search the mantelpiece, looking through the jumble of letters behind the tins of pencil-ends and drawing-pins and rubber bands, behind the bottles and pots of glue. Failing to find it there, or on the table or the window-sills, he would next search in his pockets among the sealing wax and crusts and tobacco. After that there would be nothing for it but to tackle the chaos inside his desk and begin to 'sort'. He used to say that he was an exceptionally orderly person, a claim which anyone who had seen his workroom found it difficult to take seriously. None the less, in a sense, it was true. He was *ideally* so tidy, with a special place devised for everything, special systems of filing and the rest, that it was impossible for him to live up to his own high level and, because he would never make do with a second best, he would let things pile up awaiting a time when he should be able to sort them 'properly'—a time which never came.

So he would spend the evening in sorting his desk and in the end one of his bachelor friends would turn up and they would go

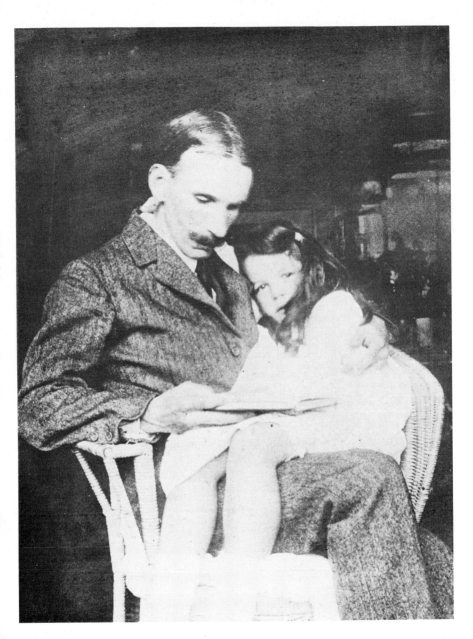

Edward and Priscilla Johnston in 1916.

ONCE UPON A TIME there was a little girl whose name was Ula: she lived with her Grandmother in a cottage at the foot of a hill on which a great forest rose up toward the sky.

Her Grandmother had a little money laid by, and they managed to live well, and happily too, with the help of some chickens, who lined the egg basket every day with white and brown, and a cow, who not only

7

She lived with her Grandmother in a cottage at the foot of a hill

'Ula and the Rabbit: A Fairytale for Priscilla' Written and illustrated by Johnston, 1918. Reduced

out to dinner together. At eleven he would return to his search, then remember an urgent letter left unanswered. He would deal with it and go out to the midnight post, his footsteps echoing through the silent square with its nocturnal jungle of trees and shadows locked in behind the railings. Climbing the stairs again and confronting his room, which had congealed in his absence into an appearance of petrified and irremediable disorder, he would reflect that one more day had slipped through his fingers. Then he would be assailed by something like despair, seeing himself going on like that for ever, snowed under by all the things he had left undone and too tired to fight his way out. Thus, he thought, he misused the gifts of God, showing himself unworthy because again and again he failed to make use of them. What was the use of resolving to do better when the end was always the same? He saw himself as 'a bundle of laziness, ill tempers, conceits and animal desires' with a 'rather wayward' heart, that 'longs so to be good'. His only comfort was in the prayer of St Simeon Stylites: 'What though I be the basest of mankind yet will I never cease to cry to God, battering the gates of Heaven with storms of prayer'. But for this and his unfailing conviction of God's mercy, he would hardly have dared to pray at all.

Then, on the last day of April, the letter came. It was quite an ordinary letter in a semi-legible scrawl, addressing him as 'Dear Mr Johnstone'—with an *e*—and reminding him that he and the writer had met once at Rickerby. It was Dora's friend, that Miss Greig, the one with the lovely voice. She had ventured to trouble him, she said, because she had a German friend visiting her who was 'very artistic' and anxious to see something of the fruits of the Arts and Crafts Movement in England. Could he advise her as to where good work could be seen?

He wrote at once offering to show them round the Central School, but there were complications and delays. The German friend suddenly decided that she must see Stratford and off they went to Warwickshire. When they got back she was almost due to leave and her enthusiasm for arts and crafts was decidedly on the

H   [113]

wane. There was so little time, she said, need they see over this school or whatever it was? To this Greta unhesitatingly replied that since Mr Johnston, whom she hardly knew, had gone to so much trouble on their behalf it would be exceedingly discourteous not to go. In fact *she* would feel obliged to do so, whether her friend did or not. Still the difficulties were not disposed of. It seemed impossible to arrange a meeting. 'You are free *till* six and I *from* six tomorrow,' she wrote to Mr Johnston, 'and next day, Saturday, my friend has to say her goodbyes as she is leaving on Monday.'

There was a will, however, and so there was a way and, whether before or after six, they did meet on that Friday evening at the Central School. From then on they never looked back. That evening initiated the lightning courtship—so astonishingly uncharacteristic—of the slow and cautious Mr Johnston.

At the Central School Greta introduced her friend and spoke of Rickerby and how they had talked there, crying out 'I remember every word you said!' That, he told her, was her Irish blarney (she had an Irish mother) but it pleased him, and the voice in which it was spoken pleased him more. It was her trustfulness that stirred him so. She seemed to confide herself to him and it felt like a sacred trust. He found himself suddenly very anxious that the school should show to advantage. When she commented that everyone in the enamelling class was Scotch like herself and said that it warmed her heart, he felt a glow of pride, as though he had been personally responsible for the students' nationalities, and rejoiced to think that he was three-quarters Scotch himself. He could not account for these feelings, they puzzled him strangely. And when she wrote to thank him and hoped that he would come and see her the following Saturday, he astonished himself by the 'daringness' of his reply: he suggested that they should go for a walk together, either at Hampstead or Kew.

They went to Kew. It was May 18, an anniversary they were long to remember. The chestnuts were in flower and the garden looked as beautiful as Eden. Edward had put on his oldest trousers, 'as a sort of test, to see if she could stand it'. She must on no account be allowed to think him better than he was, though it were only better dressed. It was as they stood under a flowering chestnut tree that it came into Edward's head that he was in love.

Afterwards they sat beside the lake and he was filled with the sense of Greta's trust in him and with it came an extraordinary peace. Because she looked to him for strength he felt the calm assurance of possessing it. She was actually a particularly independent girl, but then she had never been in love before. The capable schoolmistress had melted into the wholly feminine woman.

That night in his little attic room Edward sat writing verses about the lake at Kew and 'a new day a-dawn in two kindly grey eyes.'

Meanwhile Greta arrived exactly one hour late for a dinner engagement. As she hurried through the light spring evening and heard the birds in the London gardens pouring out their hearts she was gasping and out of breath for more reasons than one. Not only her own world but heaven, too, had come tumbling about her ears.

Next morning she received a letter from him, posted at midnight. He could not tell her, he said, what she had done for him, but perhaps some day he would try.

She answered him 'Your letter was of a sort to make me wish myself a better woman' and asked if she might go round and see his work. So she went to Vernon Place and found his little room 'stamped with his character' and with a feeling of 'peace and purity'.

She told him that his earnestness frightened her and made her feel that another person's life was far too complicated a thing to interfere with and it was better to keep right out of the way and remain safe and solitary. But already, of course, it was too late for that; things moved at such a pace. She had hardly got her breath again after the shock of his addressing her by her Christian name when she found him kissing her in a hansom. She was abashed, but he won a smile from her by gravely apologising for his lack of proficiency, explaining that it was because he 'had had so very little practice'.

Greta, 1901

Before Greta left London, in the middle of June, they were engaged. They had not met above half a dozen times but that did not trouble them in the least. To them the miracle was that they had met at all. It had taken them nearly thirty years to find each other but now that they had they both knew with certainty that this was what they had been waiting for.

Greta left London in a dream of happiness. 'Your face came between me and the fields and trees,' she wrote, 'and I sat smiling and lost my umbrella and smiled on! I felt safe and happy and far from all worries about umbrellas or anything else.'

She had gone to Wales to examine schools in French and she wrote him a delightful account of her travels, of the strange hotels with doors that would not shut and other people's belongings in the bedroom, and the inn 'furnished mostly with stuffed birds' and the inn 'furnished mostly with oilcloth'. Then there was the ever-memorable occasion when the chambermaid showed her to a room saying firmly 'You are the new young lady for the bar'. There was also the dreadful Griffin where 'I blandly confronted the Griffin's wife who regarded me with a hostile gaze and said ''We do not usually take single ladies'', and then ''Can you give me a card?'' I looked her straight in the eyes and smiled, ''No, I can't'' I said.' The she-Griffin was won over and thereafter became 'so polite that I don't know how to bear it'. Greta fled to the mountains and lay in the bracken listening to the birds and feeling that Edward's love was all about her so that neither time nor place could take it away.

She told him, too, of the children, describing them with loving sympathy. She had feared that they might be afraid of their examiner, 'though it's only *me*, if they knew!' but when she asked the little ones if they were frightened they said they had been, before they saw her, 'but not *now*'. 'All the children in Cardiff smile at me now,' she said, 'and the boys take their caps off in rows.'

She described climbing a mountain in a thunderstorm and how the lightning seemed to play round her and she 'came leaping down feeling as if St Michael and all angels were attending on me and nothing could hurt me'. Edward, with his childhood fear of thunder, was filled with admiration and longed to stand on a mountain in a storm with her. 'I feel such an accession of strength because you are on my side,' he said. 'It makes me feel quite breathless when I think how narrow the chance seemed that we met and talked at Rickerby.' Surely she was a messenger from heaven sent to 'heal his life' so that it might be made to be of some use.

Her view of him was very different from his own. To her, his *goodness* seemed his outstanding quality. 'I never thought I should fall in love with someone for his goodness,' she said, but so it had been. He grew really worried by her talk of his goodness and felt that at all costs he must disillusion her or he would be marrying her under false pretences. 'It would be strange indeed,' she said at last, 'if you "led me to think.I am loving a good man" seeing how hard you have laboured to produce a contrary impression! . . . You torment yourself needlessly, I am sure, because your life is spent to a great extent alone and you brood over things.'

She never succeeded in making him see himself differently and years afterwards he was heartened by the words of the Reverend W. H. Elliott: 'You may be clever and know it but you cannot be good and know it.'

'It makes me feel ashamed indeed to hear you speak as if I might ever dare to try to make you better,' Greta said once. 'I can't try to make anybody better, I try to make them happier and think it the best I can do for them. Remember that I am dreadfully proud of you and think you the strongest man I know.' To making him happier she was prepared to dedicate her life, but she was not to be coerced into trying to make him better, though several of his relatives felt that this ought to be her mission. She had seen the sorrow in his face and she wrote to him from Wales: 'It wouldn't matter what you ever cost me or what I suffered because of you. I should still be thankful I had ever known you, and a little proud, too, of having seen so soon. I feel as if my life would not be wasted if I could make good to you one bitter hour . . . the world is transfigured which was always beautiful to me, and I live above it because you put me there.'

By the time she returned from Wales his term was ended and they went North together. She took him to her home at Laurence-kirk, near Aberdeen, which she had already described to him as 'lying between the green ridge of Garvock, which hides us from the sea, and the Grampians behind. If you climb Garvock to the old tower you can follow the coast for miles and miles and in the evening floating, enchanted islands appear and the sea is wonderful and golden at your feet. Behind you see the great valley stretching south and Loch na Gar and Battock and Cloch na Ben. Oh, it hurts me to say it, I love it so!'

The Greigs were a very united family. James Greig was a banker, a staunch supporter of Gladstone and a pillar of almost every institution in the neighbourhood. His wife was from County Down and it was from her that Greta got her liveliness and humour. Wife of an eminently respectable bank manager she might be, but when greeted in the High Street with 'How are you, dear Mrs Greig?' she had been known to answer in broad Irish 'Sober, and sorry for it!'

They had five children of whom Greta was the eldest. She had a reputation for gaiety and humour and for making any party a success, but on this occasion her sisters complained that they could get no sense from her at all. She sat in a dream gazing out of the window until someone uttered the magic name that intersected with her thoughts like a key with a lock. In spite of this they took Edward to their bosoms unreservedly. Mr Greig deplored his financial position and his eccentricity, the incalculable nature of his work and the vagueness of his plans. His practised eye could no doubt tell at a glance that Edward not only had no money but never would have any, but that same glance would also discern his transparent integrity. It was almost impossible for people not to like him, except perhaps, occasionally, when they were in a hurry. He was so disarmingly genuine, he had such love for all created things and was so deeply concerned for the welfare of wasps and earwigs (he would not only rescue one from drowning but would spend half the morning in after care, helping it to rehabilitate itself). Greta introduced him to all her friends with the words 'This is Edward, isn't he a darling?' She assured him that he had great charm, particularly for women. The smile would come up into his peat-brown eyes, 'like a flower through deep water', she said. Often there was hardly more to it than that, with a little twist and tremble of the lips beneath the moustache. Her mother said that nobody could help loving him. As for her sisters, they said of a new photograph of her 'Greta's dear man likes it, so we must', as though he were now to be the arbiter even as to her true appearance. Only, later, when her beloved little brother Jim returned from the Sorbonne, he secretly thought Edward not quite good enough for his Greta. Their sister, Anne, confided to Greta 'He thinks you should have made a brilliant match.' 'But I have!' Greta answered laughing. 'His family is much better than ours and, besides, he is an angel!' 'But he has no money,' said Anne, and Greta answered 'Poof! I don't care a straw about money!'

The day before they left Laurencekirk Edward 'spoke' to his future father-in-law in the approved manner, but without greatly reassuring him. At this time he was thinking seriously about printing and told Mr Greig that he hoped to start a hand-press somewhere near Edinburgh in about two years' time and to print limited editions of classics. This, he said, he knew to be a very pleasant and paying occupation if properly conducted. There were obvious practical disadvantages to this scheme. It was not a very encouraging prospect for Greta to know that he intended to start a business in two years' time, on the eventual proceeds of which they might hope to be able to marry. There was also that clause 'if properly conducted'. To anyone who knew him it was clear that the operative word was '*if*'.

From Laurencekirk they went on to Edinburgh, where Greta was introduced to the Johnstons. She was at once drawn to Aunty and Olof by their obvious devotion to Edward. 'You are a king in your own land and it's an absolute monarchy!' she told him.

Greta, 1901

They brought out the family photographs to show her, Edward aged nine in a starched collar, and then his mother—'Quite beautiful,' she thought, 'but her great eyes are so pathetic,' and then 'How proud she must have been of you.'

Aunty waited on him hand and foot. Olof, quiet and pale, watched and listened silently with devotion in her eyes. Greta found herself puzzled and attracted by the girl. She was so like Edward and seemed in a way so much his own. Also, despite the fact that her petticoat was always showing and wisps of hair were always coming down, she did at times look so beautiful that Greta could hardly take her eyes off her. Although she was so quiet and appeared reserved she could be startlingly outspoken at times, because, like her brother, she was completely sincere. Later, when Greta spent a few days with Miles and Mary, Olof told her that she was not as nice to Edward at their house as at home and that she was 'rather all things to all men' and 'fell in with the Mary and Milesian point of view'. Such remarks must have come strangely from the timid and self-effacing girl of eighteen. Greta was impressed by her sincerity and reflected that with all her slowness and dreaminess she was certainly shrewd. For there was a certain truth in her observation, as Greta recognized. Greta was accustomed to adapt herself to the occasion and the company in a way that would have been impossible for Edward or Olof. They not only could not have done it, it would not have occurred to them to try and if it had they would have felt that they were practising a deception. Greta did enter into Miles and Mary's point of view, even when it was not in accordance with Edward's, so long as it did not diverge too far. When she felt their attitude to be actually opposed to his then she championed him, because she 'believed in his folly rather than in the wisdom of the wise'. When they congratulated her on having been the cause of a change in 'his old, absurd ideas' she replied fiercely that rather than cause him to lower his standards or abandon his ideals she would give him up altogether.

In September of this year the MacRaes gave up the house in

Greta, 1901

Vernon Place. Edward had taken a lease of some chambers in Lincoln's Inn but until they were available he stayed in a friendly boarding house. It was here that he described coming back late and tired one night from his Camberwell class: 'The Walters had very kindly left bread and butter and a teapot and everything for me so that I had only to boil the kettle and make tea, which I thoroughly enjoyed. You do not know how comfortable I make myself when I take my ease. I took my shoes off and my high collar and put my feet up and read the paper and drank three cups of (mild) tea and dawdled over it for an hour. Then I tied my shoelaces together and suspended them from a button, I wrapped some bread and butter in the *St James' Gazette* and put it in my pocket. Round the sticking out end was curled my collar, on my left arm reposed two bags of apples, while I held the candle in one hand and a great packet of valuable MSS (which I had been showing to the Camberwell folk) in the other, *à la* White Knight.'

In October came the eventful move to 16, Old Buildings, Lincoln's Inn. 'I have got Graily Hewitt's "laundress",' Edward wrote to Aunty, 'who came this morning at 7.30, heated water, woke me, made B'fast (4 slices bacon, 1 egg, 2 pieces toast, 1 bread, medium plate porridge, ¼ pint milk, tea and marmalade) also the fire was lit. So you see I shall be very comfortably started. . . . I should be very glad if you could do a beef roll with a little garlic and chillies, also if you could send the tongs and poker.'

Hewitt's laundress, Mrs Phelps, was a wonderful woman. She looked after Edward like a mother, did all manner of little things for him and once left a note to say that she had 'taken the liberty' of making him a rabbit pie. The magnificent breakfast described above initiated a connection between the Phelpses and the Johnstons that has continued ever since. Long after Mrs Phelps was dead when Edward, as an old man, appeared in the Honours List, her daughter wrote 'I wish my mother had been alive to hear it. She thought nothing was too good for Mr Johnston.'

To Greta, Edward wrote, 'Coming here seems a very important

[121]

step in my progress. . . . I want you so and then I wonder how, and if, I can get through the 2 or 3 years that divide us; it seems so long, and I am rather tired, you see. I think you will make Monday nights very beautiful to me and I shall not dread Mondays in future.' Again, a few days later, he wrote: 'The sunshine is streaming in at my window. The birds were singing in the great plane tree that seems so near that I could touch it, almost. Mrs Phelps woke me and lit the fire and made me a nice breakfast. Three years I worked at Vernon Place and only had the evening sun in summer. I used to long for it so and felt as if I were in a cave. . . . Let us wait "a little over a year" and I know heaven will send us light. And that is what we want, not mere money.'

Uncle Johnston came to visit him at Lincoln's Inn and 'I think he was pleased with the place because he was smiling all the time and said it would be great fun to be here "in chambers" for a day or two.'

By this time the news of the engagement, at first kept very quiet, was becoming known. Even Dora, who had brought them together, had guessed nothing and, when told by Greta, could hardly believe her ears. 'Edward!' she exclaimed, 'But you don't know him!' 'So I revealed to her by what strenuous efforts I had found you again.' Dora was delighted and swore they were made for each other. To Edward she wrote: 'I have just heard an astounding and delightful piece of news. You are a very fortunate man, Edward, for there are very few like her—she ennobles everything she touches.'

Neil, too, wrote charmingly to Greta: 'I flatter myself I know something of dear old Edward and I have always been drawn to him as one of the most lovable and truest characters I know. I congratulate you with all my heart, you have won my dearest friend.'

Uncle Johnston's comment was: 'There are two things I like about this engagement—she's not too young and not an outsider.' In other words, she was vouched for by Rickerby. He then revealed the horrid fear that had first leapt to his mind: *it might have been a girl from one of the classes!*

Greta, 1901

All the relations were delighted with Greta. They had feared that the unpractical Edward would choose some aesthete with a mind set on higher things. 'Rickerby has been quite excited!' Edward wrote to Aunty. 'I never knew I had such friends. Aunt Grace says "It is seldom one hears of an engagement in which one can so heartily congratulate *both* parties". Aunt Isa remembers travelling with Greta and says she loved her then. Aunt Pris sends £5. . . .' and so on. 'It is beautiful that everyone thinks we were made for each other', he commented to Greta. 'We thought so and you see we must be right.'

There was only one real objection to Greta, from the family point of view. Edward broke it to Aunt Pris as gently as he could, saying that after all she might get over it, but the fact was she did not *really* care for cats. Aunt Pris took it very well, saying only '*None* of the husbands and wives have, we must not expect it of outsiders.'

Apart from this the relations were wholeheartedly delighted. Never, never, with all their affection for Edward, had they credited him with so much sense. Then, with a great, unanimous sigh of relief, they thought 'Ah! *Now* there will be someone to take him in hand.'

At about the same time his bachelor friends were thinking bitterly, 'Now I suppose Johnston will be *all tidied up!*'

They were mistaken. 'I'm going to be his wife, not his governess!' Greta said.

When Aunt Johnston scolded Edward for his lack of common sense he suggested that there might be something to be said for *un*common sense. He might have calligraphic sense. She dismissed this as mere quibbling and urged him 'to seek common sense and ensue it, to *choose* it.' Whereupon he answered 'I have, I've chosen Greta' and Aunt was silenced. She had to concede his point. Greta, thank goodness, had common sense and she, Aunt, would enlighten her upon how it should be used, when she could get her to herself.

When the time came, however, the interview did not go according to plan. Aunt had done no more than touch upon her nephew's many failings when Greta rose to her feet and, observing with unmistakable finality, 'I have every confidence in Edward', left the room.

'You *are* practical,' she told him, now passionately partisan, 'and where you cease to be so you must follow your star.'

None the less it was a real problem. No one was more aware of Edward's peculiar difficulties than he was himself and he, more than anyone else, counted upon her somehow to put them right. Over and over again in his letters comes the refrain: 'It will be all right when I have you.'

What actually happened was that she left him to go his own way with an absolute minimum of interference.

At the beginning she made some attempt to introduce certain reforms. She tried to persuade him to do such things as going to bed earlier, getting up at a (relatively) reasonable hour, working regularly and taking more exercise. He agreed with her in theory, but in practice every case was a special case. She could not scold him; there had been too much scolding in the past and he felt the world against him. She was determined that he should be able to regard her with absolute confidence as the one person who could be relied upon never to scold, always to understand. In one of her earliest letters she had said to him 'I ought to scold you but I can't. You are like a child who takes one's hand so confidingly and one couldn't say anything even if there were reasons (marmalade, for instance! I have had *such* experience of it!).'

Inevitably there were occasions when she was driven to make something like a stand and even to blame him, but he was too nervous, too sensitive for such treatment. He would be haggard, white-faced, sleepless: it was all too painful to be allowed to recur. In the end the one overriding necessity became simply to protect him from being worried or hurt.

There was another factor, too, which, even alone, might have made it impossible to change him. With all his gentleness he was extraordinarily intractable. He never became angry, never made scenes—the slightest brush with anyone would leave him looking

[124]

haggard and feeling worse—but he went his own way. He was like a force of nature; there was about him that air of inevitability. Slowly and quietly, in his own time and his own way, he continued in his own direction and nothing could deflect him.

For all his lassitude he was extremely forceful, indeed dominant. It was not the active forcefulness of vitality but a kind of latent forcefulness of character. Other people had to meet him on his own ground or not at all, because he never departed from it.

It may well be that Greta took the only possible course when she abandoned all attempts to change him. It may well be that he could not change or be changed and that that terrible expenditure of time and energy and conscience, from which a more orderly life could have done so much to deliver him, was after all unavoidable and perhaps even necessary. If so, a determined effort to achieve the impossible could only have ended in disaster.

VII

Lincoln's Inn, 1902-1903

In January 1902 Greta took a post at a school in Wales where she remained for the next year and a half, up to the time of their marriage. This involved much separation and those continual calculations so familiar to anyone who has ever been in love: 'Only seven weeks, now, until I see you . . . only six weeks from next Friday', and so on—and on. Always the waiting and longing for the holidays and always when they came Edward would be behind with his work and unable to join her in Scotland while day followed day and term loomed near again. 'Come soon, soon, soon,' she wrote, 'or what am I to do—half a creature with my heart in London?'

Edward was working on the Communion Service for Hastings. Although various drafts had been done the year before the work was not actually started until January 1902. Then, when after much preparation and a slow start, he finished the elaborately illuminated first page, he was so excited that he wired the news to Greta and rushed off triumphantly to show it to Graily Hewitt. After that he got on faster and wrote that he was full of hope, had got over the 'nerves' that made the beginning of a piece of work such a nightmare and could see his way ahead.

His chambers at Lincoln's Inn were beautiful, with white painted panelling and a vaulted ceiling. 'It is the most lovely clear, cold, starry dark outside,' he wrote one night in February, 'and here in brightness and whiteness and a glow from the red grate, I have just heard the postman slam the door of the pillar-box below, and then the gate into "The Fields" shutting after him.'

And then one night, in from the roof, through the open sky-light of his bedroom, came a little black cat. This at once made the place seem like home to him and he gave her such a welcome that she very soon moved in altogether and presented him with 'a bijou edition of herself in a hamper'. Presumably it was his hamper, but she had earned it by her consummate tact in limiting her family to one. Soon both she and her offspring were com-pletely established as members of his *ménage*. The mother he called Pounce after the powder used for treating the surface of vellum and the kitten was Higgins, after Higgins's Indian ink, being of the same colour. They were made free of the place, the skylight being kept permanently open, with a mackintosh on the bed in case of rain. A duckboard ladder, devised for their convenience, led up from washstand to skylight. Once out on the intricate old roofs the cats could make their way anywhere.

At about the same time Edward was contemplating another addition to his household. 'I have been thinking about a plan to let a deserving young architect have the other half of my bed-room,' he wrote to Greta in April. 'It will make a considerable change in my *régime*, though it will not affect expenses at present one way or the other. I hope Mr Gill will earn more money presently and then he will be able materially to reduce my rent. He is the stone-mason who is cutting the tombstone for Mr Batten. I hope the plan will be good.'

Eric Gill was twenty years of age. He was one of thirteen children and his father was a curate, so his circumstances were not affluent. He lived in lodgings in Clapham, worked in an architect's office and was a student in Johnston's class, as described in a previous chapter. He was, in his own words, 'mad on lettering' and his first commission as a stone-carver, the tombstone for Batten, seems to have come to him through Johnston and the lettering class.

After the first reference to him the formality of 'Mr' is dropped and he becomes 'Gill'. 'Gill' he remained during the next sixteen years in which he was, perhaps, Edward's closest friend. Christian names seem to have been reserved almost exclusively for relatives and children. When Eric Gill's eighteen-year-old brother MacDonald, or 'Max', came to London he was simply 'Gill's brother'. Eventually, as he also became a close friend, he had to have a name and so he became Max, while Eric continued to be 'Gill'. Neither Edward nor Greta ever became accustomed to the casual use of Christian names. It continued to sound slightly absurd, to them, to hear Gill's youthful followers talking of 'Eric'.

Eric Gill moved to Lincoln's Inn in May. 'I believe his coming is a good thing,' Edward wrote to Greta, 'any small inconvenience that may arise can be made to help me and I think it will really help Gill. You shook your head, but will it not be a comfort of a sort to know that I am not all alone?' A week later he added 'Gill came on Saturday and has quite settled in. He improves on acquaintance and I think we shall get on very well together.'

To Gill the move was something much more momentous. Of his association with Johnston he wrote: 'He profoundly altered the whole course of my life and all my ways of thinking. Just as "art nonsense" couldn't stand against him so also "thought nonsense" was toppled over.' He describes Johnston as 'miraculously deliberate of speech and equally deliberate of thought' and says that he himself was just the reverse, over-hasty and ready to jump to conclusions. In the light of this statement Greta's apprehensions seem understandable, but sometimes opposites have a way of shaking down together to their mutual benefit and Gill arrived with a deep veneration of Johnston and a dazzled ecstasy at his own changed circumstances.

As to Johnston, Gill's coming provided him with an audience. It was second nature to him to 'expound', as Greta told him. ('I said to myself "Now Edward is having a lovely time *expounding*", but I knew your advice was the very best.') He found it helpful to think aloud in the form of a disquisition on the subject occupying his mind and would explain to shop assistants or railway porters that a difference in scale was absolute and not relative, or that no two objects could be identical. Now he had a listener ready and eager to drink in every word. Not that they always agreed, by any means: 'Gill has been reading *Literature and Dogma* and reading a few lines to me now and again. We have had a number of pretty warm arguments on the matter. I object to destroyers of creeds who have no equivalent ready to offer for the shelter they have pulled down. I object to the appeal to "science" combined with unscientific statement. I object to rhetoric displacing logic . . . but I will not say more till I have read the book.'

One gets a vivid glimpse of their life together from another letter that begins 'Dear Greta . . . (Here I was interrupted by a discussion with Gill on the Truth and Right and Faith! and it is an hour later! A most friendly argument and lengthy disquisition by me.).' The wonder is that it was only *one* hour later.

To Gill it was all utterly glorious. 'From Clapham to Lincoln's Inn,' he wrote, 'from scabrous rooms in a Victorian street to a room with a vaulted ceiling looking out on a noble square . . . from the kindly but entirely misunderstanding company of the church club to the society of him whom I most honoured. . . . "Light's abode, celestial Salem"—I know it must seem absurd, but it was no less than heaven to me.'

Johnston's mild hope that it 'would really help Gill' was royally fulfilled and royally repaid to lettering. The payment of the true teacher is the sight of his teaching bearing fruit and Gill, as a type designer, had a greater influence on lettering than any other student Johnston ever had.

Their most frequent visitors in Lincoln's Inn were Graily Hewitt and his friend Farrow who shared chambers nearby. There was also Noel Rooke ,'a wonderful artist and quite a boy', who came round with Hewitt one Sunday morning and cooked breakfast while Johnston had his bath 'luxuriously' and appeared when everything was ready. It detracts a little from the atmosphere of luxury when one realizes that he had a tin bath on the bedroom floor, but this seems to have been what he preferred.

Another friend was George Carter, who had spent a week-end at Johnston's cottage in Kent and often entertained him at his parents' house in Holland Park. He worked in the same architect's office as Gill and it was he who had sent him to the lettering class.

Carter and Hewitt came to tea soon after Gill moved in and they had 'a very jolly time'. They all climbed out on to the roof —by the cats' skylight, one wonders, or was there a more orthodox route? 'Then afterwards we made some very curious experiments with smoke-rings—putting out a candle about a yard away with rings tapped out on a box.' Johnston was always ready for 'very curious experiments'. He had devised and made this smoke-ring box and many similar toys. It is no wonder that he complained, when in Edinburgh, that he could not get on with his work because his young nephew, Gunnar, would not leave him alone. Even the parrot, in Miles's house, learnt to call *'Uncle Edward! Uncle Edward!'* Uncle Edward would fill a room with smoke and throw rainbows on it with a prism, extract electricity from the fur of unco-operative cats, mesmerize hens, send electric shocks through a ring of people with joined hands and do experiments with magnetism. Any boy would remain with him for the entire day unless forcibly removed. Always, too, wherever he lived, he would be surrounded by gadgets of his own devising, irresistible to a boy. They were constructed of wood, tin, string, wire, solder and sealing wax, carefully and lovingly shaped and finished.

Another visitor to Lincoln's Inn was Ernest Treglown. When Birmingham School of Art had been unable to secure a teacher for a lettering class, because none were yet qualified except Johnston and Hewitt, they had sent Treglown to London to learn the craft so that he could teach it. He and Johnston soon became great friends and Treglown used to spend his snatched visits to London at Lincoln's Inn where he received almost non-stop coaching. No doubt they slept late in the morning after their all-night sessions, but almost the whole of the rest of the time seems to have been devoted to study. They probably set out cups of tea among the manuscripts on the table and found a bit of a loaf and some cheese, all without breaking the thread of the discourse or slackening the intensity of the concentration. Johnston would have made him toast, of course; he always made people toast, and instructed them in the art as carefully as if it had been a branch of calligraphy.

Noel Rooke described Johnston as being like 'a wet rag' after these visits and they often figure in letters as a reason why other work has been neglected, but he certainly enjoyed Treglown's company as well as feeling it essential to give him a really sound, true understanding of the subject, for the sake of the craft. 'Treglown wants to "consult me professionally",' he wrote once, to Greta, 'and speaks of a fee, but that is absurd (as I have told him), there should be free exchange between all members of one craft. We must have a meeting of the three scribes. I shall ask G.H. to come to tea.' It was on this occasion that they had breakfast with Hewitt and Farrow and then 'looked at his things and talked scribeology—but mixed Latin and Greek will offend you, let it be calligraphy—till one.'

For Greta's birthday in March Edward made a tiny book of a poem he had written to her. This was for no eyes but their own, and yet when it was done he was so pleased with the writing that he dearly wanted to show it to the others, particularly because 'it had a peculiar interest to scribes as the smallest writing we have yet attempted'. In the end he compromised by showing them some of the pages, *upside down and at a distance*.

Sometimes Johnston and his friends had 'what Farrow calls "a flourish" ' and dined at Gatti's or Roche's or just at the Cock Tavern across the way, 'where, after a time, everything tastes like horse', and then to a theatre, *Iolanthe, Bluebell in Fairyland*, or *The Country Girl*. Johnston, though not musical, was devoted to Gilbert and Sullivan. Gilbert's wit, with its puns and the hint of deeper mysteries behind its paradoxes, was exactly the kind that most appealed to him. He loved the operas so much that, very occasionally, he would even try to hum a few bars of a tune.

Johnston and Hewitt worked together very closely at this

time, discussing all their work with one another and occasionally even collaborating. Thus, for the coronation of King Edward VII, Johnston wrote an address from the London County Council in which he got Hewitt to do the gilding. He also called in Hewitt to help him to write the coloured initials in 325 copies of the Dove's Press *Paradise Lost*. Sheets from the press were sent round to Lincoln's Inn in batches as soon as they were dry, 300 on paper and 25 on vellum. For each copy on paper Johnston received half a crown for the eleven initials and for vellum copies five shillings.

It was in 1901 that Johnston gave Hewitt his first commission —one that he himself was too busy to undertake. Hewitt wrote: 'I want to thank you for this most heartily and perhaps I can best do so by telling you that you are the first man who has made possible to me the earning of money by the doing of that which is pure delight. . . . Do you see, then, what you have done in handing me this thing?' Johnston enclosed the letter in one to Greta and wrote on it 'From one of my 2 best students (E.G.T.[1] the other). I value this v. much. This (his) work and this happiness would alone be far more reward for what little I have 'spent' on Teaching during the last eighteen months. He does most beautiful work—giving an extraordinary *proof* that good work *is* being revived and telling me, as mere words could not, that I have not wasted all my days.'

In April 1902 occurs the first reference to Johnston's book, *Writing and Illuminating and Lettering*. ' "They" want to publish *the* book in September,' he wrote, but in fact the Hastings Communion Service kept him busy all that summer and he did not begin to work on the book until nearly a year later.

By this time he had given up the idea of starting a press, having come to the conclusion that calligraphy was a life-work in itself if he were to 'master it' as he hoped to do and to pass on his knowledge to others. This now seemed to him to be the way in which he might hope to be of most use in the world.

He wrote to his future father-in-law saying that he had enough

[1]Ernest Treglown.

work to keep him busy for a year. 'My position is being more widely recognised and improving every day. . . . The field of letter-craftsman seems almost sure. It is small, but not crowded. There are three of us only, so far as I know. I feel impelled to go on with all my might in this present path. We have the difficulty, though it is also a great joy, of having, to some extent, to make people want the right things. . . . I have always looked on our present writing and illuminating (with few exceptions) as strictly educational (both of ourselves and the public). Mr Lethaby says that the new work is beginning to tell and that the "squirminess" and "artyness" are going. I walked across the Park with him and he was most encouraging and said "I think so much of your work—I cannot tell you how much I think of it." '

To Greta, who seems to have shown undue optimism on hearing how much work he had on hand, he wrote 'Alas! no, I'll not be "v. rich soon". I must not kill the goose that lays the gilded parchments. *The Craft* must be considered and though I take personal, passing profit from its initiation it would be lasting loss to me if its founding fell through through my fault. (Isn't it funny! This alliteration was absolutely unintentional.) It is a great difficulty not to undercharge and yet be reasonable, commending direct, good work by its cheapness. None of the sources of demand must be checked or alarmed. The adventurous must now be encouraged till they and others acquire a steady appetite. As to myself, it's better to *be* a foundation stone than "a success" and lay one!'

The problem of pricing work was clearly an important one. He had already written some notes on the subject in which he said: 'Craftsmen must cease to charge fancy prices. They must not pose as geniuses at play—they must be *workmen*, not artists in the ordinary sense of the word. . . . By beauty, by cheapness, by legibility, by force of character, we must justify and commend our work. . . . The craftsman should not set a price on Beauty, but on his work—not try to realize Beauty learnedly but *as a little child*—not cultivate a *"characteristic style"* but cultivate truth in his character.'

[133]

No doubt it was such views as this that caused Eric Gill to say of Johnston that 'art nonsense could not stand against him'.

Johnston had been profoundly influenced by Lethaby, receiving from him, not catch phrases to repeat proudly, like a young convert to the latest 'ism', but the germs of ideas for which his mind was ready and which, by much pondering, he was able to make his own. In the same way the young Gill, in this intensely formative period, absorbed from Johnston what his mind was ripe to receive.

'Only daily-work art is worth a button,' said Lethaby. 'The craftsman must be a *workman*,' said Johnston, and Gill, in his writings, never ceased to proclaim that the artist must be an ordinary man and not 'a hot-house plant'. This is only one instance of many. More important, even, than the ideas themselves, was the attitude of mind. Lethaby 'taught you how to think about things,' said Clausen, and Johnston 'profoundly altered . . . all my ways of thinking,' said Gill.

Another of Johnston's early notes on reviving a craft is headed '*High Falutin*—for personal use only'. In this he says: 'Beauty is obedience—made manifest—to the Laws of Truth, but no one knows those laws in their great simplicity or in their infinite complexity. I have therefore set forth here a number of axioms and theorems . . . as a contribution to the founding of a Grammar of Lettering in place of the lost tradition of the Scriptorium. . . . A 'rule' is only a guide to ensure good work. . . . Having gained mastery by practice you should form your own Rules.'

Johnston also expounded some of his ideas in letters to his sister, Olof. She had now left school and drawing had become her greatest interest. He sent her copies of his class sheets, got her materials and wrote her long letters of advice. Apropos of a question of hers about writing stories for children he made some suggestions about craftsmanship in general: 'As should be done in all design, when learning, you must take the simplest elements and simply arrange them. . . . Most civilised traditions and conventions run counter to simplicity and therefore people try to run before they can walk. . . . All people can make really pretty designs with a few cockleshells or pebbles, yet they will think that *designing* means doing wallpapers, tiles, metalwork and *black and white work!* . . . I have had little practice in literature but suggest these principles which are absolute in "art"—which have enabled me, with very slight talent, to "get on", for want of which there are countless art students and artists with much talent who stick—I see them every day. My two pupils who have not sought royal roads but have been "faithful over a few things" are now made rulers over these ambitious ones. Set no limit to your hopes (which may contemplate Eternity) but *every limit of the moment to your work.*'

The weeks dragged slowly by for Edward and Greta while they wondered how long their separation must last. 'I wish I were the black cat,' Greta wrote, 'why can't I come and stay with you while she teaches the second form French and Grammar?' Early in 1903 they decided to get married the following summer but now the real worry of the book began. The publishers were expecting to have it in April but by the end of February Johnston had got no further than an introductory chapter. This he dropped through Hewitt's letter-box and they met for dinner at the Cock Tavern to discuss it. Hewitt—like Johnston himself—had many criticisms to make. Johnston was grateful but depressed. He was continually tired, his faculties dulled, unable to give the book the degree of concentration it demanded.

In March he wrote to Greta: 'I have been dawdling lately till I am almost frightened into industry again. A quarter of the year is gone and I seem to have done nothing. This morning I sorted some accounts and things, wrote two short letters and then made my lunch. After lunch I sat in my chair and read *The New Atlantis* till about 4 and then *dozed* for half an hour or so. I don't enjoy the many wasted days but feel "driven" all the time. Perhaps I don't take enough exercise but I do get very lazy and tired and feel it simply impossible to touch the Book. Nearly always, when things go wrong, I think "It will be all right when I have Greta to look after me." '

Greta was worried about him. This continual tiredness seemed so unnatural to her. 'Two short letters and a little tidying up is not a day's work,' she said. She was, herself, working desperately hard that term with half the staff ill, racing from one class to another all day long, which must have made it doubly hard for her to understand his behaviour. As the days passed and no work was done the Easter holidays began to be in jeopardy. Greta would not come to London and interrupt his work but went home to Scotland and waited in miserable uncertainty while the precious holidays slipped away and the publishers grew anxious. Edward wrote that it was impossible for him to come to Scotland at all but, at the last moment, changed his mind, sent a telegram and packed a bag.

Greta had been up on the Cairn o' Mont all day among the heather, thinking how he would love it and 'longing for you distractedly, wanting to telegraph and yet determined I wouldn't.' When she came down there was his telegram. She must have felt as on another occasion when he had made a sudden decision to join her and she wrote: 'How the stars are shining in heaven, and beyond them all the angels looking down at me in circles and circles of radiant wings and faces. All the ivy growing round my window flutters like little wings longing to fly too because all the world is so gay. That is because you are coming on Friday.'

The holiday did not seem to dispel the tiredness. May came and June and Edward wrote that he had ceased to worry about the book as it did no good. He was occupied with house-hunting for they were to be married in August. They would have liked to live in the country but Edward decided that he could not travel to London every day, 'it unsettles head and hand too much'. He considered Hammersmith but decided against it and took a tiny flat in Gray's Inn. Gill was to keep on the old chambers and share them with his brother MacDonald, who, in fact, retained them for many years.

Johnston spent two days making 'a rotary fan for an experimental improvement for the gas stove at Gray's Inn' but the book got no further. He often took refuge in carpentry and such things when he felt unable to muster the energy and concentration that his work demanded, a habit which sometimes added the final touch to the exasperation of those he kept waiting. It was natural to assume that if he could mend a kettle or make a new handle for a knife he could write a manuscript, but this was not necessarily true.

Now, close upon his marriage, Johnston wrote one more desperate letter to his publishers before putting the book from his mind. 'About three weeks ago I called on you (and found you were out) to tell you I had failed at the book. I ought to have let you know before now, but my courage has failed me. . . . I hope to be married shortly and to return to London in the end of September. With someone to look after me I think there is some prospect of progress, if you are willing to leave the work in my hands.'

Fortunately Mr Hogg, the publisher, was a man of great patience. He only remarked, ruefully, that it was hard on him as this was the fourth book in the series[1] to be interrupted by the author's marriage.

Term ended and Greta left the school in Wales, travelled north and stayed at Rickerby. When Edward was able to get away she joined his train at Carlisle and travelled to Edinburgh with him. She wrote, afterwards, describing this meeting: 'Every time I see you it is such a lovely feeling, the face is so familiar, so beloved, but a hundred times more dear and beautiful. It is like meeting people in heaven. I can't tell you what I felt like at Carlisle. I didn't feel able to expect you and stood in a grey mist watching moving figures who might be alive or might not, "signifying nothing", and then the train came and you came straight through the vagueness, you real and warm and adorable and—just yourself, and I thought "Oh, I had forgotten what he was—how he draws my love to him!" '

'That is something like a love letter!' she commented at the end. The same might have been said of a good many of her letters at this time. From Wales she had written to him, when she

[1]The Artistic Crafts Series of Technical Handbooks edited by W. R. Lethaby, published originally by John Hogg, now by Sir Isaac Pitman.

escaped from the desperate overwork of school for a brief, solitary respite by the sea: 'I've been lying in a nest in the dunes looking at the stars through coarse reed grasses growing about my head. All my senses are lulled by the subtle breath of the wind, all sorrow and care, all time blown away by the wind which blows from beyond all time and carries everything that has ever happened away so that one is left nothing but a concentration of utter passive joy. I often feel as if all the world were mine, it is tonight, the creeping sea—a white line of breakers in the moon-light—the deep blue up above of which I am a part, with the seven stars of the Plough over my head. I hardly know whether I am alive and yet existence is all pleasure, exultant in a strangely quiet way, loving it all and taking it all in. I didn't want anything or anyone, not even your bodily presence, I had and have you so vividly in me. I don't long for you till I'm sick at heart as I did last week. I have you close and warm in my very heart. . . . I am a treasure if you make me so. If you love me I am a splendid creature and rich and great and happy.

'I am half asleep, the wind rocks me. Storms soothe and calm me. I love the sound of wind and rain and give myself up and lie in the arms of the wind and feel so safe and happy. Goodnight, my sweetheart, I can see, though you are so far from me, your dear and peaceful face in rest.'

They were married on August 20, 1903, in the little church of Drumtochty, near Laurencekirk, and went away together to the Hebrides.

VIII

Gray's Inn, 1903-1905

Edward and Greta set up house together in a tiny flat in Gray's Inn. Their little cream-panelled sitting-room with its carved wooden mantel and long, embrasured Georgian windows looking down upon a garden must have been charming. It could not, however, be charmingly arranged since it also had to serve as Edward's workroom. He had his desk in an alcove which was supposed to be his 'scriptorium', but in actual practice his tools and materials probably overflowed the whole room.

His ideas about furnishing were emphatic and unconventional. In his maturer years he ceased to exercise himself about such things but at this time he was acutely conscious of the principles involved. Thus everything had to be perfectly plain and functional (a very advanced idea in 1903). Exceptions might be made in the case of hand-made things but machine-made ornamentation was anathema, as was pretentiousness in any form. He was, himself, as nearly completely honest as a man could well be and he demanded this quality in things and assumed it in people. Even the hole in the carpet had to be in full view, not under the sofa where Greta had dishonestly concealed it.

Imperceptibly these strictures were relaxed. Somewhere about 1920 we even got a floral dinner set (Oh, the glory of it!) but at this time only plain white china was allowed. The kind of furniture he preferred—failing the traditional products of surviving crafts—was a straightforward piece of carpentry in unstained deal. To relax in, he had a deck-chair padded with his brown plaid travelling rug. So long as a thing was simple and served its purpose he regarded any objection to its appearance as frivolous. This was, perhaps, a combination of a reaction against what Eric Gill called 'art nonsense' and a genuine indifference to appearances. He did not really *see* things—wallpaper, curtains, carpets—any more than he *saw* his wife's dresses. Only very occasionally he would look at her and say 'That's rather pretty—is it new?' and would show no surprise upon learning that it was five years old.

If Greta had not clearly understood that in marrying him she was taking on a job of more than ordinary difficulty the fact must soon have been brought home to her. She was relatively conventional and liked a house to be clean and tidy and to 'look nice'. She also loved people, enjoyed social life and had many friends who were very dear to her. Edward rarely consented to go out with her so most invitations had to be refused and she can hardly have asked her friends to Gray's Inn when it would have meant showing them into his workroom. His friends no longer felt free to drop in as they had in his bachelor days and he never thought of inviting anyone, so visitors were few. Hewitt was sad and rather hurt at the sudden cutting off of their day to day association and at the sight of Johnston devoting all his energies to making shelves and cupboards for the new flat instead of to calligraphy.

It had always seemed that once they were really married there would at last be time for everything. They meant to learn so much from each other. Edward, being self-educated, was the more impressed by Greta's learning. He said he felt like the husband of St Margaret, who kissed her books although he could not read them. Greta found such an attitude incomprehensible and counted her more academic knowledge trivial beside his original and penetrating thought. Then there was music. When they were married, he said, he would often ask her to play to him and she should teach him to appreciate music. She was also to teach him French and he would teach her writing (he laughed at the scrawl in which her letters were written but assured her that he loved it more than any other hand). Alas for human endeavour, he remained wholly ignorant of French and almost wholly unappreciative of music, and Greta's writing—despite some gallant efforts in a cookery notebook, which showed a courageous optimism towards both calligraphy and cooking—continued to be very much what it had always been. Her music, like so many of her gifts, grew rusty for want of use, and the greater part of her life was spent in domestic work, for which she had no aptitude whatever. All her life she continued to burn her cakes and to cut out blouses with both sleeves the same way round, yet, with her ready wit and her incomparable gift for winning people's confidence and putting them at their ease she might have made an ideal wife for an ambassador. Alternatively, she might well have reached the top of her own profession. She wrote once, when acting headmistress of a school, 'I have had a day and a half! Parents and parents and parents! I love it. I've been so civil to them all that they have departed quite willing to confide their babes to me.' There is also a description of a lesson which suggests that she had a real gift for teaching: 'I told them about Napoleon and saw my dear Madge Glazebrook lying on her desk for sheer interest. There are 35 in the Fourth and you could have heard a pin drop.'

It seems, on the face of it, a waste of so much talent, but she had the kind of marriage few achieve and she would not have wished it otherwise.

She had been youthful enough, even at the age of thirty-one, to write that she was glad they were to be poor because it meant that she could do everything for him. The experiences of the next thirty years no doubt disillusioned her about poverty, but she never lost sight of the important issues. As she wrote once, in their Gray's Inn days, in words that convey a whole story to anyone with experience of marriage, 'Things *are* hard just now and I'm horrid sometimes. I was impossible about the china vase—after all, it's only a vase. But I do love you and that's the great thing, isn't it?' That was the great thing, always. Many a china vase was broken, many a meal grew cold: things were hard not only 'just now' but always, but never was there the slightest doubt or confusion in the mind of either about what came first in their lives. 'There is nothing I would not give up for your sake,' Edward wrote, after five years of marriage, '—my writing, my life and more than that—but these things show only rather painfully and fitfully in my practice and I know it is hard for you.' They may have shown fitfully—indeed, they did—but never were they in doubt.

More than thirty years later, after her death, he wrote: 'We were not always kind—especially I—but we both agreed and often said to each other that beneath little disharmonies, tiffs and other surface rufflings, always, deep down in our hearts, there was love for each other—*and knowledge of that love in each other*: for which we thanked the goodness and grace of God.

'That knowledge was, perhaps, the greatest comfort of all, that, no matter whether things went well or ill . . . each of us had one other incarnate spirit with love for one—real and certain; so that always—at the worst or the best—each had that loving sympathy to rely on.

'Love is so great a thing that I used to say to Greta that I believed that "I really loved her a little". Now I know that I love her more.'

Over all their early life together, demanding, insisting, forbidding holidays, hung the shadow of the book. '*Oh, the book, the book!*' Mrs Phelps used to say, casting up hands and eyes, in answer to enquiries about its progress. Anyone who came within its orbit, Greta most of all, must have felt the same: *Oh! the book, the book!* On and on it went, always with the desperate urgency of the last lap, yet somehow failing to achieve the goal. Always it had to be ready for the publishers either in the autumn or the spring but autumn followed spring, spring followed autumn, and still it was not done. Greta did what she could and copied out pages in her most painstaking hand. Edward borrowed a typewriter and proudly informed his publishers that his wife could 'work it', and was typing his book, as she gingerly tapped out pages with two fingers.

It is oddly touching to come across those fragments of manuscript in her handwriting. I never knew her to help him with his work and would hardly have supposed that she would have been allowed to. In my day his workroom was sacrosanct—a far cry from Gray's Inn and the shared sitting-room. But, in any case, that kind of companionship belongs chiefly to the early days of a marriage before the children come.

For them this time was brief. The small flat grew rapidly smaller round them, for they had hardly settled into it and Edward had not finished putting up shelves when prams and cots began to edge their way in. It was clear that their days there were numbered.

The prospect of having a baby did not discompose Greta in the least but it filled her husband with nervous anxiety. He could not leave her side without apprehension, even to go to his classes, and once sent a note from the College by special messenger, asking for reassurance. The messenger brought back a soothing answer, enabling him to concentrate upon his work for the rest of the evening. In the years that followed Greta became experienced in that peculiarly feminine function of foreseeing the partner's anxieties and taking precautions to defend him from them.

In May Greta went home to Scotland to have the baby and Edward reverted to his bachelor life. Hewitt was once again a frequent visitor, Eric Gill or Noel Rooke would drop in and spend a night on the sofa and Treglown came on long, working visits. 'I can see you wandering round and cooking,' Greta wrote, 'as I used to find you at Lincoln's Inn.'

He missed her intensely and worried so much that in the end she was almost assuring him that she was looking forward to her confinement. It was a year of the blackest tragedy for the Greigs, so much so that any risk she might herself be running seemed to Greta insignificant, but Edward wrote with ever increasing anxiety about timetables and telegrams. She passed on some of

[143]

the queries to her father, who seemed uncomprehending. Gently, she tried to explain: 'Edward is worried.' For answer he shook his head, murmuring 'He's thinking of Annie, poor fellow.'

The youngest of the family, Jim, had gone into a sanatorium just before Greta's wedding. By the time she returned to Scotland the following spring they knew that he was dying. Meanwhile Anne had gone out to South America to be married, knowing that she would not see her brother again. Jim was their adored and brilliant boy, the centre of all their hopes. Visiting him became an ordeal because of their fear of betraying what they knew, for he had his bed covered with guides to Paris and was planning to take his mother there in the spring.

Meanwhile they were waiting for a cable announcing Anne's marriage, but no cable came. By the time they had news of her, at last, she was already on her way home to Scotland. She had arrived at the Falkland Islands only to be shown the grave of her fiancé.

Within a week Jim, too, was dead.

'The glory is departed from our house for ever,' Greta wrote, and then, as she thought of Anne, 'I shiver and cling to your coat and wish you were here already. One trembles for what one has.'

Into this black world the baby came, a solitary ray of light to which they all turned. Her father was there for her birth. 'Our prejudices incline us to think it looks rather sweet, occasionally,' he wrote guardedly to Aunty, while Greta stated categorically that its skin was like a warm, white rose and its eyes like violets.

Edward's visit was brief. He had left Eric Gill in charge of his classes and Gill was very busy at the time, with work that took him out of London. He had been commissioned to paint the lettering on the fascia boards of W. H. Smith and Son's shops. St John Hornby of the Ashendene Press was on the board of directors and was responsible for this innovation. This was an important event, not only for Gill personally but for the whole movement. When the ubiquitous newsagents began to appear

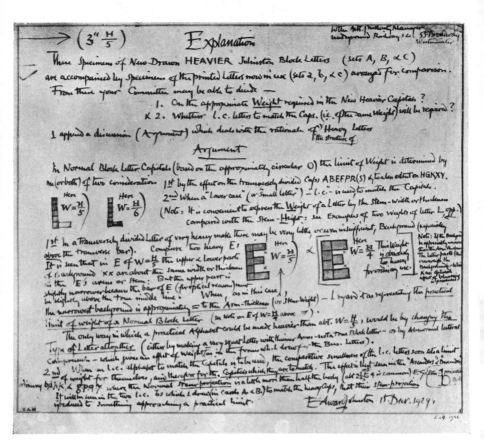

Notes for a heavier version of Johnston's sans serif alphabet for the Underground Railway. 1929. Reduced

To Rudolf von Larisch

Dear Herr von Larisch,

In this April 1952, joining my name with those of many other Scribes, I send you my best wishes & my kind regards: (With wife also) I remember with pleasure meeting you at Hammersmith, on your visit to London about 20 years ago, & your interest in the River & in Sailing boats.

The greatest interest in the work of the Scribe has for me always been, the Things themselves the subjects of our writing and how we may do them justice in our presentment of them on the page.

Here I transcribe for you what one of our poets says of the Writing.

Yours sincerely

Edward Johnston

14. 4. MCMXXII.

The Scribe. (A Poem by Walter de la Mare)

WHAT lovely things
Thy hand hath made:
The smooth-plumed bird
In its emerald shade,
The seed of the grass,
The speck of stone
Which the wayfaring ant
Stirs — and hastes on!

Though I should sit
By some tarn in thy hills,
Using its ink
As the spirit wills
To write of Earth's wonders,
Its live, willed things,
Flit would the ages
On soundless wings
Ere unto me
My pen drew nigh;
Leviathan told,
And the honey-fly:
And still would remain
My wit to try
My worn reeds broken,
The dark tarn dry,
All words forgotten —
Thou, Lord, and I.

Draft in brown of a letter to Rudolf von Larisch including transcription of *The Scribe* by Walter with fascias so far in advance of any others the difference between this and other public lettering was forced upon the attention of anyone with an eye to see such things.

Gill often dropped in at Gray's Inn and no doubt consulted Johnston about this work. One letter to Greta in Scotland describes how he and Rooke spent the night there: 'Gill shall have the sofa and Rooke the camp bed. Gill is now preparing dinner, a large tongue, toast, nice butter, etc., etc. I am going to take this to Euston, where the late fee letters are collected, and as Gill likes engines, etc., he's coming with me.' Edward always paid the late fee and took Greta's letters to Euston 'where I have a chop and read *The Westminster Gazette*.' But this particular evening he dined at home and perhaps spent his time at Euston with Gill studying the name-plates of engines, for it was these that had first inspired Gill's interest in lettering, when, as a boy, he lived above the railway, outside Brighton.

Noel Rooke was a frequent visitor at this time because he was engaged in making drawings of Johnston's hands illustrating the various processes described in his book. Anyone wishing to know what his hands were like has only to turn up these illustrations, for Rooke has shown them faithfully—spare, muscular, nervous, workmanlike, and entirely characteristic. Even his half-averted chin and moustache, in the figure illustrating breathing on gold size, could be no-one else's.

To Mrs Phelps, Rooke was always 'that lad'. She would formally announce 'a gentleman to read the gas meter' or 'a gentleman to mend the tap', but when it was only Noel it would be 'That lad to do the drawing'.

Johnston wrote: 'Rooke has been drawing me all afternoon . . . he is getting on very well on the whole and making very nice drawings. I have asked Hewitt to write an appendix to my chapter on Gilding and Treglown to write something—a few pages on miniatures. It will be an uncommon feature adding greatly to the value of the book to have three special subjects treated by experts (who have yet been my students and *on the whole take the same general view as myself*).' The other 'special subject' was carved lettering by Eric Gill, but Treglown's article on miniatures did not materialize.

Treglown spent a lot of time at Gray's Inn that summer and Johnston recounted how they dined at Roche's and then 'came back here and walked up and down Leather Lane looking at the flaring lamps and at the different stalls. We bought strawberries and salad and bread. Gill came and he has been playing the piano while I have written $3\frac{1}{2}$ letters.'

By July most of Rooke's illustrations were done but Johnston still had a great number to do himself and wrote that he would have to do ten a day—a forecast even more optimistic than his estimates usually were. Years later Rooke recalled this race against time, and the urgency with which they worked at the book. He was speaking of Johnston's capacity for sustained concentration. Before he embarked upon certain drawings, he said, they had 'a preliminary non-stop talk of seven hours. It ended at five in the morning. It had been of unflagging intensity and interest. We got down to work at two that afternoon and made good progress.'

Time went on and the term came to an end. Greta and the baby were waiting in Scotland but still the book was not done. 'I have been cutting the ''Trajan'' letters out of photographs to make up an alphabet,' Johnston wrote. 'Gill came last night and read over his chapter which wants a lot of revising.' Later he wrote: 'Last night and today I have been writing the chapter on illumination and I should say it is more than half done. I felt this p.m. as if someone were helping me as I found it comparatively easy to express my meaning, which is not always so. I shall read Sherlock Holmes (or something equally silly) and have supper at The Cock. Mr Hogg is very energetic and keen. Awfully nice to me about the book (and always speaking most highly of it in anticipation). Gill brought his chapter with some good illustrations of his own. . . . I cannot go any faster, much as I *long* to be with you. Don't think I *can* come this week, there are large matters at stake for us (3).'

They were now well into the holidays. 'We are sacrificing a

great deal to that book,' Greta commented, but she bore the delays with patience and told him of the baby's latest achievements and who had bathed her this time and what they had said —for she was idolized by the whole family. Mrs Greig lamented that all the strawberries would be over before he came, and now all the raspberries and all the peas. He had 'a merely theoretical wife and child,' she said, 'and no holiday.' Greta wrote that at least he would not miss the heather 'and we'll go up Garvock by the light of the next new moon when Bridget is sleeping'.

Anne arrived home from the Falklands and still Edward did not come. September was upon them and it began to appear that he would not get away at all before the new term began. Greta was growing desperate. The situation was not eased by the discovery that in Laurencekirk it was now being openly said that he had left her. She told him at last that she could stand it no more and if he did not come she would leave Scotland and join him, even if it meant weaning the baby. He, too, was overwhelmed by the same feeling. He wrote to Hogg, his publisher, a letter half guilty, half resentful, saying he had worked so long and so hard at the book that he was 'feeling quite queer', and with that he almost ran away, leaving the work unfinished.

The only pity was that he had not decided to play truant weeks earlier for, one way and another, the book dragged on for almost another two years. The following summer he was again writing to Hogg: 'I have not yet been able to estimate the date of completion of the MS but will let you know as soon as I possibly can. I am working *every* day at the book and at nothing else.' And again, 'I am working early and late but the end seems far off.'

Delay was occasioned by the necessity to cut down the book because it was found to be much longer that the others in the series. This seems to have occupied the summer. By the winter of 1905 it was in proof and early in 1906, 'after 45 days or more' he finished correcting the galleys. In May he was writing the preface and making the index. At last, on August 21, two years after the desperate rush of the Scottish summer, it was ready for press. 'Gill helped me to do up the parcels (3),' he wrote to

Aunty, 'and we ran to the pillar box. In my relief I told the postman it was a book I had been writing for $3\frac{1}{2}$ years. When he understood he was sympathetic and said "And you don't know yet if it will take." Now I believe the printers are actually printing the first sheets and I expect that it will be published in October.' He learned with pleasure that the printers had said that a copy of the book ought to be kept in every printing office.

Actually his estimate of three and a half years confided to the sympathetic postman was conservative. He had had the book on hand since early in 1902, if not before, and already he felt, on reading it in print, that he had changed and had learnt much since it was started. The rush period might be said to have lasted three and a half years and the relief of its being finished must have been overwhelming.

> '*When the book was ended*
> *His wife began to sing . . .*'

Greta had written from Scotland, and added 'I *shall* sing!'

Looking back, the most surprising thing is not that it took so long but that it was ever finished at all. Nearly forty years later, when he was working on another book—which seemed to bear some resemblance to Penelope's web—his daughter, Bridget, remarked that she wondered how he had ever finished the first, to which he replied 'It was comparatively easy then because I knew nothing about the subject.'

The book did not cause a sensation. The reviews were good but not noticeably enthusiastic. It sold quietly but steadily and seems to have done rather better than had been expected. The real difference between what was expected and what achieved was only revealed by time, for instead of the sales falling off as the years passed they steadily increased. Now, fifty years later, in its twenty-fifth impression, it remains unchallenged as the classic text book on the subject.

On October 24, 1906, Sydney Cockerell wrote 'Your book came this morning and I have been reading it with great interest. I congratulate you on having compressed into it such a mass of useful information and on having illustrated the text in such a complete and stimulating way. It will certainly lead to an increase in the study of calligraphy, not only in this country but all over the world, and I hope it may also lead to your being very busy in more remunerative ways than in the preparation of the book for the press, which must have been a gigantic task.'

Long afterwards Cockerell said 'I have sometimes made bold to assert that this small volume, now in its nineteenth edition, is the best handbook ever written on any subject. That is a rash claim that could only be made after a perusal of all other handbooks on all other subjects. I will now be content to declare that, with its faultless illustrations by Noel Rooke, Johnston's handbook is a masterpiece, immensely instructive and stimulating.'

Lethaby, the editor, described the book as 'astounding' and wrote to Johnston 'It is, I think, entirely admirable, clear and, of course, *right*. The schedule of the qualities good lettering should have must be right, for it would apply to architecture and all the arts.'

The 'schedule of the qualities of good lettering' referred to was *readableness, beauty and character*. Much later, after many years of experience and a great deal of thought, Johnston formulated another three 'essential qualities' of formal penmanship, *sharpness, unity and freedom*. It is interesting to note that the original qualities are all more or less general—almost an informed layman's choice—whereas the later ones are highly technical and specific, the findings of the craftsman after a lifetime of experience. They are, in fact, an analysis of the technical qualities by means of which readableness, beauty and character may be achieved. 'If there is one word that sums up the effect of sharpness, unity and freedom it is LIFE,' wrote Johnston. '(Compare the quality in blades of living grass.)'

Beauty, of course, is always a suspect word because beauty, like happiness, cannot be captured by a direct approach. Johnston came to regard it as a sort of divine grace which might be bestowed, like a reward, on work well done, but not as a thing to be aimed at in itself.

It is remarkable that *Writing and Illuminating and Lettering*, though written at the start of Johnston's career, when, as he put it, he 'knew nothing about the subject', never required to be altered in any important particular in the light of nearly forty years of subsequent experience. Already, in 1906, he had grasped the essentials. During the rest of his life he gave to the whole subject an immense amount of the most profound thought, extending and deepening his original conception, yet continuing always on the course he had mapped out from the beginning.

The publication of the book must have brought an extraordinary sense of liberation. For the first time in his professional life Johnston was free to do as he liked, to accept whatever commissions came his way. Up to this time he had always been committed to something of major importance that had to take precedence of anything else, however tempting. At first his researches and learning to teach had taken him most of his time, then had come the great Communion Service, for the sake of which all other commissions had had to be refused, and then the book. Now at last he emerged, experienced and free. Writing his book, no doubt, had taught him a very great deal. When it was finished his work gained new confidence and 'seemed to develop more in six months than in the preceding six years,' according to Rooke. The early, tentative period was over. His penmanship blossomed into a new freedom and now assumed its most characteristic and best-known form: the 'foundational hand'.

It was not without reluctance that Johnston abandoned his early half uncial hand. In particular he regarded it as useful training for students, affording a better discipline than the foundational hand and a useful groundwork for it. Increasingly often, however, especially at the College, students lacked the time for a long course, and he considered the foundational hand more practical.

This hand was based upon a late Caroline[1] minuscule as shown in a tenth century Winchester psalter in the British Museum.[2]

[1]'*Caroline*' here refers to the Emperor Charlemagne.
[2]Harl. MS. 2904. See *Writing and Illuminating and Lettering*, plate VIII.

'I doubt if there is any other extant,' wrote Johnston, 'that would make so good a strain from which to breed varieties of our excellent and readable printers' ''Roman lower-case'' as this Winchester MS which contains, as it seems to me, the perfected *seed* of our common print besides marks of the noble race from which it sprang. Indeed the links with the Roman capitals are so fresh in it that I had to straighten the back of the Winchester *a* and deglossate the *e*.' He also had to invent a number of letters which were missing .Of these, *j k s v w y* and *z* he described as

Et haec scribimus
vobis ut gaudeatis,
& gaudium vestrum
sit plenum.

Et haec est annunciatio, quam
audivimus ab eo, & annunciamus
vobis : Quoniam Deus lux est,
& tenebrae in eo non sunt ullae.

Ef. 22 February 1918. A.D.

"Heavy Italics" based on Winchester MS. Winchester MS very slightly modified.

Copy sheet. Black. 1918. Reduced

[151]

'sympathetic novelties' of his own with very little Winchester foundation and *f* and *h* as 'guesses' based on the original *f* and *n*. He also devised a formal way of making the heads of the letters where the Winchester scribe had relied upon a sort of sleight-of-hand which would, Johnston realized, be difficult to copy satisfactorily himself and impossible to teach his students.

He must have felt strangely near to that anonymous scribe at Winchester. They had both faced the same problems with the same tool in their hands and his own quill, Johnston reflected, if it could come to life, would fly very much like a tenth century bird. But whereas the old scribe had been in the full stream of a living tradition and had had a living master, Johnston's master had been dead for a thousand years. It required a process of intensive detection to discover exactly what he had done and why; how he had cut his pen, in what order he had made the strokes of each letter and at what speed he had written. Neither pen nor parchment had changed much in the time and the hand of a tenth century man was much the same as the hand of a man today, only their thoughts were different. This, Johnston felt with sorrow, must forever preclude him from being a *real* scribe. Physically everything could be reconstructed: his quill could be cut identically and his hand trained to move it in the same way but his self-consciousness must always remain an impassable barrier. However hard he tried to make a manuscript real and simple and down-to-earth it never could be just a job of work to him, as it had been to his predecessors. 'When I write I am thinking of "doing my duty", if I'm teaching,' he said, 'or I'm thinking of "doing my best", but the old scribe was thinking of the words.' The old scribe had been the true professional doing a routine job and thereby filling a real and urgent need, because, as a friend of Johnston's heard a schoolteacher telling her class, 'Long ago people didn't know how to make books and so they had to write them.'

'If we could have seen the old scribe at work,' Johnston said once, when speaking on the subject, 'the thing that would have struck us most, even more than his skill, would have been the *speed* with which he wrote. . . . You might say of these early people that while they made beautiful things they didn't seek beauty directly. They were engaged on serious work. They were writing this kind of writing as fast as they could write an ordinary letter. It was very rapid and they wrote it for their lives and everything they did primarily was for use and even these gorgeous letters they put in their illuminated manuscripts were primarily for use as book-markers. Of course they had obviously in their hearts a kind of dream of divine beauty that they were seeking, but at the moment they were doing something that was useful. But note how much of that dream was fulfilled.'

IX

Hammersmith, 1905-1912

The arrival of a baby made the flat in Gray's Inn impossibly small. Somehow they managed to get through a winter there, all three of them—at the cost of what nervous exhaustion one can only guess—but to remain longer was out of the question. Again they thought longingly of a little house in the country, but for the time being it seemed essential that Johnston should be in London. His thoughts turned once again to Hammersmith.

The Doves Press was gaining for itself an international reputation. All those interested in fine printing were drawn to Hammersmith, whether from the Continent or from America. Johnston knew that Cobden-Sanderson, with his dream of an 'allied scriptorium' would welcome him as a neighbour, and he thought that he might fall in with future clients there.

William Morris had lived on Hammersmith Mall, and, no doubt through his influence, that delightful corner of Hammersmith where it borders Chiswick by the river had come to be a sort of centre for the Arts and Crafts Movement. The river air must have been conducive to printing, for, even before the Kelmscott Press, the Chiswick Press had been established there. Now the Doves Press was installed in Hammersmith Terrace, where Emery Walker also lived, and soon Douglas Pepler, at Hampshire House, a working men's club near by, began those experiments with printing which later, at Ditchling, developed into St Dominic's Press.

Hammersmith, 1905-1912

Early in 1905 Emery Walker moved from the house where he had lived for some twenty years to another further along the Terrace. Cobden-Sanderson passed on the news that 3, Hammersmith Terrace was to let and Johnston eagerly took it. For the first time they found themselves with a real house of their own.

'We have for some time thought of leaving Gray's Inn,' Johnston wrote to a friend, 'and, a delightful house offering itself, we suddenly flitted on the 31st of March (I working on my book till 2 a.m. of that day). If you should want a house having the advantages of country (very nearly) and town combined there are one or two to let in the Terrace at about £60 per ann. They are old houses on the river and you can keep a boat or be content with watching the L.C.C. historical steamboats passing up and down.'

The old Terrace houses had basements and no bathrooms—not so much as a tap above the ground floor—but they had great charm and a wonderful view and little gardens running down to the river wall. An old bookseller in the neighbourhood who had known Hammersmith as a country village fifty years before, remarked, when Johnston gave his address, 'Some good people *used* to live in those houses.' Good people still did. Not only was the Doves Press at No 1 and the Emery Walkers at No 7, but the Edward Spencers, of the Artificers' Guild, were at No 10 and, later, the Peplers at No 14. Romney Green, the cabinet maker, had his workshop opposite and soon Eric Gill, now with a wife and a baby, came to live round the corner in Black Lion Lane. The Cobden-Sandersons were at River House, next to Kelmscott House on Hammersmith Mall, and the Spooners (Charles Spooner was an architect and furniture designer) had one of the little houses that were tucked in beyond the end of the Terrace, before the road converged on the river and became Chiswick Mall. Beyond the river was the towing path and beyond the towing path were reservoirs, so that the view was all open. Sunsets flushed the water with pink and gold and the moon spanned it with silver. (Bridget, found gazing from the window, excused her absence from bed with the wholly understandable explanation that the river 'could not be left alone'). Swans rode at anchor under the garden wall. The tugs went up and down with their strings of barges loaded with coal for the Gas, Light and Coke Company and the pleasure boats went by packed with 'trippers', to the strident notes of early gramophones.

> *Hullo, hullo,*
> *A different girl again!*

sang the gramophones, to Bridget's joy, and a factory sign from somewhere across the water continually reiterated the message: *Cocos, Cocoleum, Coco-lardo and other edible vegetable fats and oils.*

April welcomed them to Hammersmith and soon the acacia tree in the garden was hung with white clusters of blossom; summer came and they sat out in its shade, or on the balcony outside the drawingroom. And Edward wrote to his brother, Miles, thanking him for directions for fitting a blow-lamp to a Bunsen burner and confiding to him his plans for making 'a little wind-pump' to pump up water from the river into a butt in the garden. It is doubtful if the garden needed much water, shaded as it was by the acacia, but there was the river lapping, twice a day, at the garden wall. The inventor in him could not resist the challenge.

His correspondence with Miles was always strictly practical, concerned with tools and experiments, recipes for curing herrings and enquiries about how to calculate the area of a regular hexagon.

As soon as they were settled in at the Terrace and, for the first time, had some storage space, Edward wrote to Aunty asking her to send 'the tent, clubs, shelf, measuring thing, chain and zither.' He did not play golf, still less did he play that strange instrument erroneously known to us as the zither: he just felt that you never knew—he *might* want them. Greta used to call him her White Knight because any place of his was always cluttered with such a diversity of objects in the expectation that they would come in handy. Such was his ingenuity in making use of them that they very often did, although, even more often,

[156]

they did not. The golf clubs and the zither were in the latter category.

Less than a year after the move a second daughter, Barbara, was born. She came somewhat precipitately before the nurse or doctor had arrived. Edward was left to deal with the crisis alone and, as usual in a crisis, he turned for help to the Encyclopaedia. While the birth was in progress he sat by Greta's bed with the huge volume open upon his knee, studying the article on obstetrics. This he mastered so successfully that by the time the nurse arrived he had delivered the baby.

Two new members of the household had arrived almost together, for Mrs Phelps's daughter, Ethel, had come to help while Greta was in bed. A penny notebook has somehow survived containing accounts in her writing, beginning on the day that Barbara was born. When Greta took to her bed Ethel started to do the marketing and to write in a little book such fascinating items as 'butter, 2*d*., bacon, 3*d*.,' and—mysteriously —'Mr Johnston, 1*d*.'

As the eldest girl in a family of ten where money was short and the mother was out at work, Ethel had early learnt a good deal about children and a good deal about life. Life was hard but hers was a happy nature; she had found plenty to laugh at and plenty to love. Especially, she loved children and since she possessed an inexhaustible supply of patience and good humour, children loved her. Moreover she would turn her hand to anything and work, if necessary, till she dropped. For Greta it must have been rather like being able to secure the services of one of the junior angels for a matter of a few shillings a week. She had come for the period of the confinement only but for seven years she remained as an indispensable member of the family, our much-loved nannie.

The great social occasion in the Terrace was the Boat Race. Everyone gave a party and asked everyone they knew and—such is the mysterious hold of this event on the public mind—everyone who could possibly do so came. The little gardens behind the Terrace were thronged.

Greta wrote an account of one such occasion to Aunty: 'We had a delightful boat-race party. We asked 70 people, almost, and 40 came. We had the house beautifully cleaned and on the Thursday *and Friday morning* (!) the drawingroom was white-washed. It was perfectly snowie and beautiful and quite made up for the inconvenience of having men in it the very day before the party. Ethel and a girl got into it at 11 on Friday, cleaned the windows, scrubbed and polished the floor and then all the furniture was put back. Edward and I had taken away the books to his dressingroom (he did most of it) and on Friday evening we put them all back *so* neatly.' (The books were a formidable item at any time.) 'I had got a nice Chinese hanging for a Christmas present and we hung it over the sofa. The drawingroom has got old-fashioned chintz curtains with large, gay flowers on a white ground and a mirror over the mantelpiece which was a Christmas present from the Gills, so it looked very nice. We planted mauve and white crocuses and lots of flowers in the garden and on the balcony in window boxes and there were pots of hyacinths in the house. I have described it all at great length but it made such an impression on us both and we both worked so hard to accomplish it. Edward moved things and planted things and got very tired but we all enjoyed it. His room was cleared and had tea and coffee in it and the diningroom also had both.' There follows a list of guests, including the Gills, the Rookes, Anna Simons and Ernest Treglown.

'Bridget loved it all and said "Isn't it nice to go to a party?" and Barbara clasped me firmly in her arms and kissed me every time anyone shook hands with me. Bridget played at it afterwards in bed. We heard a sort of cheering and then "Good Oxford! Do it, Oxford! Good Cambridge!" She is very advanced now and Edward's shadow. He draws pictures for her and makes her toys and helps her over all her stiles. She knows that No 1 in this Terrace is the Doves Press and next to that is a little shop where the people keep fowls and we get new-laid eggs. Just now Edward is making Bridget a coloured drawing showing the river and the houses of the Terrace. Bridget said "That's the Doves

Press" and then she pointed to the next house and said "And where's the chickens' press?" It sounded so funny.'

It was, perhaps, at this same party that Bridget, gazing with close attention at Mrs Graily Hewitt, observed with interest '*You're* like a daffodil!' Everyone was charmed with the lyrical imagination of the little girl and another lady asked 'What am I like?' Bridget studied her with the same candid scrutiny and replied 'You're like a pig.'

It was the pig-lady who told the story to Greta, gallantly adding 'after all, I did ask for it!'

The drawingroom was a beautiful first-floor room with three long windows opening onto a balcony and the Gill mirror in its golden frame reflecting the view of the river—'Turning weality into a beautiful dweam,' as Cobden-Sanderson was said to have observed.

The plain, white walls must have looked strange in 1905 when the heavy Victorian wallpapers seemed set for eternity. Even within the Arts and Crafts Movement such a thing was unusual, the official decor consisting of Morris wallpapers and Morris curtains, Gimson furniture and William de Morgan tiles round the fireplaces. They had done away with the Victorian richness of plush and pompon but, because Morris loved decoration, they had replaced it with richness of another sort—at least, those who could afford it had done so. Others, like the Johnstons, the Peplers and the Gills, had plainer, barer houses than was usual at the time. No room in a Johnston house was ever papered but, because Morris and his works were loved and revered, an exception was made in the case of the stairs, which were papered with his lovely *Willow Bough*. This tradition began at Hammersmith and continued in every house where Edward and Greta lived.

Another letter from Greta to Aunty gives a description of Barbara's second birthday party, as organized by her father. 'We had three little girls to tea, they had games in the drawingroom, then tea, then fireworks on the balcony while they watched from the drawingroom. Then the musical-box was fastened to an electro-motor and played while two candles danced round and round . . . finally they fried bacon in the dolls' kitchen and set the little table and sat round and ate it. Mrs Philip said "I see no way of giving a party except by hiring this house," and I said "Oh, but to ensure success you would have to hire my husband, too." She quite agreed.'

Douglas Pepler described a firework party in The Terrace one Fifth of November: 'For the sum of twenty shillings one could provide quite a spectacle in those days and, for about fifteen minutes, my contribution to the joint display rocketed to the heavens, illuminated the earth, and sent mild tremors down the more juvenile spines of the small audience.

'It was then Edward Johnston's turn and, with the manipulation of magnesium wire, some two-penny worth of coloured matches, a box of fuses, iron filings, and a pinch of gunpowder, he kept the fun going for an hour, on a total expenditure of eightpence!

'Not for a moment were the children either bored or restless. The Pepler shillings had had their day and ceased to be while the Johnstonian coppers established a memory which no subsequent Brock's Benefit was ever to overcast . . . and the chief reason for that success was not in our seeing unusual lightings with attendant if subdued explosions, but in watching the process of their manufacture: a process which gave quite as much satisfaction to Edward Johnston himself as to the rest of us. He had discovered that the true joy of toymaking is to give away the secrets.'

Johnston had a natural gift for playing with children, whatever their ages. Many years later he had occasion to break the ice for a two-year-old visitor, large-eyed in the strange house. They surveyed each other gravely across the dinner table. Then, still with equal gravity, Johnston picked up a table mat and put it on his head. Very slowly he leant forward until the mat fell off onto the table. The child stared, astounded at such behaviour. After a repetition of the performance a slow smile began to dawn upon his face. Suddenly he seized a mat with both hands. His arms were just long enough to reach to the top of his head and, copying his

The SEARCH on which we all embark –
To find the Thing which we believe –
Flies, like an arrow. to the Mark
That all our years can scarce achieve.

No journey brings us face to face –
With these. our hope, our love, our star:
Across the ways of time and space
Our Near must be forever Far!

Yet Love divine brings these to pass;
And Love will bring all things about –
And that dim vision in our glass
Shall clear, and gloriously shine out –

For God. who loveth everywhere,
Enters wherever hearts do bow;
Love is not only Then and There
But Love is Here and Now.

Come Adam's fear or Jeptha's pain
God shall hear these words again.

For men do speak with Adam's tongue
And say that Woman causeth Wrong:
And Jeptha-like are men brought low,
When they themselves have struck the blow:

Yet. when the Pharisees brought in
The woman whom they took in sin,
Being of Adam's flesh and bone
No man dared to cast a stone.

Nor dares who holds the Newer Law
Make Women to be Creation's Flaw:
His Saviour's Mother & his own –
Helped they not Adam with God to atone!

For Eachman did a Woman brave
Pain & Death – & Women gave
The life of Earth, the Hope of Heaven:
Let our hearts the names record –
EVA – the Mother of all living
MARY – the Mother of our Lord.

Two openings from a book of his own verses made by Johnston for his wife. Above, in black, 1913. Below, in black and red, added in 1918. Reduced

Here biginneþ ye Book of ye Tales of Caunterbury.

Whan þat Aprille Wiþ his shoures sote,
Þe droghte of Marche haþ perced to þe rote,
And baþed every veyne in swich licour,
Of Which vertu engendred is þe flour,
Whan Zephirus eek Wiþ his swete breeþ,
Inspired haþ in every holt and heeþ,
Þe tendre croppes and þe yonge sonne,
Hay in þe Ram his halfe cours yronne,
And smale fowles maken melodye,
Þat slepen al þe night Wiþ open ye,
So priketh hem nature in hir corages,
Þan Longen folk to goon on pilgrimages.

Geoffrey Chaucer (c. 1340–1400 A.D.) wrote these words about 1386 A.D. probably at Greenwich (as conjectured by Skeat pp. xvii & xix). They are here transcribed in a fac-copy of an English Back Hand of about 1586 A.D.

The Prologue as given by Skeat.
Here biginneth the Book of the Tales of Caunterbury.
WHAN that Aprille with his shoures sote
The droghte of Marche hath perced to the rote,
And bathed every veyne in swich licour,
Of which vertu engendred is the flour;
Whan Zephirus eek with his swete breeth
Inspired hath in every holt and heeth
The tendre croppes and the yonge sonne
Hath in the Ram his halfe cours y-ronne,
And smale fowles maken melodye,
That slepen al the night with open ye
(So priketh hem nature in hir corages):
Than longen folk to goon on pilgrimages
[... and specially ... to Caunterbury].

Though in its size the writing is about four times as tall as the 1586 Back Hand (in Chaucer's time the twelve lines might have been written in a space of about five square inches), yet the shapes of the Letters may be taken as somewhat like the characters in which the Tales must first have been written in a Book. The text is taken from Skeat's Student's Chaucer (1897)—v. opp.—but his punctuation is omitted and replaced by fine-and marks and certain letters are changed in form to the contemporary usage: thus þ = th, ſ = s (initial or medial), but final s = δ, and u = u. or v. (medial or final), but initial u. or v. = ὧ.

We lue þees hir late Scriueyn for to relÿe,
Ewⁱ as a scribe, by ordre of þe relÿe,
In nineteen hundred twenty seven Aprille,
Wrote out Wiþ yron and Wiþ fowles Quille.

For presentation to Miss Louisa Puller this is written for the Society—Guild of scribes & illuminators by me.

Opening of *The Canterbury Tales* written in a contemporary hand in black and red, 1927. Greatly reduced

host, he set the mat there and then leant forward and, triumphantly, tipped it onto the table. Together they burst out laughing.

Another small child he knew was frightened of men. She
dated her conquest of this fear partly from the day he took her to
the henhouse to find an egg and afterwards wrote her initial on
the shell, together with a picture of a hen.

When Johnston had small children of his own this gift, though
a great joy, was also an ever-present temptation to waste time.
Greta, reared in the belief that after breakfast men went off to
work, was shocked to discover that Edward, instead, got down
on his hands and knees and built a marble-run. For the children
this was enchanting but then they did not know that time lost
now might mean their father working all night later, or being
unable to leave for Scotland on the day arranged. Greta knew it
only too well. (Mrs Greig would write again and again '*When are
you coming?*' '*Which day are you coming?*' Always the answer would
be the same: 'Edward is not sure . . .') There were times when
she could not watch these games and felt driven to leave the
room. She thought anything better than 'being a policeman' and,
rather than risk hurting him by losing her temper, would, in
extreme cases, leave the house and not return until her equanimity
was restored. 'My husband is a saint,' she remarked once to
Ethel, 'but saints aren't always easy to live with.'

Edward could never work to a routine. He would alternate
between weeks of idleness and bursts of desperate, enforced
activity, when he sometimes worked all night. If he had promised work for a given date he would deliver it by that date,
though sometimes subjecting his client's nerves to a considerable
strain by the narrowness of the margin, as when he delivered
freedom scrolls half an hour before they were to be presented,
with pomp and ceremony, to august recipients. Princes, generals,
statesmen, peers, little they knew of the history of those scrolls
that made them Fishmongers, Drapers, Skinners—Freemen of
the Livery Companies of the City of London. On one occasion
Johnston finished such a scroll only an hour or so before it was
due to be presented to the Prince of Wales, and forty miles from

L   [161]

London. It is said that he took a camp-stool and sat beside the main road, waiting for a 'motor car' that was bound that way. When one came he hailed it and, after explaining the circumstances, asked the driver to deliver the precious document to the Guildhall, which, being a loyal subject, he did—in the nick of time.

When, in 1907, Greta was persuaded to go to Wiesbaden for a rheumatism cure Edward was so much unsettled by her absence that he did no work except his teaching for the whole five weeks she was away. He worried continuously, both about his work and about her. Had she asked the doctor this? he wrote; had she asked him that? Wasn't she having the baths too often or staying in too long? He had always understood . . . and so on.

Meanwhile the only thing he felt like doing was playing diabolo. In this, at least, his efforts met with success and when Greta returned he was able to demonstrate his increased proficiency. Greta was not a diabolo enthusiast, herself. She was more concerned about paying the weekly books. She spoke of trying to get some teaching to do but he assured her that it would be all right. 'I *will* be good,' he wrote, 'and earn lots of money for you and Bt. and Ba. . . . My Manchester lectures were the direct outcome of the book and there is no doubt it will lead to other work.'

In fact, there never was any serious shortage of *work*, either then or later. It was getting the work done that was the trouble. Johnston used to compare himself to the man in the old *Punch* joke, who, when asked by the doctor what his trouble was, answered 'I sleeps well and I eats well but when I sees anythink like a job o' work I comes over all of a tremble.' This was true enough in a sense, though hardly to be explained, as he sometimes explained it, by saying that he was lazy. Such a word was wholly inapplicable to him, whether he lay in bed all morning contemplating the nature of legibility or whether he spent a couple of days soldering a pair of broken nail-scissors on to the end of a long handle and thus constructing a tool to cut a rose growing high on the side of the house. Whatever he did he pursued it further than most men and with an intensity of concentration. 'When I see the work of any good craftsman I am ashamed at my laziness,' he wrote. 'But if there has been very little doing there has been an active contemplation of principles and purposes.' Few people realized the amount, or intensity, of thought that he gave even to seemingly simple problems. His friend Robert Bridges, urging him to do a small piece of writing, said 'You could do it in half an hour.' 'I would give half my substance to any man who would teach me to do *anything* in half an hour,' was Johnston's comment. Every commission posed a separate problem and every problem was infinitely complex. He would never, he said, be guided by a man who said that there were two sides to a question, for the smallest number of sides any object can have is four, as in a pyramid on a triangular base. A polyhedron may have any number and in a living thing—or a problem—every side may have a different shape, a different texture and a different relation to the others. All these aspects had to be considered before a problem could be solved. It was this, combined with his nervous temperament and the fact that he was always tired which made an ordeal of starting a piece of work. Once this stage was past execution was swift and sure. In the words of Noel Rooke: 'His penmanship was razor sharp and rapier swift; never hurried. . . . The writing had to be deliberate *and* swift to be possible.'

Greta did not wholly abandon the idea of doing some teaching and it happened that only a few months after her return from Germany she was asked to act as headmistress for one term at the school where she had taught in Wales. It was the summer term, she would have the children with her in the country, she would love the work and, what was more, she would earn a hundred pounds—a handsome sum in those days and a very substantial addition to their income. To be set against this was the fact that it meant leaving Edward alone for three months. Would he agree to her going, she asked. He answered that he was not sure, he could not decide just yet. He was temperamentally opposed to any plan that threatened any alteration in the daily round, whether it were going abroad or going out to dinner. The school wrote again, more urgently; something had to be done. Could she say she would let them know next week? But no, Edward was not sure, he must think it over. At last, in March, she wired refusing the job. After this the headmistress must have renewed her entreaties. She was ill and unfit to carry on but she would not leave her school unless she could entrust it to Greta. Almost miraculously, Edward agreed. Up to now he had considered every possible danger exhaustively—was it right, for instance, that small children should be exposed to the infections and epidemics that might occur in a large school? Greta had answered that epidemics were unlikely in the summer term but agreed that at the first sign of one the children should be sent home.

So she went to Wales and took the babies and was thrilled to find herself in harness again and in the midst of such an active world. 'There's so much life all round me,' she wrote, 'the young birds and lambs and children, I do like it so.' It was her one regret, at home, that she felt cut off from life. Edward rarely wanted to go anywhere and hardly seemed to notice whether he saw his friends or not. 'We sit by the fire and life goes by us,' she said. In general she thought herself the most fortunate woman in the world to be his wife, but there were times when she could not blind herself to the fact that she had given up a great deal for this uneventful domestic existence.

It was bleak for Edward left behind in London. He missed his family intensely and the house seemed very forlorn. Only the cat, Tablet, met him now when he came home from his classes, lonely as himself and running mewing to the door to rub against his legs in an ecstasy. At this time he was working very hard, flourishing the Doves Press *Browning*. It was nervous work, with the precious pages so easily spoilt by the tremor of a hand. He found the monotony of it a strain, too, when he had to repeat the same initial or flourish hundreds of times, the pages laid out in rows upon his desk. When Greta was there he liked her to read aloud to him while he worked to a rhythm, repeating the same pen movements over and over again, mechanically. He had brought the long, hair-line flourishes to a remarkable degree of perfection, swift and sure as the crack of a whiplash, fine as a spider's thread.

A steady hand was so essential for this work that he sent round a note to Cobden-Sanderson, two doors away, asking him to send more sheets, saying 'I do not wish to shirk a walk but it is apt to upset my hand and that would mean delay.' There was no question of his not getting on now; he was working as much as twelve hours a day. One little note seems to testify to a night well spent: 'Parcel to Mr Cobden-Sanderson at 8.15 a.m. if possible. (The parcel is on my desk.) Please call me 11 o'c.' Cobden-Sanderson scribbled a note: 'Very many thanks—you are playing up! I will not disturb you this afternoon but will send round at six for what you have done.'

Such little notes do not often survive, but when, as here, they have done so they are able to convey an almost poignant sense of actuality such as a letter can rarely give. Thus it is with an un-dated note in Johnston's writing saying only 'Mrs Phelps. Please do not frighten the cat,' perhaps relating to one of Pounce's visits of reconnaissance at Lincoln's Inn, before she acquired official status as a member of the household. Letters may evoke a sense of their period but notes outwit the calendar. They are of the moment; they are *now*. Those exchanges between Johnston and Cobden-Sanderson seem able almost to give a fleeting glimpse of that day-to-day life flowing between No. 1, The Ter-race, and No 3. Behind them lie the leisurely chats by the pillar-box, the casual words on the doorstep, from which new projects spring (to the chagrin of the biographer) quite as often as from considered proposals in letters.

Hammersmith must have been full of these casual meetings. At the bus stop news would be exchanged of the last meeting of the Artworkers' Guild—to which they all belonged—or sug-gestions mooted for the next. They all wrote letters for the mid-night post and met at the pillar-box. There they would stand and talk or slowly walk home with each other and back again while

Greta, Clare Pepler and Ethel Gill, letter-box widows, lay awake in bed. The ultimate click of the front door, if they still had not fallen asleep, would tell them that the problems of Faith and Reason or of the Artist and Mass Production had been disposed of for the time being and domestic life could now proceed.

In this May of 1908, however, Johnston was alone and only Tablet, the cat, knew what time he came in. Greta, much as she missed him, was revelling in the springtime countryside. She wrote lyrically of the babies running in the garden on May Day morning, when 'the grass was wet with dew and the paths in the wilderness covered with white petals from the plum tree'. The babies, of course, were an enormous success at the school and must have caused unspeakable delight when they gave their nurse the slip during prayers and made a bee-line for their mother, where she stood alone on the platform and 'throwing themselves on their stomachs on it, wriggled towards me.' Another letter told how Edward's photograph had been received by his daughters, who 'shouted "My own Daddy!" and kissed and kissed it.' 'Hardly any babies had such a nice Daddy,' they said.

Then came a dreadful happening. A child at the school went down with scarlet fever. Greta immediately took the babies away and settled them in lodgings by the sea, with their nurse. She wrote to Edward that she had made this arrangement temporarily and had meanwhile written to 'Aunt Pris' (his aunt) to ask if she could have them at The Beeches, her house near Rickerby. As they would be going to Laurencekirk in a few weeks they could pick up the children on their way.

In reply Edward wired: 'I propose to bring the children back. Please tell Aunt Pris.' He then went down to Wales, fetched the children and took them back to London.

The fact that Greta was then occupying the position of headmistress in a large school must have underlined the strangeness of having her arrangements thus summarily countermanded without reference to her. 'Can't you see,' she wrote, attempting to explain her distress, 'how hard it is for a woman who was *very*

[166]

independent from childhood and married so late, to have things taken out of her hands so completely? . . . It is treating me like a child and I have suffered through it and I think I ought to let you know. You see, if ever I preferred any life to my life with you or *anyone's* society to yours I should feel I had been guilty of an awful infidelity for which I could not forgive myself and to be so *close* people must understand. We are so different that my point of view will often seem very commonplace to you.' She kept telling herself that '*Anyhow*, whatever you did or meant, *I* was on your side and if your actions were foolish the folly would belong to me because I was part of you, and if they were odd, the same, or wrong, the same.'

In answer he wrote: 'Now for my high-handedness—I am so sorry, I would almost undo it if might be and send them to The Beeches. You know how vehemently I lay down the law about all things and uphold my views as best against all my *principles* of tolerance and reverence for others. We were allowed to argue as children, we had a somewhat narrow upbringing and we in-herited a good deal of wilfulness. I told you how I used to talk to Aunty and how sorry I had been and often I have been sorry for "bossing" you as I have done. You see it in Miles very strongly: when anything is *mentioned* he gives his opinion, generally a vehement one and often practical. I have the same vice, some-what quieter and in some ways less practical. But somehow, though he sounds unkinder, he manages to be kinder than I am. I cannot tell you how much I long to be kind to everyone and everything and how I fail and seem to hurt everyone and every-thing I ever meet. I know it is that I have always thought too much of myself and thinking of others is to me a strenuous daily effort, often intermittent.'

It might have been truer to say that he thought about other people as little as he did about himself. 'Women,' he used to say, 'are primarily interested in *people*: men are primarily interested in *things*.' The Johnstons, as a couple, were certainly an out-standing example of the truth of this statement.

It was in this letter that he said 'Again, we have had *such* training in taking care of people's healths, we fancy ourselves as good caretakers and nurses, to the distrust of most others.' This, of course, was the real crux of the matter. They had been brought up to regard the safeguarding of health—their own or other people's—as a moral duty which automatically took precedence over any other, and, moreover, as something in which their family possessed exclusive rights. Although the children were far removed from infection the very thought that someone, somewhere, was having scarlet fever would have made him feel that he must have them with *him* because no one but *his* family understood how to be '*really* careful'.

He had built the children a bower of branches in the garden, he told her, and furnished it with chairs and a table and, for each, a half banana on a vine leaf. 'I thought it would be pleasant for them to remember, though the bower will wither soon.'

It would be magic to remember, but Greta could well imagine how it would wreck a day's work.

This letter, characteristically, gives a verbatim report of an attempt to get the children to send messages. Bridget said 'I'd like to tell her Daddy built a fairy house and that we've been swinging—and a kiss,' but no message could be got from Barbara. At last, much questioned and long silent, she burst out irrelevantly, 'Look at that nice colour you been painting on that picture, the red colours and the green colours.' These were the flourishes to the Doves Press *Browning*. 'But what messages?' her father asked again, 'What messages for Mother?' 'You tell her 'at we've been out in the Park,' said Bridget. 'Out in the Park,' said Barbara, and with that he had to be content.

'Don't let them hinder your work,' Greta wrote in answer, 'that is one of the things I dread. What shall I do if you don't come on Wednesday week? It will be like the day at Crewe when I threw away my ticket because you did not appear.'

On this occasion, however, he did not fail her and they all went north together, to spend the holidays at Laurencekirk.

In 1905 the Prussian Ministry of Commerce had arranged a

lettering course for art teachers at Dusseldorf, the first of its kind. Count Harry Kessler, who had been greatly impressed with Johnston's work and teaching when he had visited England the year before, saw the opportunity of introducing it into Germany and used his influence to this end. Johnston was not himself available to conduct the course but was able to recommend his former student, Anna Simons, who carried out the work with outstanding success. Great interest was aroused and from then on Johnston's teaching was spread throughout Germany by Anna Simons and her pupils.

Count Kessler was the sort of aristocratic patron of the arts more readily to be found in the eighteenth century than in the twentieth. Endowed with great wealth and wide culture, he was a truly international and civilized man of the world. He was also a man of vision, fiery, vital, impatient, swept along by the force of his enthusiasms and carrying others with him. His letters frequently ended with a whole itinerary: 'I am here at the Hotel Cecil until Monday, then in Paris (Grand Hotel) until Friday and after that at the Chateau de Ste Honorine'—or at Berlin or Weimar or staying with Maillol in the south of France.

It was in 1904 that he first met Johnston. This was before he had founded his own Cranach Press at Weimar, when he was concerned with the publications of Insel Verlag, for whom he commissioned Johnston to design a dedicatory inscription for their series of reprints of the classics. In the years that followed this led to other work and Johnston designed a number of initial letters to be cut in wood by Rooke, Gill and others.

The Germans at this time were keenly alive to new developments in printing and lettering and soon after Johnston's book was published there was a demand for a German translation which Anna Simons gallantly undertook to make. It was not an enviable assignment. Johnston's first instruction to her was that where he had used a term with 'five or six different meanings' he had meant them all and she must translate them accordingly. A less courageous spirit might have quailed but she was determined, thorough and extremely capable and she persevered. She made

[169]

the remarkable statement, afterwards, that she had been greatly helped in this exacting work by the fact that while in England she had lived for some years with a great-grand-daughter of Elizabeth Fry. This remote cousin was unknown to Johnston but something of the Quaker strain apparently persisted in both of them and Anna Simons asserted that, because of this, when she came to work on the book 'certain attitudes of mind and modes of expression were familiar to me'. In the close study of the book which this work necessitated she became deeply impressed by 'its unfaltering thoroughness and clear thinking and the simple, lucid words used to deal with intricate and hitherto unsolved problems'.

Johnston conceded that, in some ways, this translation must have been 'more difficult to make than the original', but he had absolute confidence in Fräulein Simons. She had won it by hard work and meticulous accuracy in the past and, once won, his confidence was given unreservedly. Despite the fact that he could read no German he was satisfied that the translation was as good as was humanly possible. Had he been able to read it his exhaustive precision would have driven him to a thousand queries, no matter how excellent the work, but he was spared that. In the back of his mind there must have been a sense of relief in the knowledge that he could do no more than entrust the work to her capable hands and leave it there. This confidence in individuals was a most endearing trait in his character, the more so because the sweeping statements that he would make in championing them were sometimes startlingly at variance with his usual extreme caution in the interests of accuracy.

While at Hammersmith Johnston took a share in starting two small societies, the Housemakers' Society and the Society of Calligraphers. Both began as small groups of friends meeting unofficially at each other's houses or at Lyon's Smoking Room, next to the Cock Tavern, in Fleet Street.

The Housemakers' Society was started in collaboration with Eric Gill. They were both exasperated by shoddy building and particularly by the inefficiency and bad design of domestic fittings in contrast to industrial machinery. In the first place Johnston laid down that 'the chief aim of this society is to discover its aim', saying that this was the object of any reasonable individual and so might well be the object of a group.

This little Society continued intermittently for a year or two and then gradually fell into abeyance. In 1910 Johnston, who was treasurer, issued a statement that 'Whereas the treasurer having held for it a statistical balance of £1.11.6½ since the 14th May 1907 hath concluded that as an active combination it doth appear incapable of competition with ye amalgamated IDEAL of the D***Y M**L in Olympus, therefore setting aside 1/6½ and fourpence of his own for the expenses of dissipation, he hath divided all that remainder of 30/– into 24 shares of 1/3 for each annual subscription received unto all or any of those 15 members who paid up. Signed: The Absconding Treasurer, Edward Johnston.'

One of the fifteen members chanced to be H. G. Wells, who replied: 'Your noble behaviour shall live for ever in my memory. I am sending you as a modest acknowledgement *Ann Veronica*, because I am fond of her, and in Swedish—lest she corrupt you.'

The Society of Calligraphers was a larger and more serious group. Its object, as defined by Johnston, as president, was to advance lettering and to claim for such objects as manuscript books 'a place among real things—in the simplest, yet in the best sense—as works of art.'

One achievement of this Society, with the assistance of Anna Simons, who was a member, was to send an exhibition to Germany where it met with great success. The domestic life of the Society, however, was less fortunate. After four or five years of what Johnston described as its 'stormy history' it came to an end and later its place was filled by the Society of Scribes and Illuminators which has grown to be a large and flourishing body.

It was during the lifetime of the Society of Calligraphers— upon the doubtful unity of which it had unfortunate repercussions —that an event occurred which, to Johnston, was intensely painful and disillusioning. He had expected the little group of scribes that he had brought into existence to resemble what, in his possibly idealized view of the Middle Ages, he saw a guild as having been—a close community of men united in service to their craft and putting its interests before their own. So it had been in the beginning with Hewitt and Treglown, but now there were many more people involved and even Johnston could not blind himself to the fact that some were less concerned with the good of the craft than with their own careers.

After the success of his book his publishers were continually urging him to do another and he decided to bring out a portfolio of loose cards showing different alphabets, based upon (and superseding) his class sheets. This work was in hand and going forward, no doubt in that series of desperate rushes and pro-longed interruptions to which his publishers had become accus-tomed, when the thing happened. An ex-student of his own brought out just such a portfolio, based, without acknowledg-ment, upon his class sheets and book. Johnston was bitterly hurt —so much so that when the offending author called at The Ter-race he refused to see him. Strong feelings were aroused among his friends and, in particular, his publishers. There were urgent meetings with Hogg and Lethaby and talk of legal action but this proved impossible because the plates were not facsimiles. Johnston's portfolio, *Manuscript and Inscription Letters*, was rushed ahead by the publishers and produced as soon as possible and gradually the affair blew over and was partially forgotten. For Johnston, the wound healed as wounds heal that cease, in the end, to be felt at all except occasionally, in bad weather.

Such was the state of affairs in the summer of 1935, nearly thirty years later, when there occurred a curious and interesting sequel. After all the years of silence the plagiarist author wrote to Johnston asking for permission to reproduce a piece of his work in a book that he was writing. Probability would have been in favour of Johnston leaving such a letter unanswered, not deliberately, but because the feelings it aroused would have been so complex as to brand it as a 'difficult' letter, one to be dealt with, always, 'another time'. This did not happen. He answered promptly and at great length, covering both sides of two quarto pages and with a liberal allowance of his characteristic marginal notes. This letter is of rather special interest, both historically and in the light it throws on Johnston's character. I have therefore quoted it at some length, though, but for it, the whole incident might have been better forgotten.

'I am quite willing,' Johnston wrote, 'that you should have an example of my work in your coming book—particularly as you say you will take my consent as a sign that I am "no longer annoyed or offended".

'Trusting in that assurance from you I beg you to believe that it is true that I am no longer offended and that—if the term is permissible—I have *forgiven* the brilliant pupil who (quite innocently, I believe) published about 27 years ago a good deal of his Teacher's work as though it were his own original research.

'For that is what actually happened (in regard to various examples in your portfolio). Very few people realised it because very few knew the actual facts. You yourself evidently did not and, in the interests of the truth (in case you are still innocent of the facts), I quote here two examples.

'1. The *Family Tree* of MS letters in your portfolio was in effect a copy of the 1st fig. in my book or of a similar school copy which I graphed. No one had ever before published such a tree of letters in which *the actual forms of the letters* were used for the Names. That was an original idea of mine.

'2. The "modern" or "modernized" half uncial alphabet was a v. close copy of what I gave in my book and in school copies. *No such alphabet had existed before, apart from my teaching.* It was myself that "modernized" the old Roman half uncial (as in fig. 6 of my book) and produced what was tantamount to an original design for a pen alphabet. *That* (influenced by the Book of Kells) Roman ½ uncial was the source of my "modernized" form. On comparing the two you will see that in effect mine was a new form of writing.

'I don't blame you for not having realised the truth about these

[173]

and other examples. Perhaps I was partly to blame for not having made it clearer that they originated with myself. If our revival of Manuscript is to continue, however, it is historically important that its growth from stage to stage should be accurately recorded.

'Certainly in those old days (was it in 1908?) I was *un*christianly offended and acted unkindly (for which I am sorry). There were circumstances to some extent perhaps extenuating but, as far as the issue was concerned, certainly complicating. . . . In view of the legal proceedings I had decided that I should not communicate with you. I think now that that was a wrong decision, but the breath of the law is apt to warp one's judgment.'

Johnston goes on to recall that, at the time, he had been told that the author of the portfolio claimed that he, Johnston, had said that it would be useful to him in his classes. He had commented that he 'had no recollection of saying such a thing' and could not imagine what had given rise to the idea. The letter continues:—

'About 3 or 4 years ago a strange thing happened. (This was about 24 years after the event!) I was in a reverie, thinking of nothing in particular, when it seemed as though a small patch of blue sky opened—somewhere—and I saw—somehow—a table at an exhibition (I think a private exhibition that our Society must have had) and, among other exhibits, some small, paper (?) proofs of what appeared to me to be a facsimile reproduction of my semi-uncial alphabet (I don't recall anything else) and I "saw" that you said something like "These are some little things that I wanted to show you"—or "wanted to talk about"—and that I, hurrying past (because we were late for the meeting) and with my mind bent on the meeting, said—something to the effect that they looked "all right" or "good" or what not, and that they *"might be useful to me in my classes"*. Thus that curious glimpse of a past memory came back very clearly and my impression at the time, namely that you were going to bring out *some copies (facsimiles) of my class sheets on paper*—to sell perhaps at 1d. or 2d. each—and that they might save me the great and continual labour of jellygraphing my elementary class copies. . . .

'I have been rather worried about it since and am glad of this opportunity of getting it off my chest to you. And, if you care to, you can show this letter to anyone interested in the affair. And again, for any wrong, I am sorry.

'P.S. Please do not imagine that anything above is meant in reproach to you. It is meant, as well as I could make it, as a mere statement of fact and an explanation—to some extent—of things that we—neither of us—quite understood at the time—to which I add an apology.'

In reply the author thanked him warmly and spoke of a 'lifted cloud of regret and disappointment'. He, too, had been 'hurt and indignant' at the reception of his portfolio. He recalled having shown the plates to Johnston and that he had seemed pre-occupied and uninterested. 'I'm afraid, too, that then I must have been very dull,' he wrote, 'and not at all deserving the word "brilliant", for despite our little society I didn't know—till later—the real relation between work done by you and by others and I had never heard of the word "research". . . . ' Neither, he said, had he known the facts given in Johnston's letter about the 'family tree' of lettering and the 'modernized' half uncial.

Remarkable as such ignorance seems now, in one who con-sidered himself qualified to write on the subject, it appears to have been fairly widespread at the time, even among those with some claim to be regarded as authorities. In April 1909, *The Bibliophile* contained an article on the revival of calligraphy in which the name of Johnston was never mentioned except in-cidentally, in a list of those showing work at an exhibition.

From time to time people sought Johnston's advice upon the subject of ordinary handwriting. For this reason he gave it some attention but he does not appear to have been very deeply in-terested in the subject for its own sake. Scrawled and illegible handwritings did not distress him, he viewed their eccentricities with tolerant amusement and, where the authors were personal friends, with affection. He had no desire to improve them. To

Alfred Fairbank he wrote 'You know something of my idea of non-interference with people's hands, but of course when it comes to their being *taught* either badly or well I prefer the latter.'

In 1906 he was asked to report to the London County Council on the teaching of handwriting in schools. In this report he stated frankly that he could not approve of *any* of the seven nibs and twenty-seven copy books submitted to him. He advocated the use of a broad-nibbed pen and copies based on the book hands of the ninth and tenth centuries. He also urged that the copies should be written with the same type of nib as those supplied to the children and that they should be reproduced photographically and not engraved. At this time children were being set the hopeless task of copying with pens, on paper, letter-forms made (and partially evolved) by gravers on copper plates.

It will surprise no one to learn that these suggestions were not popular and that the matter was shelved.

Nothing was done until 1913 when Johnston addressed an LCC conference of teachers and again put forward those suggestions rejected in 1906. It seems to have been as a result of this lecture—though without further reference to Johnston—that the form of writing known as 'print script' was evolved. Johnston's publishers continually urged him to do a copybook himself and he started on one, but never finished it, probably owing to the fact that the war intervened.

In 1928 Marion Richardson, who had been a student of his, consulted him about copies she was designing. After an exhaustive criticism from him she completely rewrote them and said 'I have enjoyed doing each one and watching the effect of your advice. I little dreamt what a vast difference and improvement it would make.' These copies, published as the *Dudley Writing Cards*, were described by Johnston as 'the most practical copybook I have yet seen' and later he commended Alfred Fairbank's manual. He still regarded a round hand based on the old book hands as the ideal but had regretfully decided that these would never make a rapid handwriting and that it was necessary to compromise.

Hammersmith, 1905-1912

About the time that Edward and Greta had moved to Hammersmith, Miles and Mary had left Edinburgh and settled in a large house outside Bideford. Here Miles grew orchids, kept aquaria, studied fish scales under the microscope and wrote monographs of a highly specialized and technical nature. Here Edward—on visits —and his nephew, Gunnar, would play together all day with the latter's superb railway or go on kite-flying expeditions. Aunty and Olof lived with the Miles Johnstons, which meant that Gunnar had the doubtful advantage of an elderly great-aunt who constituted herself his personal servant, running to take off his boots when he came in or to wheel his bicycle up hills for him.

Olof sometimes visited Hammersmith where she was eagerly awaited by her nieces. 'They are always talking about you,' Greta told her, 'as one of the three people they know who would make a really satisfactory angel' and, again, 'They constantly talk of you and wish for you and say how beautiful you are and how long your hair is.'

Wild flowers were Olof's greatest interest. To them she now devoted her gift for drawing, conveying with infinite delicacy the character of speedwell, tormentil, herb robert and wild strawberry and a host of tiny, little-known flowers beside. She began to make herbals and Edward wrote in them, using sepia ink and a fine, italic hand that echoed the delicacy of the drawings. These little books were received with such enthusiasm at the Arts and Crafts Exhibition in 1910 that prospective purchasers were said to be almost quarrelling over them at the private view. 'If you can do with encouragement,' Edward wrote, 'Greta likes your flower-drawings better than any she knows and she is generally right in such things, at least I generally agree with her (as I *think* I do in this instance).'

Count Kessler, also, was impressed by her work. 'I still think with great pleasure of the way in which we missed our respective trains,' he wrote once, 'and with great delight of your sister's flowers. I hope she will consent to do me a little book like the one you showed me. . . . And then perhaps she would go one step further and learn to cut in wood.' She agreed to attempt this and Kessler eagerly sent her wood blocks to work on, but it is doubtful whether she ever got beyond some tentative experiments, or, even, whether he got his herbal. She was, as her brother had once remarked, 'a faithful mirror of my own bad habits'. That is to say she suffered from the same crippling lack of energy and was vague, dreamy, nervous and unmethodical. Like him she would play happily with the children by the hour together, oblivious of time. For them she drew and painted and cut out gorgeous figures of princes and princesses which perhaps originated the host of 'paper people' who came to play so important a part in their games. When it came to undertaking a commission, however, it was a different story. At once all confidence deserted her and she felt that she could do nothing without Edward. If he were there, if she could come to stay and they could work together, then, she felt, though dubiously, that she might be able to manage what was wanted, but unless some such arrangement could be made she was liable to refuse commissions. As Greta was fond of her and the children devoted she made a happy addition to the household, to which she came on long and frequent visits. These were, perhaps, the happiest times of her short life, for, except in her association with Edward, she never completely seemed to have come to terms with life. She was something of a stranger in the world.

These long, happy visits did not begin, however, until after Edward moved to the country. Olof was nervous about coming to London, fearing what was obliquely referred to as 'The Arazaty'. Aunty, while preserving Edward's letters, went through them with a pair of scissors, carefully snipping out such portions as might corrupt posterity. Such betraying sentences remain, however—preceding yet more eloquent cuts—as 'I do not think there is any real danger from the Arazaty.'

'The Arazaty' was the name of their father's house at Kenley, which he had called after his ranch in Uruguay. What he can have done to make Olof afraid to visit her brother in London remains a mystery for, according to Edward, 'he kept himself and his second family to himself and even cultivated a sort of estrangement.' This state of affairs dated from Edward's marriage. His father had explained to Greta, in the friendliest manner, that he could not invite her to Kenley as his wife disliked her so much. Since his wife always appears to have been reasonable and friendly and Greta was the last person to arouse an insuperable aversion in anybody, one is inclined to seek for some other reason. Possibly he resented Edward's marrying. They continued to meet, but only at the club. As for Olof, she felt it her duty to let her father know if she came to London—not to do so would have been 'concealment', and that neither she nor Edward could approve—so she seems to have preferred to remain in Devonshire rather than risk the possibility of a meeting.

Some years after the Johnstons settled at 3, Hammersmith Terrace, new tenants arrived at No 14. Douglas[1] Pepler was a Quaker, at that time engaged in social work under the London County Council. He was concerned in running Hampshire House where, as has already been mentioned, he began to experiment with printing. His wife was a painter, now claimed by domesticity, and their elder boy David was of an age with Bridget and Barbara. The children soon became inseparable friends and every morning David, aged about four, would accomplish the journey from No 14 to No 3, find Edward sitting over his late breakfast and a tempting smell of bacon in the air, and open the conversation with the words: 'Mr Johnston—I've got indigestion, can I have some of your breakfast?' As soon as this sovereign remedy had been applied the next request would be 'Can I play with your railway?' and off he would go, upstairs.

Soon the parents, like the children, were constant visitors at each others' houses and Johnston and Pepler were passing whole nights in talk. 'We miss you,' Pepler wrote later, recalling those evenings. 'It is bad for me to have no one to revise my creeds and no one with whom to consume the last precious moments of the night. I wonder if we get to bed any earlier, do you?'

Johnston's conversations were always liable to last all night

[1] Later known as 'Hilary'.

and many a guest missed his last bus home and was obliged to sleep on the drawingroom sofa. Johnston himself realized that when he was tracking down some philosophic theory other considerations ceased to exist. He even occasionally took practical steps in advance, such as setting an alarm clock and putting it in his pocket before paying an evening call. When the clock went off he would explain to his startled host that that meant it was bed-time, after which they would adjourn to the front doorstep and there be irresistibly compelled to continue the discourse.

The Peplers had a little cottage in Dorset. It stood alone on the far side of a cove, deserted and almost inaccessible, and joined to it was a tiny, long-disused chapel. This cottage they lent to the Johnstons who spent the most idyllic of all their holidays there. Olof, too, joined them and found new flowers to draw on the Dorset cliffs. Before she came her brother wrote describing the place to her: 'The cottage is at the head of a small stream. The chapel is absolutely plain and I think very fine in spite of all that it has been through and what might almost be called its cottage style. It is to me, at any rate, even impressive. It is a beautiful room to sit and work in.'

Greta wrote to Clare Pepler describing their arrival: 'It is ridiculous here to call it 1911, there *is* no time and we shall never die or go back to London but always stay here in this wonderful light. It is all magic. The day is a glorious pageant all sunny and friendly and then comes the night and we see heaven open.

'It is a lovely journey. At Wool there was the "omnibus" (ordered by your kind husband) and we clambered in. The children were wild about the primroses and bluebells. Williams was waiting for us and so kind and nice and charming Mr Dorey (I hoped his name was John but it's only George) had got everything so nice and the smoke was curling up from the chimney. I never saw any water like that of the cove when first we saw it. It was very vivid and changed from blue to the most bright, wonderful green all the time. How we enjoyed being rowed across and then eagerly scrambling up the cliff to see the house.

It is a darling house but of course it owes its unique character to the chapel, which is a gem.'

Near the end of that visit she wrote: 'We're coming back on Saturday, I can't tell you how I dread it, I could cry like a child. I *love* this place so and feel so much at home.'

The following year they went again and this time took David Pepler with them and Greta described to his mother the games they had played. 'We've been doing some history and tonight had a tilting yard on the lawn. Mounted knights rode at the ring (which was made of willow and hung by a slender string) with lance in rest and tried to carry it off. Edward and I were chargers and when the clarion was blown we pranced into the lists carrying a knight and rushed past the ring.'

A later letter says: 'David . . . had such happy days with Edward, helping him to make a box, for instance, all one showery day. He was always very riotous in the evening and wanted "the rough game" or to do an adventure on the little cliffs and we had lovely games then. Generally Edward chased them and they him, with fearful shrieks.'

That year they stayed for five weeks in May and June, Edward going to London for his classes and returning again. Olof again joined them and an American student and dear friend, Elizabeth Webb, stayed at the hotel in the village, as also did Anna Simons, who came to talk about the German edition of the Portfolio.

A few months after that visit came the move to the country, but to explain the reasons for this it will be necessary to go back a little.

X

Ditchling, 1912-1916

January 16, 1912. 'The babies are all peacefully asleep. All is well in your little house except that you are not there. This is to tell you that we love you and long to have you back. I feel sometimes as if I didn't know how to bear you out of my sight.'

Thus, with a misleading air of peacefulness, came 1912, a year of change, anxiety and separation; the end of the old way of life and beginning of a new.

Once again Edward and Greta had begun to think about a house in the country. This had always been their ultimate goal and now the advent of a third daughter had made it seem more than ever desirable.

Some years before this the Eric Gills had left London and settled in the Sussex village of Ditchling. Here, in childhood, Eric and some of his twelve brothers and sisters had spent their holidays on a farm, when they lived in Brighton. Here Johnston now visited them, to look longingly at the country scene, to listen, enthralled, to tales of home-brewed ale and home-cured bacon and all the country ways with which the Gills were so enthusiastically experimenting, and to enquire about possible houses nearby. If he had hesitated before, the sight of the solid old house looking down the steep High Street to the Downs, the spectacle of family meals in the flagged kitchen and of baking in a real, brick bread-oven would have turned the scales. This was life as it should be lived and here, in the country, there were still people who did these things naturally, carrying on the traditions that had come down to them. Johnston and Gill had both passed most of their lives in towns and thus they were able to discover the country for themselves and to feel for it the enthusiasm of a convert for a new faith—a way of life more righteous and more real than any they had known. The new discovery of each old tradition was a delight to them. As craftsmen themselves they held tradition in the highest honour and here they found men who took pride in doing things 'the right way', in curing a ham or laying a hedge as well as their fathers had done.

Here, too, Johnston saw the Sussex wagon—made, perhaps, by the local wheelwright—which he described thirty years later in a letter to Sydney Cockerell, possibly the last letter he ever wrote. 'A kind of Fairy Land Ship for beauty,' he called it, '—with all its little stop-chamferred and painted banisters and beautiful time and craft shaped "parts" (I dare say it had a vocabulary of its own of anything from 50 to 100 words or more). Once, in that abysm of time I had the luck to see one: it was empty (but would have carried a whole hayrick); it was drawn by six horses, in pairs, they were slightly decked with coloured ribbons and wore their historic shiny Brass Ornaments. Three carters shouldering long whips walked at their heads—and the glorious procession passed. . . .'

This was the vision of the country with which he fell in love and he and Gill together indulged in all sorts of eager plans. They were to live together, build a house—a simple quadrangle entered by an archway—somewhere up under the Downs. There Gill would have his workshop and Johnston his scriptorium, for the wives there would be a kitchen with a real bread-oven and for the children the freedom of the wilds.

Fired with such dreams Johnston returned to London and paid little enough heed, no doubt, to a warning letter from Miles. Miles thought Ditchling too inaccessible and feared that Edward would lose touch with what was going on in London and suffer the 'petrifying influence' of lack of intellectual society. If he failed to keep to the fore, Miles assured him, he would be 'elbowed out' by inferior men. Some journalist with no knowledge of the work would write a variant of his book and he would be finished.

'I noticed when you were here much the same symptoms that I find in myself,' he continued, 'viz. considerable lack of energy and consequent distaste for settling down to work. In your case, of course, the lack of energy has the more serious result of rendering you unfit to do your work. Most of mine can be done after a fashion, even when my finer faculties are blunted. Yours cannot as you require every power to be at its best to turn out work that will satisfy you. I know that the slackness and disinclination to work from which we *all* suffer is largely a matter of health and if your comforts or time for working are diminished by living far out it will be a heavy price to pay.'

It was characteristically pessimistic of Miles to suggest that Edward would be 'elbowed out', but there was a good deal of sound common-sense in his warnings, none the less, and a shrewd appreciation of Edward's peculiar difficulties in regard to his work.

For the moment nothing was done, then something happened which made the move imperative.

In June they went to Dorset, whence Greta wrote so gaily of being a 'charger' and racing about with the children on her back, but when they returned her doctor sister, Lila, with a professional eye not deceived by tan, was shocked by her appearance. She took her at once to a specialist who diagnosed tuberculosis. Their thoughts flew instantly to Jim, their brother, a robust young man who developed a cough and was dead within two years. Greta wrote later, from a sanatorium, of how the doctor had spoken of 'consumption' and 'at that *awful* word, which cost us as a family all our brilliant hopes, I really believed for the first time that I had it and the old pain and horror all mixed up with it rushed in like the sea. I came back to my room feeling as if the old, awful grief for Jim were of yesterday. I recalled the day we drove to Glenbervie and with our own hands let him down into the grave, so living and so wonderful a creature.'

What Edward must have felt on first learning the news it is hard to guess. In childhood illness had been the enemy beneath whose shadow one lived, the danger round every corner, the threat to every hope and plan, as an occupying army might seem to a child. It had been their household devil to be placated with a ritual of shawls and sealed windows and the hartshorn bottle. This feeling, reinforced by the streak of pessimism he shared with Miles, must have conjured up terrible forebodings and faced him with a panic fear rooted in childhood's nightmares. At the same time he believed that what happened must be a part of God's plan—and that, indeed, it was 'a sort of petty blasphemy' to wish the past different—and so, though a minor crisis might find him white and haggard, in face of real disaster he was calm. This particular situation, however, probably belonged to the former category rather than the latter, since it allowed so much room for hope and therefore for anxiety.

It was at this, of all possible moments, with Greta about to go into a sanatorium and the business of moving house to be under-taken, that he was obliged to make his first and only professional appearance in a foreign country. He had—by heaven knows what perseverance and ingenuity on the part of the sponsors—been persuaded to agree to lecture at the Fourth International Congress in Art Education at Dresden. Bitterly as he must have regretted his promise, he had to go.

At this time the Germans were turning from their traditional Gothic to Roman types and were thus particularly concerned with the new movements in lettering and typography. Stanley Morison wrote that 'the school of calligraphers practising the teaching of Johnston and Gill which has arisen since the year 1905 has in its hands the whole of German type-design, with the exception of the cruder kinds of advertising letter'. Sir William Rothenstein, also, when visiting continental schools of art some years later, was impressed by the fact that in Germany, in parti-cular, 'the name of Edward Johnston was known and honoured above that of any living artist'.

It was thus particularly unfortunate that Johnston's one visit to Germany should have been at a time when his domestic anxieties were so pressing as to leave him with little time or inclination for anything else. He made the journey there and back in the shortest possible time, staying only long enough to deliver his two lectures.

The lectures did not suffer, however. They were powerfully impressive and no doubt contributed to the extent of Johnston's influence as demonstrated two years later, on the eve of the outbreak of war, at the great Exhibition of Graphic Arts at Leipzig. Here Bernard Newdigate recorded that 'I seemed to see, in the German pavilions, the hand of Johnston on every stall and on every wall'. At Dresden Johnston relied chiefly upon blackboard demonstration as internationally understandable,[1] but he also had the help of Anna Simons who stood by him on the platform and translated what he said, for the benefit of the German-speaking section of the audience. His blackboard demonstrations were immensely impressive and this one, said Anna Simons, 'made a sensation'. Through years of practice he had achieved such mastery that he seemed to write on a blackboard with almost the same vigorous, easy flow with which he wrote on vellum. Indeed, he might have claimed to have invented a new art, being probably the first man to have used chalk on a blackboard as a medium for expressing his art itself and not merely for explaining something about it.

He not only told his audience, at this lecture, about the technical side of his work, the history and development of letters, he also expressed for them his own philosophy, the very heart of his message. After quoting from Goethe:

Dass wir uns in ihr zerstreuen
Darum ist die Welt so gross.
(Only through our freely faring
Is the world so truly great.)

he went on to say 'This expresses my sentiments not only in

[1]See illustration facing page 96.

regard to writing, but to life itself. Life is the thing we all want and it is the desire for life that is behind all religion and all art. I do not care what nation the art belongs to, or to what "school", as long as it is alive. I think I can claim that, poor as they are, the letters on the blackboard are alive: this is not due to myself—I am only a superior kind of motor or engine—it is due to the pen (which brings life to letters) and to all the life and the spirit of men that were before this. Our aim should be, I think, to make letters live—we can bring life to our poor letters—not merely for the sake of art, not to make advertisements of them, not for the sake of their beauty, but that men themselves may have more life.'

Four days after his return from Germany, Edward took Greta to the sanatorium at Midhurst and left her there. The following October he and Ethel Phelps packed up the things at Hammersmith, left the house empty, echoing to the tramp of removers' feet, and took the children to Ditchling. The new house was not at all what Edward had intended, nor was it at all like the Gills' house in the High Street, being a red brick villa on the outskirts of what was then an almost entirely unspoilt village. Outside it had gables, verandahs and white woodwork; inside it was freely garnished with *art nouveau*—that very 'squirminess and artyness' that Lethaby had said were vanishing partly as a result of Johnston's work. Here there was not a gas bracket but had its foliated curves, not a door handle but was decorated with twining water-lilies. However, the house had practical advantages and it was a foothold, a place from which to reconnoitre. Above all, it was somewhere to bring Greta.

When she came home in October it was to this new house with the smell of paint and distemper still fresh in it and, outside, the immense view of the Downs.

Noel Rooke, who was seeing Johnston frequently at the time, said that his health benefited greatly from the move to the country and that he became noticeably more robust. None the less, it did put an added strain on him and, as Miles had foreseen, tended to cut him off increasingly from the London life and the friends he had known there. The village was a mile and a half from the nearest station. An old horse-bus, with the word *Victoria* thinly painted out, made occasional, leisurely trips between the two, and a 'Fly, Omnibus and Wagonette Proprietor' in the neighbourhood boasted a 'National telephone number', but in spite of these amenities Johnston often had to make the journey on foot and his Mondays at the Royal College were made considerably more arduous by the additional hours of travelling. He gave up his class at the Central School, finding it impossible to continue both. His choice of the comparatively impersonal Royal College, rather than the Central School which had meant so much to him, was decided by the fact that Lethaby was still at the College. A tightening up of controls by the London County Council, an insistence on the importance of diplomas and regulations which made it impossible to continue the more elastic and imaginative methods of the past, had finally driven Lethaby to resign from the Central School which he had created.

In the new house Johnston fitted up a bedroom with a north light as a workroom and went on with the type he was designing for the Cranach Press, urged on by a stream of letters—anxious or enthusiastic as occasion warranted—from Count Kessler. That autumn Kessler paid one of his many lightning visits to London, staying, as always, at the Hotel Cecil, and taking Ditchling in his stride. There, when Greta was gardening with her hair in her eyes and a sack tied round her waist, he appeared, to her amusement, like a being from another world, faultlessly turned out from head to foot down to the spotless handkerchief in his breast-pocket which, if dropped, would be used no more.

It must have taxed Kessler's powers to the utmost to persuade Johnston to design his type, for principles were involved. Nevertheless he had triumphed, as he usually did, for his dynamic character contained a potent blend of autocrat and diplomatist. Johnston was won over, though, even with Kessler, he could be adamant in defence of a principle. In the early days he had designed initial letters and headings which were engraved on wood by other craftsmen, both for Kessler and for the Doves Press. Later, however, he refused to do this and insisted that the letters must be designed by the craftsmen who engraved them. Kessler, though 'rather pained' (his own words) accepted this refusal simply and without protest. The work was eventually done by Eric Gill.

Johnston's objection to designing type was based on the same principle that had prompted this refusal. He held, with Lethaby, that an object could only properly be designed by the craftsman who made it because the design should be an outcome of the craft itself and not arbitrarily determined on a drawing board. Thus he considered that the proper person to design type was the punch cutter. In the end he came to terms with his conscience by regarding himself as the collaborator of the punch cutter, equally ready to take advice or to give it.

Johnston's work on designing type for the Cranach Press had begun almost by chance. Shortly before he left Hammersmith an italic type had been designed for Kessler under the supervision of Emery Walker. The punches were being cut by Edward Prince, who had cut the *Golden* type for Morris, but Kessler was not entirely satisfied with the results and he asked Johnston, informally, to 'explain' to Prince certain aspects of the letters which, he felt, needed to be more clearly brought out. This Johnston did, with the help of large chalk drawings on blue paper, so effectively that Kessler asked for more 'explanations', this time 'on a business basis'. Soon he was asking Johnston to redesign certain letters and was so delighted with the results that he finally asked him to do the whole fount and had new punches cut. It says much for Walker's generous nature—as well as, perhaps, for Kessler's experience as a diplomatist—that he continued to co-operate on this work and to supervise the cutting of the punches.

This was the first modern italic type to be based on the Italian chancery hands of the fifteenth century. Kessler had planned to use it with the capitals from his Roman type but this proved unsatisfactory and he decided that it must have capitals of its own.

Before Johnston could start work on these, however, all Kessler's drive and enthusiasm was suddenly switched over to his *Hamlet*. He and Gordon Craig were planning an edition of *Hamlet* with Craig's engravings and for this they wanted a black-letter type. Johnston seems to have made some attempt to refuse this commission, only to be overwhelmed once more by Kessler's energy and determination. 'I am most keen about our programme,' he wrote, 'and look on every item much as I believe an Alpine climber looks upon some unexplored peak. But unfortunately I cannot do the climbing myself. I am like the old lady in a Bath chair waiting to be hauled up Mont Blanc. She is, of course, much more keen and adventurous than the man who has to pull her along.'

There was no gainsaying this old lady and Johnston duly embarked upon the black-letter, while the italic capitals and a proposed Greek type were shelved, awaiting a more favourable time. Time, as it happened, was short—for once even shorter than Kessler supposed it to be. Suddenly the full flood of his letters—sometimes two or even three in a day—was brought to an abrupt conclusion. A wire from the Hotel Cecil, '*Will you and Mrs Johnston give me pleasure witnessing Joseph*[1] *Drury Lane tomorrow night? Kessler,*' is dated July 20, 1914. It was his last communication with Johnston for ten years.

Already, as early as 1912, Kessler had had a rival claimant for Johnston's time and attention, an equally dynamic man: Gerard Meynell. No two men could have been more unlike, yet there was a certain similarity in their relationship with Johnston. Both were driving forces, dynamos of energy. Both had the power of persuading him to undertake work and of driving him to get it done. Both, too, succeeded in overcoming certain conscientious scruples on his part. Kessler had persuaded him to make designs for another craftsman, at least in the field of type design: Meynell, in turn, persuaded him to do work for reproduction and remained the only man for whom he would do this. Johnston used to call these lapses from principle (as he regarded them) 'bowing in the

[1] A Diaghileff ballet, the theme of which was by Kessler and Hofmannsthal.

house of Rimmon', a reference to the story of Naaman, whose very human request for a dispensation on this count touched and amused him. His objection to working for reproduction was based upon the fact that the processes ordinarily in use could not give results that would satisfy his high standards. He spoke of 'Two great modern illusions—Reduction and Reproduction' and pointed out that differences in size are absolute and not relative and that 'Nothing is reproduced, something different is produced.'

Gerard was the nephew of Wilfred and Alice Meynell and first cousin of Francis Meynell of the Nonesuch Press, one of whose first ventures in printing, a selection of the poems of his mother, Alice, had been rubricated by Johnston. Like his cousin, Gerard Meynell was a printer, but there the resemblance ended. In appearance he was small and dark with a hooked nose, a blue chin and flashing spectacles. He resembled the popular idea of a newspaper man, cocking his head like a sparrow, his hat pushed back and—almost—his thumbs hooked into his waistcoat. He and Johnston together made a most improbable couple. Meynell was a master of the pregnant, unfinished phrase, eked out with a wink or a jerk of the head. Johnston, to whom this kind of shorthand dialogue was a foreign language, would watch him with the close attention of a boy at a conjuring display and having, after some unequivocal interrogation, guessed at his general drift, would say 'I'm not quite clear whom you intend by *"the boys"*, but if, as I gather, the matter is confidential it might be best to say no more'.

Meynell acted upon impulse and with such energy as to force other people to fall in with his plans. He would burst in with the announcement: 'It's all arranged. . . . Nonsense, of course you're coming! We'll motor down to see him and discuss the whole idea. I've hired a motor, it's at the door now.' Even Johnston, under such pressure, would usually go.

Meynell saw the possibility of harnessing Johnston's gifts to his own energy and becoming a sort of business manager for him. Their association would not have been surprising had it been founded simply upon his business acumen and flair for spotting talent, but it was not. This incongruous pair was united by deep, mutual affection. One of the most surprising things about this surprising man was that behind his hail-fellow-well-met exterior, the reckless generosity and the aggressiveness to which it could give place—for he made enemies as well as friends—was hidden an unimagined depth of sensitivity and understanding. Equally unexpectedly, he possessed psychic qualities which afforded him occasional flashes of foreknowledge or telepathy.

It was Meynell's generosity which first touched Johnston. About the time that they became acquainted, in the summer of 1912, Johnston was going through a difficult period. Greta's illness and the move, together, put a considerable strain on his small income. It was at this juncture that Gerard Meynell, whom he hardly knew, sensing his difficulty, spontaneously offered him a sizeable loan. Johnston did not accept it but the incident made a lasting impression upon him.

The friendship ripened quickly. Johnston's diary becomes suddenly peppered with the initials G.M.—letters from or to him, wires, appointments, meetings in London, and then his visits to Ditchling. It was while Johnston was at Laurencekirk with the children in August 1912, that he received a wire from Meynell saying simply: '*Have chosen the simplest title—The Imprint.*'

The Imprint was a periodical concerned with printing which Meynell started with J. H. Mason, Ernest Jackson and Edward Johnston all named as co-editors. The first number appeared in January 1913. Johnston's father wrote, in his curmudgeonly way, 'As to yr. editorship I can't say I thk. the mr. o' you for that. Too many cooks spile the broth.'

There was something to be said for his point of view.

This journal set out to deal with every aspect of printing and the making of books including calligraphy and illustration. Its object was 'to benefit and, if possible, elevate the printing and allied trades and to show the place for craftsmanship in the printing trade'. Mason, who had been with The Doves Press, was an expert on typography and Jackson on lithography.

Extracts from two poems by Chaucer in brown with red and one blue
initial. Reduced.

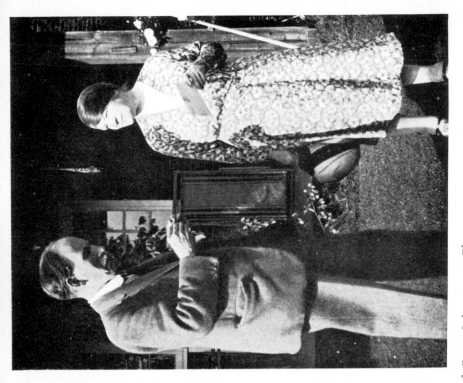

Edward and Greta Johnston at Cleves, 1930

Ditchling, 1912-1916

A new type face, *Imprint*, was specially designed for this publication. It was adapted from an eighteenth century model by Mason in collaboration with Meynell 'in an incredibly short space of time' according to the preface, probably with advice from Johnston, but without his taking much active part in it. He did, however, design the cover and contribute a series of articles on lettering under the title *Decoration and its Uses*. In a number devoted to books for children he also reproduced drawings by Bridget and Barbara (then aged 8 and 7) with a verbatim report of an interview in which he elicited their views on illustration.

The Imprint appeared for eight consecutive months, then faltered, missed two numbers, appeared once more and finally faded out. It met a sad end, beset by financial difficulties and disagreements among the editors. Johnston, fortunately, was not directly involved in the controversy but was probably torn between loyalty to Meynell and the suspicion that the other two might have some grounds for their resentment. It must all have caused him the most acute distress. Such things wounded him to the quick. He would be white-faced and silent, unable to bring himself to speak of them.

So *The Imprint* died. One more eager enthusiasm, beginning with so much excitement, such high hopes, so many plans and meetings, had faded into silence and disillusion.

The whole of this period was a time of great anxiety to Johnston for in the spring of 1913, while the first numbers of *The Imprint* were appearing, his wife's health had broken down again. Once more she was sent away to a sanatorium. Meanwhile he was very busy; besides his *Imprint* articles there was a genealogical tree with coats of arms and two illuminated addresses. 'You have done such a lot of your own work lately and I'm so glad,' wrote Greta, and again 'How much you've earned in the last six weeks!' She thought sadly of him sitting alone in the evening when the children were in bed. 'I have been imagining you at supper,' she said, 'and trying to pretend I was standing behind you kissing your dear, dark head as I so often do, till you are moved to some acknowledgment and move it gently under my lips.'

Ditchling, 1912-1916

In August she was allowed out temporarily, in the charge of her doctor sister. They rented a cottage on the top of Garvock, the hill above Laurencekirk, and there the family spent a very happy holiday, Edward and Greta camping out in a tent as they had done once before in Glen Esk.

In the end of August Greta went back to the sanatorium and found her room full of flowers and her friends eagerly awaiting her, for she had the faculty of making friends wherever she went. She wrote to Edward, 'You are a faithful darling to endure my crossnesses and my awful tracts of stupidity as nobody else would. I'm very stupid to be as clever as I am, aren't I? Send me a nice kiss and say it doesn't matter. You're the only person who can always find my scissors. I shall sit beside you all day and hold your hand—both your hands.'

He wrote telling her of the ambitious summer-house that he was building in their country garden. He designed and built it himself, to the intense interest of his children, adding a strange new smell to my experience of life and a strange new word that went with it: creosote. The summer-house had stairs leading up to a flat roof with a magnificent view of the Downs. When it was finished he took us up on the top for an official opening which included refreshments (he thought of everything, when dealing with children). 'What a lovely picture it makes in my head,' wrote Greta, 'to think of you four sitting on top of the new summer-house and eating blackberries.'

Early in October she was home, looking better than she had for years. This time the cure was complete.

While she was away Edward had been seeing a great deal of Gerard Meynell, who came to Ditchling and flew kites with him on the Downs. Later Meynell brought his wife to stay. They were a surprising couple, the vigorous little man with the indefinable air of Fleet Street about him and his tall, self-contained, intellectual wife, Esther, with dresses from Liberty's and shoes too elegant for our muddy lanes. She was musical and literary and became well-known later as an author of great versatility. Nelson, Bach, Miss Mitford, Hans Andersen and William Morris

[194]

all occupied her in turn, as well as novels and other works. It was for a book of hers, *Grave Fairytale*, that Johnston did the only book-jacket he ever consented to design. He scribbled what he intended as a rough sketch and was then so taken with it that he let Meynell reproduce it as it stood knowing that he could never recapture quite that carefree dash again.

The Meynells immediately fell in love with Ditchling—a sentiment not shared by their infant daughter. During their stay she expressed her dissatisfaction freely, while I sat on the stairs with my head in my hands repeating desperately, over and over, *'Oh, Joanna Meynell, don't cry so!'*

After that first visit they always came to Ditchling for their holidays and eventually settled there. Other people, also, followed us to the country. Soon after we moved Douglas Pepler wrote 'Can't you think of any work that I can do at Ditchling? We want an excuse to follow the prophet (you) into the wilds.'

Edward stayed with the Peplers whenever he spent a night in Town. After one such visit, when he had been teaching the boys to make darts, David remarked to his father 'If there hadn't been flying machines Mr Johnston would have made one'. Gerard Meynell seems to have agreed for he wrote Edward a postcard saying: 'Dear Sir, I am sending two sardine tins. Please make me a motor bicycle and a telescope.'

At the end of one of Pepler's letters was a p.s. 'David was seven yesterday.' In reply Edward sent him some verses beginning:

> *David was seven yesterday*
> *Goliath's years can scarce be told . . .*

It was a prayer that their seven-year-old champion ('little lion of Hammersmith') might deliver them from the ever-present forces of evil. This and some other verses of his were afterwards published by Pepler in a little book, *A Carol and Other Rhymes*.

Twenty-two years later, when David died, his father wrote to Edward: 'I tell you as one who loved him as a son, so that our sorrow may be shared and the joy in it divided', and Edward answered '. . . I think of the grave young shepherd climbing up my stairs at Hammersmith and of his good life. I think of him that now—or soon—he will be serving under Michael, helping to save us from the Dragon. If we are ever to be helped by angels how we should like to be helped by him.'

Pepler was an adventurous man, and it was not many years after we moved to Ditchling that he gave up his job and followed us, having decided to take a chance on printing. The Gills had moved out of the village to a remote spot on Ditchling Common, about two miles away. The Peplers moved into their old house in the High Street and there, at once, Pepler started experimenting with printing in the coach-house that had been Gill's workshop. Both Johnston and Gill were in the thick of the printing from the start and both had much to contribute. Gill, who was experimenting with wood engraving, provided blocks, and Johnston provided the fruits of over ten years' thought upon the subject. He had given a great deal of consideration to the problems of printing, both when he was working with the Doves Press and Count Kessler and when he was contemplating starting a press of his own. All his experience and his ideas were now poured into this new venture.

On January 16, 1916, his diary records: '*E to Sopers abt.* 3.30–9.20 *printing*' and the next day '*E to Sopers abt.* 6–8.30 (*Gill there*) *printing.*' On February 4: '*At press abt.* 7.25–8.15. *Gill and Douglas gave me a copy No 7 of first book.*' On February 8: '*To press abt.* 6 *found G and P nearly finishing* 2nd *edn. on to Crank,*' [Gill's house] '*LATIN, supper and talked Mill and Farm.*' So it went on. Almost every day he would be round at the press and often they would meet again in the evening. 'Talking Mill and Farm' was talking of their plans, his and Pepler's, for moving out of the village as Gill had done, to find a *real* country life. 'LATIN' was the Latin Club (with a membership of three) which they started, to teach themselves the language. They played a game with innumerable tiny cards written out by Johnston with an English word on one side and the Latin equivalent on the other. The fact that Gill had recently become a Roman Catholic and that Pepler joined him at about this time gave both a special interest in the subject. Johnston's study of early manuscripts and his intense interest in etymology had long since bred in him the same enthusiasm.

In October of this year the three men started a little magazine together. It was printed by Pepler at St Dominic's Press, as it came to be called, and illustrated with wood engravings by Gill. Johnston contributed little except to their Christmas number that year, when he wrote in each copy a full page *Gloria in altissimis Deo*.

GLORIA in altissimis Deo et in terra pax ho‑ minibus bonae voluntatis

From *The Game*, 1916. Red. Actual size.

This, with a beautiful nativity by Gill made up their 'Christmas card', as they called it—a bargain, at half a crown! This periodical was called *The Game*, probably because they produced it for fun. They had decided, according to Pepler, 'to print our views about things in general which we regarded, as all men regard games, as of supreme importance.' It gave Gill his first opportunity to express himself in print on those subjects of which he was to write so much later. In *The Game* there appeared his early essays on *Art and Industry, Slavery and Freedom, The Factory System and Christianity*: all those questions, in fact, upon which they were accustomed to spend so many midnight hours in talk.

Gill was the kindest and gentlest of men (in contrast to some of his more dogmatic pronouncements) but his early work gave rise to some hostility. It was criticized as 'modern', indecent and even blasphemous and his views were equally suspect. In Ditchling some of the more respectable matrons refused to call upon Greta because we were known to be friends of the Gills. He was said to preach socialism at the cross roads as well as carving nude figures and, in fact, to be highly undesirable. This ostracism of Greta, however, was ironic, for she was conservative, decidedly not 'modern', and had even been known to be shocked by his work herself. My own view, at the time, of this controversial figure was, if not very discerning, at least outstandingly original. I was probably prejudiced by his partiality to long, incomprehensible discussions with my father when, at the age of six, I described him to my grandmother as 'Mr Gill— a *most uninteresting* man.'

At the time that Pepler set up his press in Ditchling, Johnston was occupied in designing his block-letter alphabet for the Underground Railway.

A surprising thing had been happening in London in the past year or so. Suddenly, and already with conspicuous success, the Underground Railway had assumed the position of pioneer and patron of the arts. A new kind of poster had begun to appear on their stations, notably the work of MacKnight Kauffer, confronting the traveller with a daring modernity which at first bewildered him. There was also MacDonald Gill's 'Wonderground' map of London, that first decorative poster map which led to so many others, both of his own and his followers. In the realm of architecture, too, the Underground was preparing to give a lead to the rest of London with the new stations designed by Charles Holden. Behind this revolution was one man: Frank Pick.

Pick was the Underground's strong man, a man with a mission. He had a vision of better towns, cleaner, more beautiful and more human and he was determined to use his position to educate the public and raise the standard of taste. Like most strong men he seems to have had his detractors and some called him a dictator, but he knew how to be generous as well as forceful. Above all he was far-sighted and possessed of determination and patience—an almost irresistible combination.

Pick had begun to think about a new alphabet for purposes where large lettering was required, such as notices and station names. He wanted it to have 'the bold simplicity of the authentic lettering of the finest periods and yet belong unmistakably to the XX century', and to this end he experimented with compasses and a set square, aiming at an alphabet based on squares and circles. He was looking for someone to embody what he had in mind, someone who could do for lettering what Kauffer and Holden had done for posters and station architecture. Gerard Meynell found the man.

To begin with, he actually found two. He persuaded Johnston and Gill to agree to co-operate. For Johnston the subject was thorny with conscientious difficulties, moreover he much preferred doing his own work to making these anxious excursions into designing. It is doubtful whether there was another man in England who could have persuaded him to do it, but Gerard Meynell did. Casually the suggestion would have been thrown in, through a haze of tobacco smoke, as the three men sat together. After some account of what was wanted Meynell would have tossed it off, as though inviting them to scribble a design upon a postcard: 'You two could do something, couldn't you—h'h? Course you could!' Somehow they eventually agreed, though Gill later dropped out, saying that he had too much on hand and that 'It was Johnston's business.'

It was in June 1913 when Greta was in the sanatorium and *The Imprint* was in full swing, that Meynell first persuaded John-

ston to go to London with him to see Frank Pick. It was also in
1913 that Gill began to make preliminary sketches for the first
really big job of his career: the Stations of the Cross in Westminster
Cathedral. For him this must have been an immensely exciting
event. Years before, when they were living together, he and
Johnston had wandered in the gaunt shell of the then unfinished
cathedral in the dusk. 'It is a magnificent building,' Johnston had
written then, 'and the size and breadth of its conception is vastly
impressive, especially in the dusk which darkened the walls and
hid the roof. Far up the windows faintly lit by the evening
sky, or London's light perhaps, shone out of the blackness.
We stumbled about and examined and felt what we could
not see. Far away a party of people were being shown about
by a man with a lantern—a picturesque group in a spot of
light.'

This other, more exciting claim on his attention would have
been reason enough for Gill's refusal of the Underground work,
but it seems possible that, knowing Johnston as he did, he
realized the extraordinary difficulties which collaboration with
him would entail. Johnston was incapable of adapting himself to
other people because, with all the good will in the world, he
could not compromise. Such a collaboration would have been
like the partnership in the Kelmscott Press that Morris is said
to have offered to Emery Walker with the words 'Of course I
shall want to have it all my own way.'

Preliminary arrangements with the Underground hung fire for
over two years, meanwhile Gill set to work on his new commission. Early in 1914 he wrote asking Johnston to go out to the
common to see him. 'I'm getting ahead with the Stations of the
Cross now,' he said, 'so if you *can* come you'd confer a favour on
me by your criticisms. I've also got a particularly beautiful
inscription to show you, a regular snorter.' He was having a hard
struggle with his name as yet almost unknown and a family to
support. There were times, when he had to go to London to
supervise the erection of one of his Stations of the Cross, when
he had not the money for the railway fare and was obliged to

Ditchling, 1912-1916

bicycle or to borrow a few pounds from Johnston, whose private income, small as it was, made all the difference.

The outbreak of war no doubt caused the work for the Underground to be shelved for a time. Just before Christmas 1915 Johnston began work on the designs for the block-letter alphabet and from then until the following June he was working on them fairly continuously. During this time he was seeing Gill and Pepler almost daily and when he went round to Sopers to help with the printing he took his preliminary sketches to show them. Thus, though Gill took no part in the work himself he was in constant touch with it all the time and must have discussed it very fully with Johnston.

The first essential quality of this type was, of course, legibility. (Johnston considered that Pick was too much concerned with appearances, with what would *look* well. He himself approached the problem with the austerity of an engineer.) Legibility was a subject to which he gave an immense amount of thought. Many entries in his notebooks refer to it. One, pointing out the essential connection between legibility and familiarity, observes that if, instead of the letters ABC, we were accustomed to write 123, then 312 would not only spell CAB but would *look like* cab to us. 'It would look like the sound, the word, the thing meant.'

'The basic idea of this UD alphabet,' he wrote, '(Block letter mono-stroke being the only prescribed conditions) was to combine the greatest weight or mass with the greatest clearance of letter shape. The lower case o is the key letter. It is circular and has a *counter=twice its stem width* (giving approximate ideal mass-and-clearance). *Ascender and Descender projection=3 stem-widths* giving 7 *stem widths* for the b, d, etc. and hence for capital ABC height. . . . I have reasons for supposing that the $\frac{\text{height}}{7}$=Weight Ratio is approximately the best for *Reading* matter in larger size letters, particularly for printed letters on posters etc and particularly for block letters. (Note. An official of the UD Ry. said they could put *more on a poster* in Johnston type than in any other type they had. I took this to mean that they could use Johnston type smaller than their other types without becoming illegible.)'

Johnston laid great emphasis on the importance of spacing and complained that people spaced these letters badly because 'They think of the Letters apart from Background (which cannot be because letter and background are a complex).' On his drawings he wrote detailed notes calling attention to almost indetectable subtleties of proportion and arrangement. In certain labels that he afterwards designed for the Underground he measured the spaces between letters to a hair's breadth and spent days in experimenting with minute adjustments.

This block letter, which was to exert an immense influence upon the future of lettering, caused a stir among typographers when it appeared. 'It was a breathtaking surprise to nearly all who could be interested,' wrote Noel Rooke, 'the very lowest category of letter had been suddenly lifted to a place among the highest. We can scarcely now understand how revolutionary a proceeding it seemed. In this definite "Utility" letter he had used subtleties till then only found in the best of the Roman inscriptions.' Johnston himself maintained that the secret of the success of this type was simply that he had gone back to classical Roman capitals for the proportions. Once this basis had been established 'the alphabet', in his own words, 'designed itself'.

In speaking of the almost universal badness of block letter before this type appeared Rooke specified one exception. He recalled a certain rainy evening when he, in company with Gill and Johnston, had been walking through the dark streets, perhaps returning to Lincoln's Inn. The pavements gleamed in the lamp-light and so did the waterproof coverings of the tradesmen's carts that went rattling by them. As they walked they became engrossed in studying these carts, with enthusiasm and even excitement, for here on their covers, in one small backwater of the lettering trade, tradition had preserved an otherwise extinct species: a really good block letter.

The schedule of his life's achievements which Johnston composed for *Who's Who* in 1937 listed only three main items in his career: 'Studied *pen shapes of letters* in early MSS, British Museum'

Ditchling, 1912-1916

—'Teacher of *the first classes* in formal penmanship and lettering' and 'Designed block letter *based on classical Roman capital* proportions (for London Electric Railways).'

In a characteristically long, explanatory letter he asked the editors not to curtail these entries although they might seem 'a little unconventional' because the exact wording was important; the reference to the block letter, in particular, would be 'pointless' without the reference to the basis of the work. 'They have a historical and technical value,' he said of these entries. 'In fact they connote the most significant features of my biographical-professional record. I claim no particular merit in myself but—historically—it happens that I have been the pioneer in three rather simple and, indeed, rather obvious, ideas, which—technically—have become of some importance.'

In a letter to John Farleigh at about the same time he wrote: 'The only thing of mine for mass production which is fairly (i.e. truly) representative is the Block Letter Alphabet which I designed for the Underground Railways. . . .

'I might add that this particular design appears to have become of considerable historic importance (in the world of Alphabets). It is in fact the foundational model of *all modern*, respectable Block letters —including those painted on the Roads and Signs for Motorists and Eric Gill's very popular sans-serif type. It seems also to have made a great impression in parts of Central Europe—where I understand it has given me a reputation which my own country is too practical to recognise.'

Once again the Germans had been quick to follow Johnston's lead. While in England there was a time lag of twelve years before a comparable block letter became generally available, Germany was forging ahead producing her own types on the *Johnston* model and these, in turn, were crossing the Atlantic, while the original *Johnston* remained quietly underground.

The reason was partly that *Johnston* was a private type face, the exclusive property of the Underground Railway. When, some years later, the Monotype Corporation made what was virtually the same alphabet available under the name of *Gill sans* it ran like wildfire through the whole printing industry, with a meteoric success that eclipsed its predecessor.

'I hope you realize,' Gill wrote to Johnston, 'that I take every opportunity of proclaiming the fact that what the Monotype people call "*Gill*" *sans* owes all its goodness to your Underground letter. It is not altogether my fault that the exaggerated publicity value of my name makes the advertising world keen to call it by the name of Gill.'

'E.J. merely drew attention to classical proportions of Rom. caps,' Johnston noted. 'Gill (or anyone) could not avoid similarity.'

Thus, in the spring of 1916, in the back bedroom of the house at Ditchling, Johnston designed his block letter alphabet which has been described as having brought about a revolution in printing.

He continued to do work for the Underground over a period of nearly twenty years. During this time he designed a heavier version of his type for special purposes[1] and a compressed form for use on buses, of which he told his students: 'If you know where an omnibus is going you owe that to me because your fathers and mothers did not ever know where an omnibus was going: you could not read the letters on the old omnibus.' When he was engaged in designing this latter alphabet he spent his spare time on Mondays (his day in London) standing on the curb and studying the buses as they came towards him, their destination boards crowded with a type so heavy as to appear almost solid black. In the end some passer-by took pity on him, an obvious countryman with his brown tweed coat and his walking stick and that remote, lost look in his eyes, stranded there on the pavement's edge while the crowd eddied round him. The bus stop, he was told kindly, was further on; it was no use waiting there.

His work for the Underground included other, minor items, labels, initials and borders for posters, also he redesigned the UD bull's eye. This originally had a solid red disk crossed by a label.

[1]See illustration facing page 272, which shows notes for this.

Ditchling, 1912-1916

Pick, who had been struck by the Y.M.C.A. triangle, asked Johnston to design something like it 'but more balanced'. He produced the now-familiar red ring, calculating its thickness and that of the label across it with his usual minute exactitude.

In addition to the condensed type for buses he also designed numerals for them and it was while he was engaged on this work that he had experience of Meynell's telepathic faculty. It was a small enough incident in itself, but it made a great impression on those concerned. Johnston was working desperately on designs which were needed at once when he was suddenly brought to a halt by a difficulty about one particular figure, which could have been either a nine or a six. Urgent telephone calls were put through to London but Meynell could not be found. When at last he was located Johnston began to explain that there had been a hitch but before he could say more Meynell asked 'Is it something to do with nines and sixes?'

Country life was a joy which even the coming of war at first did little to tarnish. There were idyllic years of expeditions and picnics on the Downs; years when Johnston accompanied his family more often than he ever did afterwards. He would be in his old Norfolk jacket with his mackintosh slung over his shoulder from the crook of his cherrywood walking stick. At the top of the Downs one's climb was rewarded not only by the immense view but by a most beautiful dewpond, very large and perfectly circular. The Army did away with it in the second war, but in those days it was like a small lake, reflecting the sky. Johnston made matchbox boats to sail on it. There was a match for a mast and a piece of card for a sail, then out would come the sealing wax that was always in his pocket and he would fasten mast and sail in place. Then we would set the little boat on the dewpond and watch it sail away.

Once, in a beech wood that clothed the steep hillside, he found a large flint, curiously shaped, rounded and knobbly with a sort of head. It was an old monster, he told us, which lived up there and kept a little shop. Then he showed us the hole where it lived and gave us a penny, suggesting we might buy something, as we were there. We were doubtful. Even I did not wholeheartedly believe in stone monsters that kept shops upon the Downs. However, he turned out to be quite right, for when we looked in the monster's hole there, sure enough, was a bar of chocolate. We pushed the penny into its chalky lair, among the fallen beech leaves, and left the old monster alone with its earnings. Perhaps they are there still.

Once he helped us to build a miniature castle on the flat grassy bottom of a chalk-pit. It was inspired by Pevensey Castle which we had lately visited and was built of flint, a ruinous quadrangle of walls and towers. To complete its likeness to a real castle he made a little notice board and on it wrote an injunction against leaving litter in the precincts. This he erected in the middle and then, to add the final touch of realism, collected tiny scraps of orange peel and paper which we carefully arranged within the walls.

If we showed signs of flagging on the walk home he would bring from his pocket what he called 'shabby old toast' and share it among us. I think he must have carried toast in his pockets habitually, in the same way that he would often carry meat for the cats in matchboxes, or titbits for the birds. The toast was certainly tough—*leathern* was our highly descriptive word for it —but it was so cheering to have food when we were tired and hungry that this did not worry us.

In the early days at Ditchling he used to work with his door open and put a board across the bottom to prevent me from straying in. I could not surmount this obstacle so I used to stand outside and bleat to be taken in until he left his work and lifted me over. The board was thus merely an inconvenience to both of us. In later years his workroom door was invariably shut. Perhaps at this time his excessive nervousness about his children made him think it essential that he should be able to hear a wail or a shriek—those very sounds, in fact, which most men engaged on exacting work would wish to exclude.

Inside his room it was like another world. Even the smell was different; the musty smell of old papers, the exciting smell of varnish and the beautiful, clean smell of newly planed wood all mingled together. The room was full of everything in the world, racks of tools and shavings and shelves of books and piles of newspapers and cups of tea and crusts and bunches of turkey quills and all sorts of objects waiting to be mended. Over it all hung an aura of mystery, of wonderful secrets. Those crowded cupboards and shelves and that capacious desk left room for unlimited possibilities. There were always, somewhere, unfinished presents and toys that no eye dared look upon, waiting to burst forth in glory on some future birthday or Christmas. Sometimes they stayed there for years, waiting till the spirit moved him to finish them. The wonder and the richness of those toys was indescribable. They gleamed with paint and smelt gloriously of varnish, and varnish has smelt glorious ever since. There were marvellous shops, one for each of us, grocer, greengrocer and fishmonger.[1] Only the fishmonger's has survived intact, with a beautifully lettered fascia board announcing the partnership of Benjamin Bunny and S. Henny Penny and painted wooden fish hanging up, rather unconventionally, by loops in their noses. He brought to such work the same meticulous and loving craftsmanship with which he wrote a manuscript and, like his manuscripts, his toys were as near perfection as he could make them. One beautiful example was the dolls' house that he made for Bridget and Barbara. Unlike most dolls' houses, which are urban or suburban in inspiration, this one was entirely rural, being modelled upon the Peplers' cottage in Dorset. One of the most satisfying aspects of this and other toys was that everything really worked: the doors had real hinges and real latches, the windows opened and shut and had real glass. The stairs, too, were negotiable: the inhabitants could get up or down or even out onto the roof by means of a ladder and a trap door. The inhabitants, however, were not dolls.

In 1910 some verses by Patrick Chalmers had appeared in *Punch* under the name *The Puk-Wudjies*. This word, quoted from

[1]See illustration facing page 113.

Hiawatha, means "little people' and Chalmers described these creatures as he imagined them:

> *They live 'neath the curtain*
> *Of fir woods and heather,*
> *And never take hurt in*
> *The wildest of weather,*
> *But best they love Autumn—she's brown as themselves—*
> *And they are the brownest of all the brown elves. . . .*

Edward was delighted with the verses and painted some puk-wudjies on small blocks of wood—little brown creatures with smiling faces, sitting cross-legged and clasping huge nuts or fruits. A few months after the verses appeared he wrote to Aunty: 'The most successful toy ever known has been my 'puk-wudjies'. . . . They have been played with every day—sometimes all day—for *months* and their names are drawn from *Morte d'Arthur*, the saints and many other sources. They are always dying or being put to death, and buried, and coming to life again. All their acts and words are said aloud the whole time, thus, for example:—"Launcelot, get up out of your tomb and make room for Bedevere." Their houses are always furnished with prisons and generally with tombs, now they have your charming tables and chairs as well so they have a greater air of comfort.'

Not only were these creatures played with 'for months', they were played with for years and became a family institution. They multiplied rapidly, emerging from Christmas stockings or being discovered in the course of birthday present-hunts or even in railway carriages, where they were found perched on racks or window sills during the more restless periods of the annual journey to Scotland. When, therefore, a dolls' house was made it was made for them and was known as Puk-Wudje House. The steps of the stairs were right for them to stand on, the doors were of their height, even the chimney was made to measure so that they could be dropped down inside it, with a satisfying rattling sound, and appear in the fireplace below.

It was not only toys that he made for us but books and pictures

Book jacket in black and red. See page 195.

My dear Mary

Ditchling
Xmastide
(æ.C.Err.
mcmxlii)

Thank you for the beautiful little book of Essays and your kind letter of the 8th Dec. You sh'd have been ans-wered sooner but for my rather feeble head.

The Essays (the 1st 30 or so at least, wh. I have read) seem to have a special value in that they are so very reminiscent of the Writer — and the 2 large Engravings the great ornaments to the Book (the first, es-pecially, going even utterly inimitable by any other hand).

continued 11 January, mcmxliii

That it is say'd totally inimitable, it is un-copyable by any (I've known how tries practised & tried & tried by this Bourel), who had the same master of course.

(Some aspects of this art are seen in works of R. Austin's items when printing — & it's engravings on "to swift a line."

Swift is a good word for him; he hurts swiftly — dividing swiftly — and leaves swiftly. When that happens he very much forgoes you and, for that he had left who had so much depends on him and had found him expendable.

But somehow that made to write them (and was sure that you would know I was not indifferent). It seems to me a national loss that he died so young — (but for such as for young children) there is consolation in the thought that they are wanted elsewhere, that Life is fuller.

(Just as I am sure that all [the] mortals must know of certain children: That an man of little boy cousin — who made a great friend of me; the R. Thomas's [have] a much loved little girl, both last drowns abundant life. Our National Biography is full of such great names — here are some a few cases, Chatterton 18, Keats 26, Shelley 30, Sir P. Sidney 32, Byron 36)

Continued Mar 43.
Death & disease of Spirit commonly goes together with the fullness of power. Brief life is dependent on actual age; and his best work (such as the engravings on P.2.) has the Spirit of Life itself.

P.S.
The lapses of Time in this Letter you will reproach (some lapses in my health combined with the difficulties of time at least of an attempt to make the Script good). With Love

(P.S. The Writer may not have caught this Spirit, but, if one man alone could and now made good use of one who knew flour might know it, it is so.)

too. He wrote out *The Puk-Wudjies* for Bridget with a border of pine trees on either side with elves climbing in them. Two of these were Bridget and Barbara, the taller one dark, the smaller red-haired. They often appeared like this in pictures and illuminations of the period. There was no attempt at realistic portraiture, the figures were simple, even naïve, their relative size and colouring being used as symbols to indicate their identity. Without any conscious attempt to be primitive he achieved a sort of innocence that was in the spirit of the early illuminators, though his figures were quite unlike theirs. Even to say that he achieved it is perhaps misleading for it seemed to be natural to him.

He made me a little book with a story, composed by himself, of a child whose pet rabbit escorted her to the animals' nocturnal fair in the forest. This was made to teach me to read and was, according to the colophon, 'Written in odd times and ways, by day and night, with cold hands and hot hands: the writing therefore varies much from poor to passable'. The illustrations of this book had something of the jewel-like quality of illuminations, particularly the frontispiece,[1] which showed a cottage at the foot of a tree-covered mountain slope with a blue sky behind pierced by rays of burnished gold from the rising sun. The trees were outlined in gold where the sun caught them and in their midst the careful eye could discover a tiny rabbit.

These illustrations were much more elaborate than most of the drawings he did for us, which were simple and childlike in spirit. Sometimes he would draw a panorama, mountains and a river, here a little town, there a few cottages and a church, linked by winding roads which the eye was drawn to follow and the child to traverse in imagination. One of my earliest memories, at the age of not quite three, is of his making me a picture book of shops when I was ill in bed. There was a new picture every day, a toyshop kept by a rabbit, an ironmonger's in the charge of a cat, and so on. These were almost too successful, for they did not come until evening and no one awaiting the return of a lover

[1] Facing this page.

O

could have struggled through the long hours of the day with a more feverish impatience than I. The first, dazzling impression, when the picture was revealed, was one of richness and glory. Next came an excited scramble to discover and identify the details—the hoop, top and kite in one shop, the dustpan, trowel and hank of bast in another. When I look at them now I am astonished by their simplicity in comparison with the richness I had remembered, but they clearly gave the two-year-old child exactly what she wanted and inspired her imagination to supply the rest.

Once he suggested to me that I should write a book for my mother's birthday. I was five years old and saw no difficulty in such a project, so I readily agreed. The first essential was, of course, a book; clearly you cannot write a book until you have a book to write. He got out a big sheet of what was probably hand-made paper and showed me how to fold it, in folio, quarto, octavo, and how to cut the pages. Then he ruled lines for the text and margins for the pictures and I got to work. The pictures I drew and painted myself, the words I dictated to him. All the work was done secretly, up in his room, and when the book was finished he bound it in blue paper, over boards. It was called *The Mill Book* and was inspired by a visit to the windmill on the hill behind the village, which in those days was still working, though now it is ruinous. This book had something of a success (the dialogue had a certain bold simplicity); Douglas Pepler saw it, took a fancy to it and published it, illustrated with wood-cuts based on my drawings by his son, David, and another boy. This incident confirmed me in the impression that writing books was child's play and when, some twelve years later, I started writing in earnest, it was with the same happy confidence and, once again, everything went like clockwork. My father helped me then, too, reading the manuscript, making meticulous lists of notes and queries and paying to have the book typed. (*Father's Faith in Manuscript* was the way the *Daily Mail* put it.)

He believed, always, in teaching us to make '*real*' things, such as that first book of mine. To his students, also, he laid great emphasis on the importance of real things—on the things they made being *real* and being really *things*. On this point he waged a continual battle with his students who always wanted to be doing 'practice'. 'Practice,' he said, would only teach them to practise. There was no way to learn to make things except by making them. The first thing he asked on looking at a student's manuscript was 'What is this?' Too often the answer was that it had been intended for something specific but now 'I've turned it into practice.'

Over and over again, to new generations of students, he tried to convey his vision of the exciting adventure of making a *real thing*. This, above all, was what made him a great teacher; that he had never lost the view of the young medical student, gazing longingly from afar, seeing calligraphy as thrilling and glorious. Indeed with every year that he practised it this vision increased in splendour and I suspect that it did so right to the end of his life, even when he was old and ill and blind. To no one, he told me sadly, had he been able to hand on that vision, but some of his students would tell a different story.

As to the teaching of his own children, in the main he left that to look after itself. It was our mother, later, who chose a boarding school and sent us there—a proceeding in which he showed no interest whatever. To be with him, however, was an education in itself. He discoursed upon mathematics, politics, astronomy, etymology, philosophy and a hundred things beside. We made what we could of an immense amount of miscellaneous information, often above our heads. More important than the facts was the view of life conveyed, the sense of a universe immensely rich in possibilities, of vistas always leading out beyond the range of human imagination. He kept an open mind towards all manner of speculations, to theories about dimensions beyond the obvious three and explanations of the nature of time that set one dizzily upon the edge of some discovery beyond one's power to grasp.

My diary gives a brief outline of a conversation held one evening in 1937 when I and a young man—a stranger to my father—were alone with him. 'We talked about the craters made by meteorites, the necessity of pain as a warning [of injury], the unreality of mathematics, the reality of tangible things—a thing to hold onto, he said—and the fact that without a religious outlook the problems of religion—predestination and free will and so on—would be just as acute, in fact more so. . . . Afterwards D. said "What a darling that man is!" '

This discourse would be fairly typical, its seriousness being enlivened by unexpected touches of humour. That endearing quality which so impressed our visitor showed itself in the combination of this humour with deep sincerity and gentleness.

His way of thinking about things was infectious. He thought aloud so much—and by the Socratic method of question and answer obliged his hearers to emulate his own mental processes —that one would find one's own mind working along similar lines, sometimes to quite a comical extent. He encouraged us to think for ourselves by making us work out the answers to our own questions. There was, however, no attempt to impose his *ideas* on us (as distinct from his *method of thinking*) and he received our contributions to a discussion with a courtesy which assumed us to be rational and independent.

It was undoubtedly questions of method which most strongly brought out the pedagogue in him and this applied to many of the practical details of daily life. Thus, no one knew how to fry an egg, mend a fire or tie up a parcel *'properly'* except under his surveillance. Even his students were liable to receive instruction in these subjects and members of his household were often guided by a running commentary of minute directions while engaged in any such undertaking. As these directions frequently included the command 'No—wait!' they were apt to make the process somewhat lengthy and there were times when it seemed that one might have managed well enough—and a good deal faster—in one's own unenlightened way. Looking back I realize how much of what I know was learnt from him—what we learnt at school was negligible compared with what we learnt at home—but instruction is a blessing more readily appreciated in retrospect.

Ditchling, 1912-1916

The art of writing was not one of the subjects on this domestic curriculum. Perhaps that law obtained which decrees that the architect's house shall be damp and the doctor's family, *in extremis*, told 'You can take that stuff if you like—it probably won't do you any harm'. He believed that children should be taught to write with a broad-nibbed pen and a copy based on the book hands. I worked away quietly at school with a copperplate copybook and a pointed nib. I knew I could have it stopped if I lodged a complaint at home, but I found it rather an agreeable occupation and kept quiet, as we early learnt to do about quite a number of things. Occasionally on wet Sundays (too wet for our mother to take us to church) we were given quills and had a writing lesson, but I do not remember any other attempt to teach us or have us taught according to his ideas. He did more, if anything, about our drawing. He believed that we should be left to develop in our own way and he therefore decreed that we should not learn drawing at school. He provided us with materials and tried (unsuccessfully) to banish indiarubbers. We all drew all the time and we were left to ourselves except when we applied to him for help. We did this rarely as the result was apt to be a little overwhelming. If, for instance, we asked for some card to draw on he would go away to his room and look for card, bring down a sheet, a steel ruler and a penknife, find something to cut it on, arrange it on the diningroom table, measure it out and then, perhaps, decide that the card was not good enough and go off up to his room again to hunt for something better. These preliminaries could occupy a whole morning, by the end of which time our original interest in the subject would have declined.

We were two years at Ditchling before the war began. During that time and for a little longer we continued to go to Laurence-kirk every summer, travelling in the real Johnston tradition with sixteen pieces of luggage. To us children this was the greatest event of the year. We were intensely alive to the *drama* of the long journey. We could not wait to return to that magical other world, to see again the chandelier in the drawingroom, the glass-fronted cabinet, the beadwork firescreen, the gong with its velvety thunder, the potted ferns, the lumps of gum on the cherry tree, the incongruous grate against the garden wall where the papers from the Bank were burnt and the white raspberries by the rubbish pit.

We never went to Laurencekirk again after 1916. By then the war was making its impact felt and travelling was more difficult, but probably the real determining factor was that we had moved to another house and a different way of life.

XI

Halletts, 1916-1919

The advent of war at first made little difference to our lives. Johnston was over forty and not robust in health. Moreover, although he could wholeheartedly admire the young men who rushed off to enlist, for him becoming a soldier would have involved negotiating a labyrinth of conscience and principle, of the nature of war and the meaning of right and wrong. He did finally come to the conclusion that for him, feeling as he did, it would be wrong to fight, but his reluctance to censure other people's actions made it impossible for him to lay this down as a general principle. In any case, when he was eventually called up he was rejected upon medical grounds.

Throughout the war he continued to attend his classes and this, as usual, involved having long conversations with strangers in the train. On one occasion his fellow passengers were recounting atrocity stories, each capping the others with one supposedly more horrifying. Johnston intervened in this conversation to question the authenticity of their evidence, most of which rested solely upon the fact that the story had appeared in a newspaper. If only they could get at the real truth of the matter, he said, and cut out all the lies and propaganda, that in the end would not only be the right course but by far the most effective one. One man had remained silent through this conversation, a clergyman sitting unnoticed in a corner. In the rush at Victoria he and Johnston were the last to leave the carriage and when they were alone he spoke. He was not much good at talking, he said, and for that reason had taken no part in the discussion but he wished to thank Johnston for what he had said. 'If I had my way,' he added, 'I would make you Prime Minister.' By now they had descended from the train and were standing on the crowded platform together. 'I can't do that,' he said, 'but there is one thing I *can* do.' He raised his hand. For a moment Johnston remained uncomprehending, then 'I tore off my hat,' he said, 'and there were we like an island dividing the stream of people pressing toward the barrier, and we in another world.'

His comment on the incident was that it had been humbling. 'But you must have felt some elation?' suggested a friend. 'Well,' he answered, 'I did not exactly turn cartwheels, going down the Underground to South Kensington.'

As it continued, the war gave an added sense of urgency to Johnston's idea of the real country life, of growing food and trying to be self-supporting. In company with Pepler, who had enthusiastically fallen in with his ideas, he began, in the autumn of 1915, to tramp the countryside in search of suitable farms or smallholdings, a place where they could keep a few cows and pigs and grow their own food. They would walk all day in the bright, frosty weather, lunching on bread and cheese at some wayside inn and visiting remote farms and even a water-mill. They were sometimes accompanied on these expeditions by Gill, at others they so planned their day as to end up on Ditchling Common and be welcomed to the little farmhouse by the railway bridge, to the sudden warmth and brightness after the wintry dusk and tea by a real country fire while they gave the latest news of their search.

Rarely before this, and never after, did Johnston see as much of anyone outside his own family as he did now of Gill and Pepler. Hardly a day passed without their meeting. Whole days were spent in tramping the lanes together, long hours with the printing press, and in the evenings they met at each other's houses for the Latin Club, for 'talking mill and farm' and discussing the next number of *The Game* together. At Johnston's house they saw the latest designs for the Underground alphabet,

Halletts, 1916-1919

at Gill's they followed the progress of the Stations of the Cross and at Pepler's there would be fresh sheets, damp from the press. Even on Mondays, when Johnston went to London for his classes, he would often have the company of one or both of his friends.

House-hunting continued for nearly a year while Johnston and Pepler became fascinated by one remote, broken-down homestead after another. Finally, in the summer of 1916, Halletts Farm, on the edge of Ditchling Common, came on the market. This had the great advantage of being near the Gills, which none of the other places seen could offer. Johnston and Pepler crowned a winter and spring of house-hunting by buying it on August 1, after which we left for what was to be our last visit to Laurencekirk. For my birthday, which fell during our stay, my father made me a set of tiny farm buildings. Clearly the idea—and ideal—of the farm permeated all his thoughts.

Halletts was a small farm comprising a few fields and three sides of a quadrangle of farm buildings; cowshed, stable, barn, coach house and pigsties with a midden in the centre. They had dreamed of it, no doubt, as an entirely communal venture, but when the time came to translate the dream into terms of reality, of actual fields and buildings, it became clear that joint ownership was not practicable. The house was barely big enough for one family, impossible for two. The same might have been said of the farm. Somehow it was arranged that we had the house and the Peplers the farm buildings and most of the land. Johnston, finding himself with only one field and no barns, felt disappointed, but this in fact proved rather to be a blessing in disguise. The Peplers built themselves a house in a field adjoining the road. Their garden was separated from ours only by the track to the farm, known to us—from a faded notice that the gate still bore— as *Beware of the Dogs*. Their house conformed to the ideals of the three men and had one large livingroom for all purposes with walls of rough plaster and a huge, open fireplace at the end. It smoked, inevitably, and failed to warm the large, draughty room. I preferred our little villa, though the company of the Peplers offered ample compensation for the discomforts of their house.

[217]

Halletts, 1916-1919

Halletts was a decidedly less disastrous choice than some of the other farms, not to mention that alluring water-mill—as fatal, at a guess, as an alluring water-maiden. It was, at any rate, not bogged down at the end of a long mud track but on a good road and only about a mile and a half from the village. Also it had water laid on (in a kind of way) and drainage (of a sort). But even a mile and a half is a long way when there is no transport and tradesmen do not deliver. It means a three-mile walk to send a telegram—for of course there were no telephones on the common. Added to this all drinking water had to be carried in buckets from a house down the road. The bath-water, which was pumped by hand from the well to the cistern, was heavily impregnated with iron and chemicals. The bath in the dark little lean-to bathroom was stained brick-red up to a high-water-mark, with an additional streak beneath each tap. (In a story I wrote while we were there I specified that the children described lived in a house with a nice, clean bath, with no red marks on it.)

Uncle Johnston had wisely made Edward promise to tell him before selling any shares, as he would certainly know more about their prospects than his incurably unworldly nephew. Thus Edward had to tell him his plans before he could actually buy the house. He wrote enthusiastically of Halletts and farming and proudly announced that the six hens he had got from the Peplers in exchange for a child's cot had already paid for themselves.

Uncle Johnston replied: 'Gentleman farming is a mere way of getting rid of money, quicker than keeping a yacht or a grouse moor,' but added, resignedly, 'Thank God you are buying, not building.' Realizing that Edward was not to be dissuaded he advised him to be cautious and suggested that 'If you make your chickens pay *all the year round* you might then try pigs and possibly, later, a cow.' To this Edward answered 'It is my intention to go ahead carefully and, if money has to be spent on the land, only to spend small sums until I can see my way quite clear.' He went on to say that he had already bought a pig and a goat and his hens had already laid enough eggs to pay for their keep for a year and, anyway, he would probably kill them when

[218]

they stopped laying (they were old birds) and start again with pullets, which would give him a handsome profit. What he did not foresee was that by the time those birds ceased to lay they all had names. They were practically members of the family and one, at least, survived for hard upon ten years. Even the best-laid plans have to take account of such incalculable factors, and his were not the best, although no doubt they looked convincing enough on paper. It is one of the most treacherous elements in amateur stock-raising that it always does look good on paper. Animals breed fast and grow fast; you reckon that your increase will be so much and that you can sell them at so many months old, but they perish of unidentifiable diseases, they get gape worm and tape worm, they pine, scour, overlie their young, eat poisonous plants and even strangle themselves.

Pepler wrote: 'I return your wonderful letter to "Uncle Johnston" which I hope he will understand (none of my uncles would!). . . . Completion will be sometime between Michaelmas and St Luke's (about the same time I expect the Germans to retreat to the Rhine). The Greens came yesterday. They will, I think, put up his sleeping-hut in the old cottage garden at Halletts and build one room! We had a tremendous jaw last night until about 3 a.m. chiefly on the point of whether one material can be more noble in itself (irrespective of use) than another. Green seems convinced that organic substances are more *noble* than inorganic. It is such a rum adjective, somehow. He is thinking of approaching Branfoot with a view to part-time teaching work. How they would fight!'

This was Romney Green, the mathematician-cabinet maker who had been our neighbour in Hammersmith. He had been a schoolmaster and Branfoot was the proprietor of a preparatory school in the village. Both were vigorous, outspoken and dogmatic and Pepler's forecast was probably correct. Romney Green, though a great friend of Johnston's, appeared to suffer acutely from one particular limitation inherent in his company. When there was a break in Johnston's discourse it was only a pause between one phrase and the next and Green, with much of great moment to say, would lean forward and utter a sound which would fade away in a sort of groan as Johnston, serene and oblivious, continued his exposition. It was a familiar sight to see these victims—for there were others whose sufferings were manifest—rocking back and forth as if in pain, at each pause lunging forward with a desperate gleam in the eye, only to sink back defeated. They all had plenty to say—Gill and Pepler and Green and Philippe Mairet and all the other idealists and philosophers who gathered round. We used to puzzle over the popular belief that *women* talk so much. How, we wondered, did they get the chance?

The Greens did not come to Halletts in the end and Pepler's account of the proposed plan is surprising. The 'old cottage' was presumably the house that we had, since there was no other, but to describe it thus evokes an old-world charm to which it could lay no claim. Perhaps the wish was father to the thought. In fact, it was a little, square, brick box with one bow window, in autumn crimson with virginia creeper. There it stood, four-square, staring down the road to Ditchling, uncamouflaged save by the creeper, which rather emphasized than concealed its suburban nature, and unapologetic. It would not have dreamed of trying to look like an old cottage. To us it was home, haven for dragging feet, log fire, oil lamp, tea, toast and eggs—but picturesque it was not.

We children came off best there; I, as the youngest, in particular. I did not go to school and was not old enough to feel the shadow of grown-up anxieties. I was as free as air, running wild in company with Mark Pepler. We had unlimited country to wander in, the farm and the fields and the bracken-covered common, limitless, as it seemed then, stretching away beyond the railway cutting, beyond the half-forbidden lure of the 'big pond', to *terra incognita* and the ultimate, haunted mystery of Jacob's Post, the reputed site of the last-used gibbet.

For our elders there were troubles in plenty. To be a successful gardener it is necessary to have that attribute described as 'green fingers'. For the management of stock some comparable quality is even more essential. Handbooks, certainly, will not provide it. It comes from long years of experience. It was something we had not got.

We had a sow but when she farrowed we lost the whole litter. I think that was the end of our pig-keeping. We had bees but Greta turned out to be allergic both to their stings and their honey. The only person who seemed able to deal with them was Barbara who was thirteen and 'v. calm and capable' in some apiarian crisis recorded in her father's diary. (She also won my respect by eating the pink bee-candy that was marked 'unfit for human consumption'.)

We also had goats, which provided us with endless pleasure and amusement. Beautiful milk we had, too, in abundance, but it came from the Peplers' cows. It was set in pans overnight and in the morning the cream would come off, buckling like thick chamois leather. (That was how they meant it all to have been— idyllic country life; but, alas, how right Uncle Johnston had been about 'gentleman farming'!)

The white goat, Rosie, gave birth to a kid one bitter, bright night in February when the grass crackled underfoot. In the case of goats the answer to the hymn's question as to whether the mother's tender care can cease towards the child she bear is an unhesitating affirmative: it can. With the utmost determination Rosie turned the kid out of doors. There it stood, steaming and trembling on its untried legs, and would have been dead before morning. Edward rubbed it down, wrapped it in a blanket, took it upstairs and put it into bed beside his wife. After that it used to sleep regularly in a basket in their room. In the morning, early, we would hear it get up and clatter across the landing and into our room on its little horny hooves. There it would go round from bed to bed, bleating a good morning to each of us in turn, before it clattered off downstairs.

Edward loved playing with the kids and used to teach them to leap on to his back when he stooped down. He also played hide-and-seek with them. When the kid was not looking he would dodge behind a tree and when it found itself forsaken it would bleat piteously. Then he would make a little sound and, on the instant, the kid would go scampering off to look behind the tree and they would have a joyful reunion.

The hens were the one venture that really did yield returns. Whether they continued to pay for themselves or not we did at least have eggs. Edward spent a lot of time with them, watching them and setting them simple problems, speculating on their possible intelligence and reluctantly deciding that they had none. After fruitless attempts to keep their drinking water clean as the handbooks said, he crystallized his observations in one sentence: 'If a hen wants to get to the place where it is already it goes through the drinking water and back again.'

His thoughtfulness for the hens was such that he would, said Greta, have 'read aloud to them, if they could have understood'. One thing he could never do, however, was to get up early. For this reason he invented and constructed a water clock to let them out in the morning. It was set in the evening and the water was timed to drip into a tin at a given rate. By morning it weighed down one end of a lever, the other end rose, and down fell the hen-house door. When it was completed the family was assembled to see a demonstration, and very effective it was. With this, however, as with others of his inventions, the chief interest lay in devising the thing. Once it had been made to work, problems of maintenance proved less attractive. The life of the water clock was not a long one.

Beyond the garden was our single field, but agriculture prospered no better than stock. One field is not what is described as an 'economic farming unit'. For a market gardener it might have done well enough, or even for fruit farming, but Edward grew corn. He dreamt, of course, of home-made, wholemeal loaves from our own wheat, a fascinating idea, but one fraught with a multitude of practical difficulties of a kind with which he was constitutionally unfitted to grapple. One field of wheat and then trying to get it cut and trying to get it threshed—such a thing is not a practical proposition. When, at last, it was threshed the question arose, what was to be done with it? He may have imagined getting it ground at the local windmill but probably transport was not available, or it may have been then that the mill went out of business. The corn lay out in the rain—we had no barn. At last Greta grew desperate, borrowed a tarpaulin from a farm down the road and staggered back under its weight, to be bitterly scolded by Edward for overstraining herself. No doubt the feelings of frustration and guilt which are bred by a sense of inadequacy had told upon his nerves, but it always worried him intensely to see her doing too much. It was one of the very few things that could even make him appear quite angry with her. In general, she solved this problem by doing too much *un*seen, for there was far too much to be done. In the end the corn was brought into the house. I suppose he had borrowed sacks and then had to return them; at any rate the picture I recall is of the sight of his dressingroom with the entire floor knee-deep in corn.

A man of limited strength and vitality cannot do two jobs at once and it was fortunate that when one had to be neglected it was usually the farming. After all, it was necessary to earn money and even the modest sums that he charged for his manuscripts did something towards keeping three pairs of growing feet shod and meeting the other necessities of domestic life. It is surprising how much of his work was done during this harassed period with its far from ideal conditions. Some people, indeed, regard it as his vintage years, when his skill had come to its full maturity and he was still content with the perfected 'foundational hand' in its pristine innocence, before he began to experiment with newer forms.

During this time, in particular, he did a good deal of work for the Livery Companies of the City of London. There were four young princes to be made freemen of various companies and the war threw up its own great names. Haig, Beatty, French and Jellicoe all became Fishmongers with his connivance. He used to bring these scrolls from his workroom to show to the family before they were despatched—always at the last possible moment and sometimes after working all night. They were gorgeous things, rich, and splendid with burnished gold, with coats of arms and helmets and manteling. His heraldry was never woolly nor his lions fat and tame. It was all sharp and vigorous like his penmanship.

These and other commissions—addresses and wedding presents and all the rolls of honour that came after the war—were always finished on the last possible day. The negotiations followed a recognizable pattern, beginning in one of two distinct ways but leading always to the same conclusion. There was what one might describe as the Municipal Approach, brusque and impersonal, specifying that the work was to be in his best style of writing and only first class materials were to be used. In contrast there was the Reverential Approach, the 'just write anything you like, I know it will be perfect' manner. Of the two he preferred the first, for he hated vague commissions. Whatever the approach, however, soon the familiar pattern would begin to show itself. 'You may remember that we wrote to you some little time ago . . .' 'It is now some months since we approached you. . . .' 'I fear that my last letter may have miscarried. . . .' Sooner or later would come the letter containing the pregnant phrase: '*While not wishing to press you* . . .' Beyond this point the tone would change a little, 'anxiety' would be mentioned openly and 'an early reply' would be hoped for—in vain, one fears—and then a reply by return. After that the telegrams would start.

This may partly explain why Johnston made such a study of the *Post Office Guide* and became an expert on little-known methods of expressing letters with whom no ordinary village postmaster could hope to compete. On one occasion he took an urgent letter to the post office in Ditchling and explained the particular method by which it was to be expressed—one involving telegrams and messengers. The postmaster said that it would be all right and the letter was handed over. There should have been an immediate telegram in answer but none arrived and Johnston began to grow anxious. The next day came and still there was no word. He went to the post office to make enquiries. Ah, yes, said the postmaster, that letter—he had been going to look up how to send it but it had slipped his mind. However, he had it there safely—he brought it from a drawer to prove the fact.

For three years Johnston remained at Halletts but the association with Gill and Pepler had probably reached its zenith when he went there. As often happens, the whole venture had been more buoyantly enthralling in anticipation than it proved in fact, with its unforeseen problems and disappointments. Moreover, it soon became apparent that the greatest problem of all was nothing to do with agriculture. It was the problem of religion.

Gill, and later Pepler, had joined the Church of Rome with the same wholehearted enthusiasm that they had given to the ideal of the country life. The loose-box at the farm was now turned into a chapel, very clean and bare, smelling of whitewash rather than incense, with a small piece of sculpture by Gill as almost its only decoration. Priests came to stay with the Peplers. Bells rang and long-skirted figures with thick boots were to be seen striding from the house to the farm and back again.

To Gill and Pepler it seemed wrong, of course, that their little brotherhood of three should be divided on so important an issue. Here, now, was matter for midnight arguments of such urgency and moment as to overshadow all else. In some ways the idea must have tempted Johnston greatly. A community of craftsmen with a chapel at its centre, bound together by a common belief, probably seemed to him about as near to a perfect way of life as was possible in the modern world. The issue seems to have been in doubt for a time; certainly Greta thought so. As she lay awake far into the night or woke to find herself alone and the hands of the clock pointing to three she had ample opportunity to speculate on the course that things might take. She and Edward agreed completely about religion in all essentials; it was the very heart and core of their relationship. If they had been divided on that issue it would not have been a little rift within the lute, it would have been more like shipwreck. Actually she had already gone so far in sacrificing her own interests that she would probably have thrown in the rest to save her marriage, but not without a long and bitter struggle. She had grown up in Scotland where there was no liking for the Catholic Church.

Even in such tribulations her sense of humour stood by her. 'Anyway,' she said to her sister, after a night spent in listening to the murmur of men's voices from the room below, 'he'd never get up in time to go to Mass!'

Some years before, Edward's sister, Olof, had become a Roman Catholic, in the face of some opposition from the rest of the family. On that occasion he had written to her: . . . 'The only thing that matters, I think, is that we should hold and persevere in a desire to be at one with God. And believing that to be your desire I should not attempt to dissuade you from joining any "church" that you felt would help to that End. *All* men, I think, have this desire, but few, if any, seek with their whole hearts—I, for one, very little with mine. . . .

'I hope that you may be shown clearly before you take so great a step as you propose. The R.C. "Church" is no freer of faulty men than other "churches" (I suppose) but these men by virtue of their office may control one's will (or action, at least) more strongly than saints without that authority. That God does use the "faulty" is obvious in their existence alone. . . . I have only warned you how I think one might stumble over that step. I write as a sinful man hoping that even because I am far off I may see the true light (not even in "warnings", which I hardly have the right to make) but in the strength of my conviction that we must seek first the Kingdom of God. If in that search you are led to join another (or The) church, I will pray with you, if I may.'

In any issue deeply affecting someone's life he could be relied upon to be tolerant, and to bring to the problem this gentle humility. Even if the step taken were actually in opposition to his principles, his watchword was still 'judge not that ye be not judged'. 'Broken marriages,' he wrote, in one such case, 'have (partly because of my own very happy one) always seemed to me to be tragedies, but I have never presumed to judge anyone concerned—we do not possess the data and we have been warned not to judge anyone.'

Johnston undoubtedly thought that there was much to be said

for the Roman Catholic Church. It is hard to believe, however, that so intractable an individualist could ever have been persuaded to accept a ready-made scheme of things or to allow his own philosophical speculations to be overruled by a priest.

O GOD, who hast prepared for them that love thee such good things as pass man's understanding; Pour into our hearts such love toward thee, that we, loving thee above all things, may obtain thy promises which exceed all that we can desire; through Jesus Christ our Lord. Amen.

Collect. Black and red. 1919. Actual size.

The little magazine, *The Game*, was now becoming increasingly

Catholic with every issue. Finally, in January 1918, Johnston felt it necessary to have a note inserted dissociating him from certain views which had been expressed under the sanction of the editorial 'we'. After this incident he resigned from his position as joint editor and had no further connection with the magazine, which was thus free to become openly Catholic. It later became the official organ of the Guild of SS Joseph and Dominic, a Roman Catholic community of craftsmen which grew up round the Gills' house on the common.

The war ended and we were still at Halletts. Then, one day in the summer of 1919, Greta returned from Ditchling with her dilapidated bicycle groaning, as usual, under rations for five. I remember her bursting in at the front door and the sense of excitement in the air that made me prick up my ears as she spoke to my father. I did not understand what they said but I knew that it was important. She came in with her eyes alight and she said '*Edward! Cleves* is for sale.'

In his calm, unhurried way he answered simply 'Do you want it?'

It was the house of all others that she did want. When we had first come to Ditchling, to Downsview, Cleves had been the house next door, its beautiful garden glimpsed through the thick hedge, mysterious and unattainable. The original owners who had built it were now trying to buy it back, as we afterwards learned. With wholly uncharacteristic swiftness and luck we got in ahead of them.

Once, at Downsview, Edward had had a dream in which we had left the village to live somewhere else but had returned again to the same house and 'been very glad to get back'. It was the same house and yet not the same, being changed in ways he could not specify. One difference, however, he knew for certain: the street lamp in the road opposite was *in a different place*. Actually we returned, not to the same house, but to the house next door. The lamp was now on our right, for it remained where it had always been—opposite Downsview.

Halletts, 1916-1919

In August 1919, Edward wrote to Uncle Johnston: 'We are contemplating moving back to the village and are negotiating the purchase of a house. Greta has found the work too hard and I am anxious that she should have a more comfortable house—one with water and gas laid on and within easy distance of the shops. . . . My notion of food raising, even if I could live up to it, is now out of the question as the wage for a labourer (when you can get one) is £1 or more a week.

'A friend, a printer with a London business, has been urging us to this move and has promised to guarantee me £100 a year for five years for a MS "magnum opus" and an additional £100 a year for mixed work. It is perhaps also reassuring—and no doubt you will be glad to hear—that my book seems to be selling better than ever (after nearly 13 years) and the other day I had a cheque for Royalties (June–June) of over £54.'

The 'printer' who had urged the move and promised Edward work was, of course, Gerard Meynell. He had seen what the life at Halletts was doing to Greta, to whom he was devoted. Other people seem to have worried more about her than Edward did. As has been said, when he saw her doing too much he was distracted but he lived in a world of his own and there was a great deal he did not see. From his private world he would emerge at unexpected moments, seeming to become suddenly aware of what was going on. Thus, when a travelling salesman kept her standing at the door in the cold, Edward suddenly appeared behind her, white with indignation and almost shaking, and put him to instant flight, saying, 'Sir, you are annoying my wife!'

In general, Edward preserved the same kind of optimistic attitude to household matters as towards his own work. Just as he continued, despite the lessons of experience, to price his work on the assumption that it *ought*—ideally—to be quite straightforward and not take long, so he felt that housekeeping was largely a matter of organization and was perfectly simple *really* and that making bread was very little more trouble than buying it from a shop.

For Greta, Cleves was like paradise. For Edward it was different.

He had made his bid for the good life as he saw it and the retreat to civilization must have been a sort of defeat. When the Gills left the common, a few years afterwards, it was to plunge into a far more primitive and self-supporting life in the mountains of Wales. Edward must have felt at least a passing wistfulness on that day in the summer holidays of 1924 when Eric Gill came into the village to say goodbye to him. He realized, however, that what had happened was inevitable. Neither he nor Greta had the strength to battle with that hard life any more.

XII

Cleves, 1920-1927

We moved into Cleves early in February 1920. It was an exciting time of year to move to a house with such a garden. As the season advanced flowers appeared of which the very names were unknown to us, flowers we had never seen. In May, the blossoming trees that met over the gate were alive with the humming of bees and so spectacular in their glory that passers-by would stand in the road to stare.

Many who visited Johnston there carried away memories of that garden, the wide lawn flecked with sun and shadow, the line of the Downs rising up beyond the trees. Herbert Steiner, re-calling a visit from Germany, wrote: 'I still see the evening light in your garden, scarcely fading, almost spectral, as if it were the soul of light that still gleamed somewhere between the hedges and shone out of the lawn—a sort of light unknown, I believe, to the Continent.'

The Ditchling to which we had gone in 1912 had been entirely unspoilt and rural. It was the Ditchling of Mr Turner driving down the High Street in a smock-frock and top hat and of stout old Mrs Bourne with her bonnet and cape who always used to cook our Christmas dinner (and give Johnston the flight feathers of the turkey to hang in his window in a bundle from which to choose his pens). It was the Ditchling of old Cave, our gardener, with his contempt for the instructions on the seed packets: 'I don't take no notice of half their chatter' and of the shepherd on the Downs who showed Johnston how to use his crook and told of a lady who had supposed that he carried it 'to set meself arf, like.'

It was to a different Ditchling that we returned. It had lost its first innocence—and, indeed, it was already beginning to be spoilt, even then—but it had, at that time, gained something in exchange. It had become a rather remarkable village. Through Eric Gill, directly or indirectly, there had come a number of people concerned with the revival of the crafts, and—what is important—they were real craftsmen. I stress this because the crafts, and sometimes the village, have been derided as 'artie-craftie' by people who often fail to differentiate between the work of trained craftsmen and those products of amateurs which have tended to give even the respectable word *handicrafts* a dubious sound.

Of these newcomers, the one who most influenced the life and feeling of the village was Ethel Mairet, pioneer of the revival of handloom weaving. The Mairets built themselves a beautiful house with a great, barn-like weaving-room with stairs up to a gallery at one end. Here among the looms and the big, rough hanks of hand-spun wool dyed with madder, indigo, crottle, fustic and weld that hung from wooden pillars supporting the gallery, were displayed lengths of wool and silk, scarves and caps and jackets together with pottery and other things that Mrs Mairet brought back from abroad. Here informal lectures were sometimes held, the audience sitting up in the gallery on piles of Eastern rugs or below it among the looms. Johnston once spoke there and 'gave a most lovely address', according to his wife, who wrote that 'standing there so gravely, giving an address on his own subject, illustrating it so ably on the board, he seemed quite a stranger to me'.

Mrs Mairet was an indomitable woman charged with energy and zest for life, always just back from Czechoslovakia—or Hungary or Finland—and always it had been '*so* interesting'. She was never ill herself and never believed that anyone else could be so until a disastrous accident which befell her late in life when she was knocked down by an army lorry and her skull was fractured. The next time I saw her she was again just back, not this time from her travels but from hospital. I expected to find her changed, but no—undefeated and unquenchable, with the springy step of an athletic girl, she was what she had always been. The moment I asked after her health she burst out, with all her old zest: 'You know, it was *so* interesting. . . .'

The last time I saw her, not long before her death, she said how fortunate she had been in knowing so many interesting people in her life and that, in particular, she counted it a privilege to have known my father. He would, I am sure, have said the same of her.

Her husband, Philippe Mairet, of Swiss descent, was a remarkable man of diverse gifts. He was her second husband; she had been married first to Ananda Coomaraswamy. Mairet was what, in the theatre, they call 'a natural' and, after gracing the platform of our village hall, he offered his services to the Old Vic and was appearing as Polonius in no time. He was also a philosopher and later gave up the stage and became editor of one of the more intellectual periodicals of the time. Mairet and Johnston used to have discussions which threatened to occupy the whole night. When, at last, they decided it was bedtime, Johnston would walk home with Mairet, a distance of about half a mile through the silent, sleeping village and they would stand talking so long outside his gate that in the end Mairet would see Johnston home again, while they continued their conversation. When at last they managed to break off the discussion they would sometimes notice, with vague uneasiness, that it was not nearly as dark as they had supposed and even, inexplicably, that birds were singing.

Ethel Mairet's brother, Frederick Partridge, also lived in Ditchling. He was a jeweller and a magnificent craftsman. His rings and necklaces of gold and precious stones, brooches of enamel or boxes of inlaid wood were all made with the same minute and exquisite care. He also made all the buttons for the clothes produced in his sister's workshops, turning them upon the lathe in his attic workroom. Here a mass of fascinating tools, many made by himself, littered the bench in the dormer window that looked towards the Downs. Among them might be lumps of crystal or amber, slender gold chains or inlaid wooden handles for a cabinet. Always there were buttons of many coloured woods, brown, red, black or grey, speckled or streaked or patterned with a die. He was a wild-eyed, wild-haired man of great charm with a powerful, interesting face, his bright glance, as it darted this way and that, giving him a startled, even a desperate look. He wore a Norwegian pullover as handsome and as shaggy as himself. Johnston loved to compare crafts, either with him or with his sister, and discover with fascination how closely the same rules applied to all. Between penmanship and weaving there was even a verbal bond to emphasize their relationship. 'My Text was once your Textile and my writing *Line* your Linen thread,' he wrote to Mrs Mairet.

The most important person of all, however, from the point of view of the village, was Amy Sawyer. She was a painter with a paralysed arm and she lived alone in a little house with a studio mysteriously tucked away behind it. She had been there long before the Gills came; she belonged to Ditchling and Ditchling, in a way, belonged to her. She was a beautiful, romantic figure with her dark, curling, cropped hair, her weathered face and her coat of skewbald ponyskin. If there had been a story about gypsy ancestry and a little-known exploit of Byron's one would have accepted her appearance as conclusive proof. That would have seemed to explain her; nothing else could. She seemed essentially solitary, alone with her cats in her little house that looked like a tiny museum of the arts that had been ransacked by burglars. Brilliant silks and leopard skins were heaped upon carved chests with velvet cloaks and Chinese embroidery—a chaotic welter of fascinating riches. At least that is how I think of it, but perhaps I am recalling an occasion when she was dressing a play. For, as well as painting strange pictures, she wrote strange plays. Then, because plays cannot fulfil themselves without actors, she, who was by nature a recluse, went out into the village and picked her cast and produced her plays. Everyone acted in them, the builder's men and the grocer's family and anyone else whom she elected to choose. Philippe Mairet was not the only 'natural' in the village; we had a half-French bricklayer who could have held his own on any stage. He was also a great reader and used to discuss philosophy with Johnston, while building on a workroom to his house.

The vintage years were the early nineteen-twenties, immediately following our return to the village. It was then that Miss Sawyer produced her unforgettable pageant in which half the village appeared. It was then, too, that Gerard Meynell ran a weekly village newspaper called *The Beacon*. Posters were printed announcing its debut and Johnston wrote labels to stick across them claiming that it had the '*Largest circulation of any Ditchling weekly!*' This was just the kind of joke he loved, for of course there was no other Ditchling paper, whether daily, weekly or monthly, and never had been.

It was then, too, that Ellen Terry came to the village. She was an old lady then and nearly blind and she came to stay with an old friend who had rented a cottage there. Under the auspices of Gerard Meynell, Johnston wrote out a tribute to her, a poem by Arthur Waugh (father of Alec and Evelyn) who was living in the village at the time. This was presented at a function in the Meynells' garden. Some years afterwards, when Count Kessler was producing his edition of *Hamlet* with type designed by Johnston and engravings by Gordon Craig, he wrote: 'By the way, Teddy Craig [Gordon Craig's son] told me today that your book was one of his grandmother's, Ellen Terry's, favourites and that she used to sit up in bed reading it over and over again!'

It must have greatly pleased Johnston, who had delighted in her work in the past, to think that his work, in return, had given pleasure to her. When he and Greta offered to put her up during her stay in Ditchling (her friend's cottage was very small) he assured her that he would write her name over the bedroom door in letters of gold and no-one else should sleep there. Such remarks were the more delightful from him because they were so unexpected.

Cleves, 1920-1927

The Gerard Meynells moved to the village during this period and we long cherished the memory of a certain tea-party at our house at which they were present. Our big dining table was surrounded by guests, packed as tight as the chairs would go, with Edward and Esther Meynell sitting together at one end. He chose this occasion to extol to her the virtues of algebra. Mrs Meynell was an intellectual woman, but her subjects were music and literature; mathematics was, emphatically, not among them. Edward explained his favourite algebraic problem: 'A fish is five inches long plus half its own length, what is the length of the fish?' Faced with this problem most people give the answer seven and a half inches, but, if it is stated algebraically, $5 + \frac{x}{2} = x$ it becomes obvious that the answer is ten—at least it becomes obvious to anyone with any grasp of such things. Johnston used to quote this to his students to illustrate his contention that a problem which has been correctly stated—whether in algebra or calligraphy or in life itself—is halfway to being solved. One student's notebook is adorned with drawings of his showing whole and half fishes in scale pans.[1] The student confessed that even after this demonstration the problem eluded her, but Johnston resolutely refused to accept the fact that some otherwise intelligent minds are paralysed by figures. He was a teacher of inexhaustible patience, always ready to go back to the beginning and explain the most elementary facts again in the simplest words. If this was still not understood then he would explain again with diagrams or match sticks or anything else that might help to make the problem clear. He would cheerfully have spent a whole morning explaining that two and two make four but he would not and could not accept the idea of an unteachable student. Thus it was with Esther Meynell. We heard his voice at intervals, above the sound of general conversation, repeating yet again: 'But, Esther, it's *perfectly simple*. Now, let *x* be the length of the fish . . .' Mrs Meynell, who had no intention of allowing herself to become involved in a subject she could not handle, resolutely refused to be drawn. 'It's no use,

[1]Facing page 288.

Edward,' she repeated blandly, 'I *never* understand that sort of thing.' He was determined to make her understand; she was equally determined not to commit herself. In tenacity they were about equally matched. 'But, Esther, just look at it this way . . .' 'It's no use, Edward . . .' So the dialogue continued, punctuated by comments from her two schoolgirl daughters at the other end of the table, who, at intervals, interrupted another conversation to interject, '*Oh, mummie, it's potty!*'

This contest no doubt ended in a draw, with the conclusion of the meal. Mrs Meynell, having held out so long, might be said to have won on points. She certainly had not allowed herself to become flustered as some visitors were inclined to when obliged to do mental arithmetic during meals. This recreation was not as universally popular as their host seemed to suppose, and he allowed no quarter. The guest's predicament was made no happier by an oblique glance, now and then, from one of the three daughters of the house, who sat at table as silent as three sphinxes. Only occasionally they addressed asides to one another in a manner so composed of allusions and family sayings as practically to constitute a private language. At the first chance of escape they vanished into air, to the mutual relief of the visitors and themselves.

It would be wrong, however, to give the impression that such visits were an ordeal. For some they may have had their difficult moments but there were many for whom they remained as treasured memories. One such was a girl whom Greta brought there when she was on the verge of a breakdown. 'The extra-ordinary sense of utter timelessness healed me,' she wrote, some thirty years later. 'To others, it must often have been annoying, letters not answered, not even opened. . . . But for me at that time it was most wonderful.'

It was true that letters were not always opened at once. One air mail letter from America, commissioning (or attempting to commission) a manuscript, was marked in Johnston's hand-writing: 'R sometime in August, opened by E.J. 14th Septr.' The disadvantages of such an arrangement are obvious; it is good to be reminded occasionally that it may have its advantages too.

When Johnston was present at a meal conversation was apt to take the form of a monologue and many a meal-time became a lecture. These were often very interesting but there were times when one would willingly have dispensed with them, as when a special friend was paying a rare, brief visit and was only able to say 'Hullo' and 'Goodbye', the precious interval between being wholly occupied with a disquisition upon the evolution of technical terms or the less known services of the Post Office.

Johnston would not have realized, of course, that the visit was to be so short—such practical details eluded him—or, alternatively, he might simply have been carried away by his interest in the subject under consideration. When the time came for the guest to leave he would be shocked and distressed. Often he saw little of visitors, spending the day in his workroom and coming late to meals after other people had finished, but he liked to feel that they were there. He hated anyone to go away.

When we were young mealtimes were often enlivened by games and stories. One famous story was entitled *Under the Weight of the Soup Tureen*. The phrase occurred in conversation and Johnston said it sounded like a title and at once embarked on the story which opened with a description of a man hanging over a precipice supported only by his false moustache which had caught in a gorse bush, and contained the memorable line: '*Would seccotine hold? It did!*'

The real mainstay of our family life was reading aloud. Johnston gave his 'recreation' in *Who's Who* as 'Being read aloud to by my wife' and this reading had always been an important feature of their life together. Greta enjoyed reading aloud and did it extremely well. Her voice was warm, soothing and yet animated. Reassurance and security were in its rise and fall, no more regarded than the air we breathed but almost as important. When we were small she would read to us for an hour or more after tea, and to our father for as long again after supper. Later she read to all of us together. Edward played patience on a board on his knees by the fire, game after game, while she read him all Scott and Trollope—some over and over again—and Dumas, Malory, Jane Austen, Thackeray, Dickens. Occasionally, too, they read contemporary novels, but this was usually only when a book was lent to them.

The book Edward read most often of all, to himself, was *The Innocence of Father Brown*. It was particularly the philosophy behind it, and in all Chesterton's work, that appealed to him. He read it, altogether, nineteen times, entering the dates upon the flyleaf. When I was a small child it was always on the table by his bed in a jacket showing a large face and part of a priest's wide-brimmed hat. I could not read the title and had no idea what it was but conceived for it the same intense antipathy that one comes to feel, when abroad, for a ubiquitous but incomprehensible advertisement. He avoided murder stories when reading aloud to us but *The Blue Cross*, *The Flying Stars* and *The Queer Feet* we must have heard over and over again. We three sat round with our drawing-books and some of our drawings became saturated in the strange, Chestertonian atmosphere and would seem to give off whiffs of it when our eyes fell upon them again.

I cannot leave the subject of reading aloud without a mention of the little paper-bound books about Dick Turpin and *The Followers of the Fang* that Edward used to buy for twopence at the bookstall on his way to London and bring home to read to us. The characters in these stories never spoke but always 'hissed' or 'gritted' and the evil hordes were always utterly routed by a few bold words from the hero. 'Back, ye dogs!' he would shout, and 'reeling, cursing . . .' and so on, down they would go like ninepins. We read these books aloud and laughed at them but with a certain affection, as we did with Jeffery Farnol, whose latest work we bought each year for the purpose.

The Meynells were our chief contact with current literature; indeed, at Halletts they were probably our only one. One daring importation of theirs was *South Wind*. Unfortunately Greta conceived so violent an antipathy to this book that she—least destructive of readers—used it for cleaning the lamps. It was only when the Meynells asked for it back that she realized it had not been a gift but a loan!

For years this story was told against her—usually *by* her—as was another of an incident some years later, at Cleves. One Sunday evening she and Edward, being alone, had decided not to trouble about a meal but to make do with bread and butter and their usual cup of tea. On this occasion Laurence Christie, one-time student of Johnston's, dropped in, as he sometimes did. Greta offered him a cup of tea and afterwards retired to bed, leaving the men together. She had undressed and was about to say her prayers when an appalling thought flashed into her mind: '*I asked that man to supper!*' Horrified, she caught up her dressing gown, wondering what she could possibly say to him. Then, as she reached the stairs, she remembered that Edward had been discoursing all evening on the subject of asceticism, speaking of its virtues but emphasizing the fact that it was valueless unless self-chosen and must never be enforced upon others. The thought of the hungry guest, whose asceticism was so far from voluntary, expressing his heartfelt agreement, proved too much for her sense of humour. By the time she entered the room she was almost speechless. Rocking with laughter, she pointed at the astonished visitor and gasped out 'I asked you to supper!' for all the world as though it had been a glorious practical joke.

Cleves was so ingeniously designed that every bedroom commanded a view of the Downs. It followed that there was none with a north light, suitable for a studio. Johnston therefore built on a wing with a carpentry room below and his own private stairs leading to his workroom, above. He did not employ an architect because of his belief that things should be designed by the men who made them—in this case the local builder. Another of his beliefs was that additions (or corrections) should not be disguised to look like part of the original. He believed in things being what they were frankly and openly and he therefore designed, in collaboration with the builder, an addition that bore no resemblance whatever to the rest of the house. Inside, the

Sample alphabet. Reduced.

The peace of
which passeth all
understanding be
with you always.

Benediction in black and gold. Reduced.

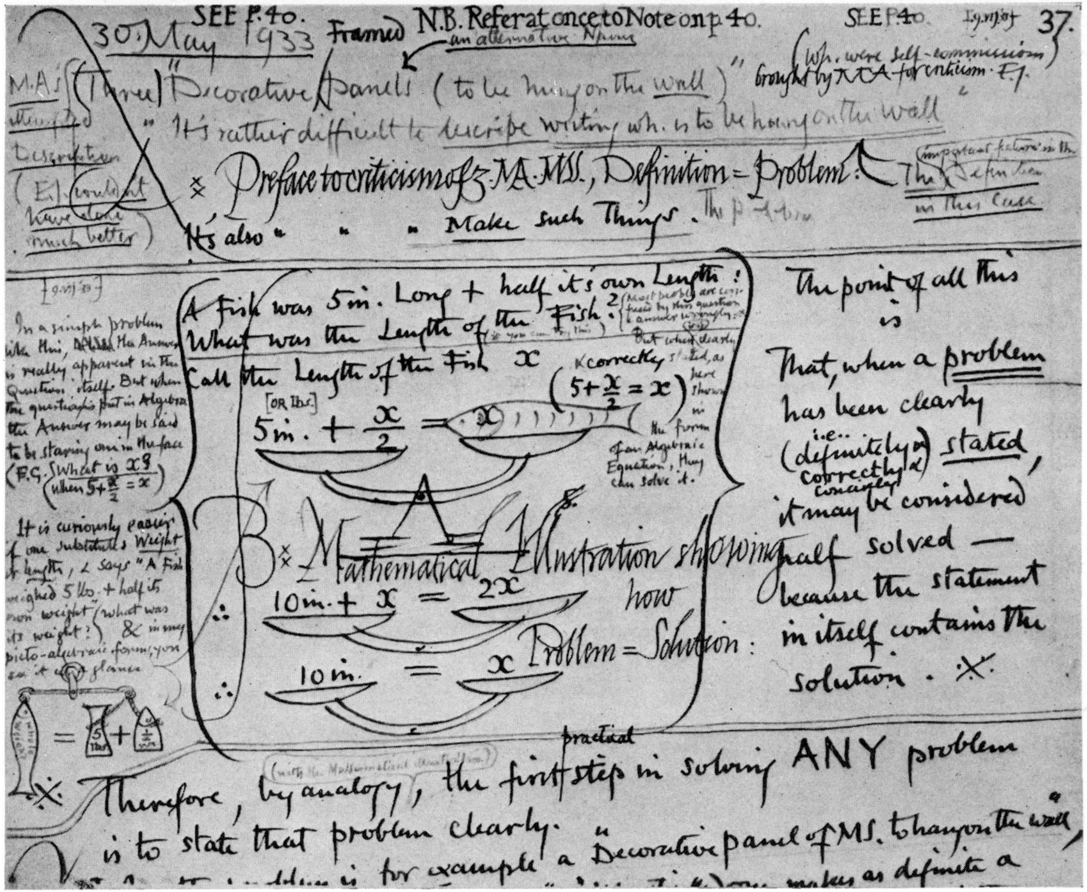

Notes made by Johnston in a student's notebook. 1933. Reduced.

stairs and doors were of unstained deal. So were the cupboards
with which he most ingeniously filled every spare inch, making
many of them himself and fastening them with his beautiful
wooden latches.

In August 1923 he moved in and Greta wrote from her
mother's: 'We shall have been married twenty years by the time
you get this. I wish I were with you to spend the anniversary.
I send you a little bathmat with my love for your new room which
I hope is ready for you now with gas and water. It feels so sweet
and peaceful and, as Priscilla says, there's such an atmosphere of
Daddy about it. You can go into your kingdom and shut the door
in our faces, like the prince in Andersen.'

At Vernon Place she had spoken of the feeling of 'peace and
purity' in his room. Here it was the same. Wherever he was he
imposed his personality upon his background absolutely. Whatever was his, his invisible signature was upon every part of it;
all this with no thought for appearances, the only considerations
being practical ones. (He always maintained that, in dealings
between artists and business men, it was the artist who was the
practical one, concerned with fitness for purpose, and the business man who was the romantic, wanting things to 'look nice'.)

The gift of a bathmat is explained by the fact that he used his
workroom to dress in and had his bath there. He never used the
bathroom, preferring his own elaborately organized system of
gas-rings, enamel cans, home-made towel rails, slop pails and, of
course, his old tin bath. This process was apt to take rather a
long time, particularly as it seems to have stimulated mental
activity; indeed he had a notebook which he sometimes called
his 'ante-bath' book. There he would stand in his dressing-gown,
lost in thought, noting that 'Familiar inaccuracy is more clear
than accuracy. Sunrise is vividly clear, Earth-set (or dip, or
down) most wd. not guess implied the dawn' or: 'Do runner
beans in Australia reverse turn, following the sun?' or: 'I rather
suspect or fear (?) that there are intervals in sensation—sight,
sound, smell, taste, touch and others—and that (like as the space
exceeds the solids in matter) the interval times exceed the

sensations time. . . . Are time and space themselves continuous or discrete? And if they are discrete, what great clock ticks out their instants?' or, again, perhaps most characteristic of all:

'Rediscovered series sum of $1/\ 1,2/\ 1,2,3/=\dfrac{(N+1)^3-(N+1)}{6}$.'

By now the bathwater would be cold and the whole process of cans and gas-rings would have to be set in motion again. What wonder that he shrank from the effort of getting up?

His room was indeed his kingdom. He went in and shut the door, as Greta had foreseen, and nobody disturbed him. No one, as a rule, even tiptoed up those private stairs to knock upon it. Nevertheless, when he particularly wished to remain undisturbed, he used to put a wooden slat across his door, on which one word was beautifully inscribed. Much thought must have gone to the choice of the exact, right word: a word which would still be entirely truthful and accurate whatever the circumstances, which would never mislead or suggest that he was working when, in reality, he might only be thinking. One word had to be found and he found it. *Preoccupied* said the notice outside his door.

For the first time, now, he had a really suitable workroom, and this may, perhaps, have contributed to his growing reluctance ever to leave home. The main cause was no doubt increasing years, but there were others also. There was no longer the same reason to go away. Mr Greig had died and the family had left Laurencekirk, so visits to Scotland were not resumed after the war. Neither were there visits to Devonshire any more, for Miles and his family had come to Ditchling, moving into our old house, Downsview, when we moved out to the common. At first we actually saw less of them after this move than before. Miles, who was something of an invalid, explaining in a business letter why communication with his brother was impossible, said: 'My brother has a small farm about two miles away. The farm and his writing leave him very little time to come here. I am unable to go to him and he rarely answers letters.'

This lack of communication between the two houses once had a tragic result. One February morning in 1917 the builder from Ditchling called to see Johnston before he was up. He came down in his dressing-gown saying 'How good of you to come so promptly about that pigsty', but was brought to a stop by his visitor's expression. 'Haven't you heard from your brother?' the builder asked. Two letters from Miles were waiting on the table. One was to say that Olof was ill, the other that she was dead. The builder, who was also the undertaker, had come to arrange about the funeral.

So Olof ended her sad, solitary life, without ever having taken root in the world or made herself a habitation in it and with most of her beautiful drawings bundled away in portfolios.

'Aunty' survived her, anxious and active as ever, a little old lady in grey with hair cut to the shoulder beneath a Victorian bonnet. Even when we were living next door at Cleves, however, the two families saw little of each other. Edward, continuously nagged by the knowledge of work neglected and hoping, vainly, to make up lost time, shrank from any commitment which might prove an interruption. This partly accounted for his chariness of holidays, expeditions and even meals. They always gave him the feeling that just at that psychological moment he had, at last, really been going to start some important work. One of the things he feared was getting involved in conversation (particularly his own) knowing how it led him to forget the time. Thus he rarely called upon his brother and once, at least, when he saw Miles coming to see him, he fled upstairs to his workroom. He had really decided that day, at last, to begin some important work—or so he thought—and he could not risk such a delay. But having safely escaped he was probably filled with compunction and certainly unsettled by the rush. In the end he sat in his room and read all afternoon, feeling quite unable to work.

Miles also lived a secluded life, seeing little of anyone outside his own household. Occasionally he was to be met with in the village, a tall, stooping figure with a bony face, peering through steel-rimmed spectacles under a panama hat grown brown with age. He pored over his microscope and aquaria much as he had as a boy and wrote occasional papers for learned journals. He was also a martyr to cats. They obliged him to get up in the night to attend to their needs and forced him to skin their mice for them. One spoilt, handsome creature who had been ours but had found both the catering and the service next door far superior to anything we could offer, used to compel his adopted master to walk up and down the garden for long periods, carrying his considerable weight, hind feet lodged firmly in a waistcoat pocket. 'They take me for an ornamental catstand,' Miles remarked in his dry, sardonic way. He spoke of his tormentors with resentment and bitterness, never affection. A letter that he wrote from Devonshire about a kitten we had sent him is so typical that one can almost hear his voice: 'The kitten is all right, quite a nice little beast if one can forget that he has neither morals nor manners. He causes a lot of trouble. Olof sits up all night with him, I don't know why. Kitten does not care for me at all. You need not fear the kitten will not have a good time, the question is whether anyone else will.' Had he not been seriously ill at the time Olof would have had no need to sit up all night with the kitten as he would almost certainly have done so himself.

In the early days at Cleves the two brothers occasionally went on an expedition to some pond together, to get fish or water snails for Miles's aquarium, just as they had when they were boys, except that they now had a small girl in tow. I was keenly interested in pond life and, with my sisters away at boarding school, I was alone at home and was more of a companion to my father at this time than at any other. He taught me carpentry and heraldry and we played 'crolf' together. This was a game of his own invention played with a croquet set which had somehow come into our possession, but on principles slightly more akin to clock golf—hence the name. When the light began to fail and he had to stop work he would go out for a gentle round of crolf, often alone. Sometimes, in the dusk, we would hear the crack of mallet on ball and, peering out, discern a shadowy figure pacing slowly round the lawn.

The only member of the next door household whom we saw

frequently, at times, was Miles's son, Gunnar. He had contracted tuberculosis in the trenches and was obliged to spend the winters abroad, but he returned home in the summer, in the intervals between his three marriages, and spent his time writing thrillers. He always came in when we were having meals—most people did, for we always had them late—and he would stand over us and make us work on some problem in his current book. When he was young he took the part of Jaques in a village production of *As You Like It* and during this period he used to come in and tell us how extraordinarily like Jaques he was in character. Jaques, he said, was recognized as being a study for Hamlet and his own resemblance to Hamlet was really remarkable. He brushed aside flippant diversions with a perfunctory laugh and a firm call to order: 'No, but seriously . . .' until, at last, his uncle said gently, 'In fact, you are a sort of Jaquelet?' That, I think, was the end of that particular conversation.

Our one real family holiday during this period occurred in 1925, when we went to Yorkshire. Greta had written from her sister's (whose plan it was) suggesting this and pointing out that it would be a great treat to all the family, but 'I know it's an effort to you and if it's too great that's enough—no more need be said.' It was her policy that the interests of the family must always, unquestioningly, be sacrificed to his; indeed this was probably unavoidable.

On this occasion he actually agreed to the plan and we were lent a house near the village of Reeth in Swaledale, surrounded by heather-covered hills and rocky mountain streams. It was our favourite country and to have him with us gave a triumphant sense of achievement, of completeness, and even brought back something of the glories of those fabled holidays before the war.

Even so he rarely found time to accompany us on our expeditions. The first part of the holiday he spent in renovating an old table and making it suitable to work on, the latter part in an immense number of experiments with gold size. Before we left he actually began work on the manuscript itself, the address to John Monteath which he wrote for D. Y. Cameron.

Cleves, 1920-1927

This and the following year were a bad period during which, for various reasons, he found it particularly difficult to work and in which he achieved very little. The Monteath address was almost the only work he did in 1925, apart from teaching, yet he had to do it in the one family holiday we had together in eight years. This can hardly have been entirely due to chance. Certainly the demands for the address were becoming urgent, but that was a more or less chronic state of affairs. If we had stayed at home during those three weeks it is more than likely that he would have done nothing. It really seemed that a nervous compulsion to work was induced in him by the fear of being prevented from doing so.

During the whole of this unproductive period one of his best clients, who had also come to be a dear friend, was trying to get a promised manuscript from him. This was Frank Rinder who was commissioned to buy works of art for the National Gallery of Melbourne. This work had been promised for years, but still he pleaded in vain. Finally, in the autumn of 1925, he became so insistent that Johnston promised that it should be the very next job he did. This seemed hopeful, on the face of it, but as the autumn passed and then the winter it began to appear that such an assurance could be interpreted in two different ways. It might be a promise to do the work but, alternatively, it might simply be an undertaking not to do any other. Rinder grew restive. Johnston explained, in an unhappy letter, that he could no longer get the good vellum he needed, he had had 'flu, his workroom was cold and the anthracite stove, long ordered, failed to arrive. Worst of all, he now had to wear glasses for his work and he found it impossible to get used to them. 'The result of this conspiracy of circumstances (or weakness of will, which might have got the better of it) is that I have done no work since the summer . . . but I have at least faith in faith and some hope left.'

Rinder's impatience vanished in face of the picture of frustration and wretchedness this letter conveyed. He divined that Johnston felt some particular difficulty in regard to the work for Melbourne and assured him that 'It is not only ungenerous but

[246]

absolutely wrong to hold you to your proffered promise. . . . One or two straightforward jobs would inspirit you.'

In the beginning of March, like a first tentative bud of the cold spring, a little manuscript appeared for Greta's birthday, the first work Edward had attempted for six months. It was a rhyme about the blue tit composed by himself, with an illumination of the bird in an initial O showing the line of the Downs behind. (He fed the tits so sedulously on the verandah, hanging up coconuts and bits of fat, that the gardener, ruefully eyeing the ripped pea-pods, observed with a certain bitterness, '*Some* gentlemen's gardens aren't *troubled* with tits.')

This little manuscript brought a faint light of hope and encouragement into the gloom of what was, all told, nearly a year of inactivity.

A few months later Rinder wrote that he would be leaving for Australia on July 14 and would be 'woefully disappointed' if he could not take a manuscript with him. Johnston answered 'Thank you for the kindness—surprisingly not yet cut off—of yours of May 31. *I shall do what I may.*'

Weeks passed and nothing happened. Then, on July 11, three days before Rinder was due to sail, Johnston wrote guardedly: 'I may have an MS which I can bring up tomorrow to the R.C.A. I have not time to go into any details but hope you will not be disappointed (either by O[1] or) by the MS being something quite different from anything of mine that you have seen hitherto.'

When a manuscript was wanted for a particular reason by a specified date Johnston never failed to deliver it in time. He could be relied on to rise to an occasion, even when it meant working all night. The mistake some clients made was in their failure to insist upon the absolute necessity of having the manuscript by a particular day. Where there was no real urgency they naturally wished to spare him the anxiety of being pressed for time. They could not know that the sense of urgency, the pressure and even the anxiety were almost indispensable. He could not be 'spared'. 'I have suffered much mentally over it,'

[1] Nothing.

he wrote of one manuscript, 'and spent a good deal of time for which there is little to show. Perhaps these stresses and strains are essential to creation, however mouse-like the result.' When at last he was driven to make the immense effort of tackling a job, of daring and surviving the 'sort of panic' that he always felt on first putting pen to paper, the actual execution often took no more than a few hours. He sometimes thought that he worked best when pressed for time. Often it seemed to be the only way he could work.

The work for Melbourne, after four years' delay, was carried out entirely in one day and finished about midnight. Next day, having left the manuscript at the College to be collected, he wrote to Rinder: 'By now you know the worst and are, I hope, recovering from the MS. I have been doing most of my work in heavy italic for the last three years and developing the hand, but the present MS is not a good example as I am out of practice (this being the first work I have done since D. Y. Cameron's MS last summer). When I have got my hand in, if all's well, I can do you another to replace this present one, if Melbourne will send it back.'

'Hurrah and hurrah!' Rinder's answer burst out, in understandable relief and triumph. The manuscript was, he asserted, 'a glorious piece of work'. 'When I characterize this piece of writing as noble in plan—imaginative plan—and vital in execution I defy you to convince any reasonable and responsive person that the word expresses one whit more than bedrock truth.'

Johnston replied that he was 'unfeignedly grateful for all the kind things you say and even believe them, as coming from you: my doubts beneath my gratefulness like little mice play in and out only in regard to them applying to *me*.'

Johnston's casual reference to having done most of his work for the last three years in 'heavy italic' announced a change of far greater importance than the words suggest. It was, in fact, the second major change of his career. Just as, about 1906 or 1907, he had discarded his 'modernised half uncial' alphabet and devoted himself almost entirely to the foundational hand, so in 1923 or 1924 he made a second great change.

Now, when past his prime, almost at the point when his sight and health began to fail, he produced the most spectacularly vital and original of all his work, 'the first major change in calligraphic form for many centuries' in the words of Noel Rooke. Life, rather than beauty, was his inspiration and this new hand was keen as life itself. Like life, too, it was dangerous; students were warned against it. Johnston had reached a stage where he could afford to take risks. Being able to control the pen completely he was also able to set it completely free. Here, in his latest development as in his earliest, the pen was the arbiter. With all their dash and vigour and display these were the lean hard bones of letters and their shape was never arbitrary, always inevitable.

Verses from Psalm CXXXIX. Black. 1926. Actual size.

[249]

Johnston stated that this hand had, in the course of his working life, 'grown directly' from the tenth century Winchester Psalter upon which he had based his foundational hand some twenty years before. This suggests that he regarded it as a development of the foundational hand though it shows little resemblance to it or to the Winchester manuscript, having more affinity with the book hands of the sixteenth century. 'However influenced,' he wrote, '[it] is actually the product of the "Edged Nib".' This casual reference to influence seems to imply that the answer was unknown even to himself.

Why this hand should have been what it was or appeared when it did are questions to which there can be no more than the most fragmentary and imperfect answers. It is part of the incalculable working out of an artist's development. Sir Sydney Cockerell, however, has pointed out that Johnston, in one lifetime, did to some extent follow or reproduce the course taken by lettering in nine centuries. He began with the half uncials of the seventh century, went on to the Caroline hand of the tenth and finally arrived at this compressed and Gothic type of hand having more relation to the italic writing of the sixteenth century. It is interesting at least to speculate on the possibility that there may have been something inevitable in this progression. It is also interesting to remember that (as already described) his ordinary handwriting, developing gradually, independently of his formal hands, had followed a parallel course, from a round, open hand to a more vigorous, compressed and angular one.

Johnston's new, 'compressed hand', as it has been called, was described by himself as a 'heavy italic'. Noel Rooke, however, wrote of it that 'It is not in any sense an italic . . . the origins are deeper and more structural.' He had discussed it with Johnston and he says: 'He saw that more compressed forms, getting more letters into the same length of line, could be an economy not only of space but of legibility. The distinction between a straight stroke and a curve is always a vital one. So he evolved a compressed hand which preserved the curves and avoided the width and slowness of the round hands, yet was as economic of space

and therefore of "eye-travel" as the Gothic hand. . . . It seems
most probable that, appreciating the reasons for compression, he
set about obtaining the advantages without the disadvantages.
That was, as I remember it, his line of discussion at the
time.'

Rooke also said that, though palaeographers shook their heads
over it, all the younger scribes acclaimed this new hand with
enthusiasm. They, of course, wanted to copy it, but were warned
against doing so by their master 'because it breaks rules' and
bidden to remember that he himself had been a 'respectable
scribe' for years before he broke rules. This seemed hard, for
had he not told them again and again that rules were only
'jumping-off places' and were there to be broken? 'The true
criterion is *success*,' he said, 'transcending our attempted limits,
that success which breaks or infringes many or all the rules.' He
always feared that some pronouncement of his might limit his
students unduly and make them afraid to follow their own
intuition. The danger of cramping or misleading them was ever-
present in his mind, as is shown by a half-humorous remark at the
beginning of a session, when some new students had appeared at
his afternoon class and he referred to 'the unspoilt half-dozen of
you who did not hear what I said this morning.'

Sometimes, in moods of depression, surveying the floods of
illuminated addresses that he had let loose upon the country, he
wondered if his teaching had not done more harm than good.
'Now that my working days are limited,' he wrote in 1936, 'I
see no successor who will put his life and heart into the work
that I love. There are plenty of *good* scribes to whom it is an
occupation and a profession but apparently not a preoccupation
and a dream.'

The first important manuscript in the compressed hand seems
to have been the magnificent roll of honour for Keighley which
Johnston wrote in 1924. He did few real books in his life and
few large, important commissions such as one could list as
'principal works'. The majority of his manuscripts were booklets
or single sheets for framing. The Keighley roll of honour was an

exception. It was a large book and must have been one of the biggest pieces of work he ever did. It was when this was being bound by Douglas Cockerell that Emery Walker wrote: 'Spooner says Douglas Cockerell is binding the most magnificent specimen of modern calligraphy that he has ever had the good fortune to see.' Cockerell himself must have written in the same vein, for Johnston replied to him 'I greatly value your encomium of the MS, judging you to be a fair and experienced critic. I feel curiously unresponsible, however, for its virtues (such as they are) which come mainly from the pen and the vellum (such as it is). Had the vellum been better the MS would have been better and I happier. Nevertheless, you encourage me.' In another letter he said of this great work 'I believe it is all there but I myself am scarcely so, after about three months of work, getting intenser and intenser.'

In the same year, 1924, Johnston made an intensive study of a fourteenth century book hand which made a great impression on him. It would be natural to assume this to have been the inspiration of the compressed hand but that the Keighley manuscript had already been written, earlier the same year. Dr Kellas Johnston, a dealer in rare books, had in his possession a fourteenth century manuscript copy of Gower's *Confessio Amantis*, valued at a thousand pounds, from which the last page was missing. He asked Johnston to write this final page on a fly leaf of contemporary vellum. This, of course, necessitated a very close study of the particular script. The days spent in discovering exactly how this writing had been done and then in mixing inks to the right colour, practising the hand and finally writing the page, naturally aroused a keen interest in the subject. So, too, did the satisfaction of achieving a hand hardly distinguishable from that of Gower's original scribe. Shortly afterwards Dr Kellas Johnston again asked him to write a missing page, this time for an early printed book, a Cicero printed on vellum by Schoeffer in 1466. Johnston had already made a thorough study of Schoeffer's type when designing his black-letter type for Kessler, which was based upon it, and he wrote that 'I know fairly well what the MS from which Schoeffer very closely copied his type must have been like.'

These two essays in fourteenth and fifteenth century hands had interested him so much that when, shortly afterwards, he was commissioned to write a passage from Chaucer and, later, one from Barbour, he decided to do them in the contemporary manner.

Of the Barbour he wrote to his friend and client, Frank Rinder, 'Now I am very keen about a 14th century hand which I learned to imitate in 1925.[1] (This is *quite* different from imitating 14th century architecture in 1925, as I can explain sometime when we have more leisure but now, briefly, thus: that Book hands are so much the product of the pen's Nib that if the scribe *thinks* 14th century straight he produces *matter* having an immediate relation, whereas the architect who can think 14th c. can at best reproduce its spirit by coincidence of its good qualities with the qualities of his own spirit: that is, if he is good enough he can be as good as the 14th c. But the scribe needn't be really good—he can be moderately bad, like me, and yet make a passable *forgery* of antique writing because the spirits of all natural penmanship are in the Nib—if my Quill might come to life it would fly very much like a 14th c. Bird.) And when you mentioned Barbour I hoped we could agree about it—all *three*, I mean. Barbour does because he died in 1395 and my fancy hand is about 1380. . . . I have just written 12 lines from Chaucer in the hand referred to[2] and am rather pleased at the moment (feeling that I appreciate Chaucer better through it and hope others may). Now I want to write Barbour like that . . . let me have permission to make hay of this MS in my own way!'

Rinder agreed to this suggestion and the Barbour was written in the manner of *Confessio Amantis*. This manuscript, intended for a wedding present, had an adventurous history. Rinder collected it from Johnston at the College of Art and took it away in a suitcase. He was delighted with it and was no doubt

[1]Actually 1924.
[2]See illustration facing page 225.

congratulating himself on having persuaded Johnston to do it, and in time for the wedding, too, when he had one of those almost incredible lapses from which no one is immune. While waiting for a bus he put down his case on the pavement and, when the bus came, went off without it. When he discovered what he had done he was distracted. The police told him that the chances of recovering the case were very small. The situation was such that Mrs Rinder wrote secretly to Johnston confessing the truth—which her husband could not face doing—and imploring him to write the manuscript again.

There were still two days left before the wedding and Johnston replied to her 'Your letter came yesterday and I trust you had my wire in reply fairly early. . . . Tell dear F.R. that I am not unhappy but feel, when pleased with my work, like a hen that has laid an egg, the happiness of creation (that fact remains to me even if the egg is lost). But, as human beings, we should feel most sorry for the thief.' He set to work instantly, wrote the manuscript again and delivered it in time for the wedding—an achievement which the Rinders never forgot.

In the end, when it was all over and the bridal pair had gone off with their present in happy ignorance of the anguish it had cost the giver, the police recovered the suitcase after all, and in it the original manuscript. Perhaps it was as a kind of thank offering that the Rinders decided to present it to the Royal College of Art. Johnston told Rothenstein that he thought it fairly suitable for exhibition there, firstly because it was 'a noble piece of British verse' but also because it was '*not too easy* for them [the students] to copy with an appearance of success' (without the necessary technical knowledge).

The Rinders, at first known to Johnston only as clients, had become friends for whom he felt the warmest affection. Perhaps the quality that had first endeared them to him was their understanding appreciation of his work. The affection was mutual. Rinder described Johnston to a friend—who was trying unsuccessfully to get a manuscript from him—as 'quite unique—a lovable original'.

Cleves, 1920-1927

The two men had a special brand of nonsense with which they enlivened their letters to each other. One of the forms it took, on Rinder's part, was a pretence of haggling over money. He was driven to this by the attitude of Johnston, who never named a price, however small, without explaining that it was really far too much and that the work was not worth it. On one occasion when Johnston had written out three words, *The Night Cometh*, and apologetically explained that he was afraid he must charge ten and sixpence, Rinder replied 'The present market price of those three words in 2½d. per letter, total 1s. 9d.'—and enclosed a cheque for a guinea. Another time, when Johnston had asked for a guinea and a half and feared that it was 'an awful lot', Rinder replied: 'Unfortunately I have once again to draw your attention to the exaggerated value you place on little bits of writing. My view is that 1s. 6d. would be ample.' He enclosed a cheque for two guineas.

Once, when writing about the manuscript for Melbourne, which was to be a collection of the sayings of artists on art, Rinder addressed his letter to E. Johnson, Clives. Johnston had probably been telling him of his perennial battle to keep the *t* in his name and of the many variants of *Cleves* supplied by his correspondents, among which '*Olives*' and '*Clever*' were favourites of his. He replied, on this occasion, with a very badly type-written letter—in place of the usual vital and characteristic hand-written one—saying 'Dear Sir, Your note of the 9th inst. addressed to Mr Johnson of Clives has been opened by me, but I judge by its contents that it is intended for someone else. I gather, however, that you want some views on Art typed for a Mr Melbourne; as it seems Mr Johnsin's views would be unfit for publication perhaps I might fill the bill. I have always been a pretty good typewritex since I was anoffice boy. Yrs respectfully, E. Johnson.'

He wrote to Rinder with particular freedom because of the certainty of sympathetic understanding. Once he wrote 'How can I send in bills in face of such letters? Complete appreciation —such as yours—is probably the nearest thing we know or can have to poetic compensation. Let it be understood, then, that my 'bills' to you are not for 'work' done—which you always 'settle' promptly with words of understanding and encouragement—but are the wildest guesses at the market price of the Bread and Butter which my family have eaten while the thing was happening.' Again, in another letter, he said: 'Your appreciation has most decidedly helped to keep me 'going', if it comforts you to know that. But I should go further—it is a pet idea of mine that appreciation, or rather "to see that a thing is good" (v. *Genesis*) is the final *creative act*: in fact, that a thing is not completely created until it has been appreciated. Now that may sound a little mad but, mad sounding or not, I believe it: then mark that for me you have helped to create a number of my works.'

Much as he valued such praise he found it hard to accept it wholeheartedly because, judged by his standards, there were so many faults in every manuscript and these, though they might be invisible to other eyes, were inescapably obvious to his own. Sometimes he even rejected praise outright and on one such occasion he wrote rather anxiously to Mrs Rinder: 'After his most charming and warm encomium a fortnight ago and my remarks—almost like a cold criticism—my heart smote me lest I should have hurt dear F.R. . . . But I was thinking of my students all the time and of Truth—or, say, what the Truth may be (seen by me darkly) but after I thought of F.R. and did hope that there was nothing in my words to hurt—you see, I forget other things when trying to clutch one Thing.'

Some of Johnston's letters to Rinder give detailed accounts of how particular manuscripts were written and of all the difficulties and set-backs which were such a common occurrence, yet one he never learnt to anticipate. In 1930 he wrote some lines from Shelley's *Prometheus* for the Rinders, with a Greek quotation at the top, and here is his account of it: 'Enclosed are the beginnings of three actual attempts on vellum—with some later experiments. Each group (I & II) and (II & III) represents a point arrived at when the light was beginning to fail and the day seemed lost—a rather sharp, unhappy point. With I, I knew the

Letter to Mr. and Mrs. Fletcher. Reduced.

Notice for a church entrance. Part of a draft manuscript; black lettering written with a bamboo pen, vermilion with a steel pen. 1938.

instant "Man" was written that it was no use and there was time to cut another vellum and prepare it and rule it and begin II. There was an interruption of two days—with a sense of fear and gloom about the chances of this MS. On the 3rd day the *experiment* IIa, however, encouraged me to prepare a third vellum and attempt it. But it chanced, by careless thinning, my ink was too thin and No. III failed also.

'Next day I found that though erasing one line of III spoilt this thin vellum there was enough depth in the piece to let me move three lines down, and you have the result (finished, i.e. a few touches and the Red MS added—on the 5th day).

'I hope these details will not worry you or make you feel that the MS should be *priced* (as distinguished from *prized*, let us say) highly. I go as far as conscience permits—and perhaps a little further—when I stick on a percentage charge for my own mistakes. You don't buy a "Mistake" from somebody. Nor can such mistakes be entirely defended as part of, or "all in" the day's work.'

He goes on to outline what the ideal transaction would be, the client saying what he wants and the scribe, after making some preliminary experiments on paper and 'brooding over the work a little' going straight ahead and doing it. 'A small thing should almost be "done while you wait" (as they say) instead of you *waiting till it's done.*'

'As to the Greek, intended, as you surmised, partly for a balancing ornament, but partly to fill or *hedge* the gap which I always feel haunting an *extract*. I know no Greek but found this, from Sophocles, quoted in Mrs Shelley's notes as expressive of Shelley's feelings. His translation is given thus: "Coming to many ways in the wanderings of careful thought." You may have observed that I wished to extend that line and that the ornaments attached to that (and to *each*) end somehow formed themselves quite naturally into inverted commas. Many small and perhaps even some large good-haps seem to attend the wanderings of careful thought in points of arrangement, ornament and special treatment. This is, of course, a common experience among

R   [257]

craftsmen. For example, take the left-hand flourishes marking the second rhyme in each verse. Usually I keep a *straight left edge* but this time played with the idea of a concession to the normal *set-in-and-out line treatment* and got the fun of those flourishes out of it. . . . I get some *Fun* out of those little playings, where the game is to combine the *intellectual* with the *aesthetic* in forms in harmony with the Word(s)-and-the-Thing-Itself.'

'Coming to many ways in the wanderings of careful thought' is so apt a description of Johnston's own mental processes that it is hard to believe he chose it only for the reasons given. There must surely have been another—that it found an echo in his own mind.

The Rinders were probably the only clients whom he allowed to keep these trial attempts, or 'spoilt copies', as he called them. On another occasion he wrote: 'My first attempt did not satisfy me so I did another distinctly better and felt very good and what they call "bucked"—as I always do after a moderately successful attempt. The moderately good one is in the blue cover, the passably good in the white. I tell you which is which because my MSS seem to hypnotise people who don't write quite as clearly and they like the sheep and the goats with equal enthusiasm.' The bill he sent for this manuscript was 'For one passable sheep four lines long, One guinea. A goat of the same quantity *free*. I ought to be able to sit down and dash a thing off but I don't and nearly always boggle at it. . . . The third scrap [of vellum] had a much better surface (which is mainly responsible for its having turned out Mutton while it was largely due to the capriciousness of the vellum that the other became a goat).' For the benefit of those readers who do not share his passion for etymology it should perhaps be explained that the word 'capricious' is derived from the Latin for a goat, its current meaning being a commentary on the supposed temperaments of these animals.

In referring to people who 'don't write quite as clearly' he may have been thinking of Rinder himself, who described his own handwriting as a 'hideous scrawl'. 'This "hideous scrawl",' wrote Johnston, '(as a critic has more than once called it) is a

[258]

thing the mere sight of which gives me a keen feeling of pleasure.
Now I, claiming to be a Master in Scrawls (having the rather rare
degree of MSS) declare it to be funny and lovable but not hideous.
Hadn't you better point out to the critic that he may be mistaken?'

Actually Rinder's writing was second only to Cobden-Sanderson's in illegibility. Even Johnston admitted on one occasion that
'Your letter is not very clear (e.g. there is one word which my
wife reads as "Rainbow" (that's how we get through my Monday
a.m.'s correspondence, i.e. while I eat breakfast and put on my
boots) but I am convinced it is "Number"—anyhow you were
thanking me for it and, as you know, I always appreciate your
thanks).'

Rinder was the one client for whom Johnston would consent
to do 'specimens', just as Gerard Meynell was the one client for
whom he would consent to do work for reproduction—both
things he disliked and of which he disapproved. 'What a dreadful
world it would be,' he said, 'if it were filled not with things
themselves but with specimens of things' and, again, 'Imagine
being asked to give a "specimen" of your smile!' This illustrates
the difficulty very well; the specimen, in his view, was bound
to be an unreal, self-conscious thing, like the smile of the photographer's model. To him, the whole point of the manuscript was
the words. If the client did not care what the words were then
the manuscript was meaningless. The Rinders, like other clients,
were accustomed to have to wait months and even years while he
resolved the various problems raised by their requests—para-
doxically, raised most of all by the request to do 'just anything
you like'—but while the Rinders waited a young friend of theirs,
with great initiative, addressed herself to the legendary Mr
Johnston on her own account, saying simply: 'I am fourteen and
this is my favourite collect. Please write it out for me.' He did so
at once and probably charged her about seven and sixpence. This
was the sort of commission he really liked.

When Frank Rinder went to Australia in 1926, taking with
him the *Sayings of Artists on Art* for Melbourne, he appealed to

Johnston to do 'something' for his wife's birthday, which fell shortly after his departure. The Rinders—like the Johnstons—were a devoted couple and he wanted her to have something to console her in his absence. Johnston chose the passage from the Psalms containing the words 'If I take the wings of the morning and remain in the uttermost parts of the sea, even there shall thy hand lead me. . . .'[1] He made a little book of it and added at the end, as a colophon, a rhyme he had himself composed for them, called *The Five Elements*.

> *If toward the Southern Cross*
> *One should again repair;*
> *If, biding 'neath the Bear*
> *Another one should stay;*
> *Neither sustaineth loss*
> *Of the Four Things they share—*
> *The all-seeing Sun by day:*
> *The all-embracing Air:*
> *The linking Waters: yea*
> *The giant Earth so gross*
> *Shouts 'Here!' when men say 'There.'*
> *Yet there's a clearer light*
> *Concealed by no night,*
> *And Air; a gentler Wave;*
> *Earth more than Eden brave.*
> *So sings this morning star—*
> *'HE IS! Rejoice! We are!'*

He had copied into his diary a sentence from Chesterton: 'There is at the back of all our lives an abyss of light—the fact that things truly are, and we ourselves—real, shouting for joy.'

This was his vision of life, a vision to be apprehended in flashes and, in the times between, clung to by faith. It was the meaning of Truth for him and the reason why Truth was 'the one thing I care most about'. Truth was Reality—that which *is*.

[1]See page 249.

XIII

Last Working Years, 1928-1935

In August 1928, Edward and Greta celebrated their silver wedding. A group of admirers of Johnston's work presented them with a cheque and suggested that they might use it in spending part of the winter abroad, in the hope that it would benefit his health. Johnston had always had a tendency to bronchial trouble and he now suffered much from a cough which gave him bad nights, leaving him exhausted and unable to work the next day. For the first time in his life the routine of Mondays had lapsed; for more than a year he had not attended his class, leaving it to his assistants. Moreover he was now developing cataract in one eye and, although an operation was advised, the state of his health at the time precluded it.

Greta's health had also been giving cause for anxiety and, perhaps for her sake rather than his own, Edward actually agreed to go abroad. It was an astonishing event at the time and it is hard to imagine, looking back, how he could have been uprooted from the intricate paraphernalia of contrivances with which he surrounded himself and persuaded to go to a country where there was not even porridge for breakfast. In the past thirty years he had only left Britain twice, and then on the briefest excursions possible. However, they went. He left long directions and warnings about gas, oilstoves, fires, frozen pipes and the winding of clocks, full of capitals, underlinings and marginal notes. Ironically, we had the finest March that I can remember. We were having all our meals out on the verandah and the Downs were smouldering with grass fires while he, on the Riviera, complained of a 'draught'. It was the same draught that had beset the sealed windows of his childhood. He never escaped from it. Even when he had tea with us in the garden that draught was always there, often imperceptible to us but haunting him like a familiar spirit.

So, at Ospedaletti, there was a draught and no porridge and bacon had to be specially ordered for his breakfast. Greta got some fun out of the holiday, enjoying the rest and the sun and laughing with the chambermaids as they tried to teach her Italian, but whether Edward could be said to have enjoyed it was hard to determine. At any rate, two good things came of it. It was there, on a cheap writing-block bought in San Remo, that he started a second great work on calligraphy, which occupied him, on and off, for the rest of his life, and his health really did improve. The cough never entirely left him but for some years it was kept at bay. He was even able to return to the College and his class again. His Mondays in London once more became a regular feature of the week, and continued to be so for several years.

That summer a presentation was made to him, perhaps partly in celebration of his return to his classes. Admirers of his work joined together to give him a portrait drawing of himself by his friend Sir William Rothenstein, then principal of the College.[1] In this drawing Rothenstein has captured exactly the remote and visionary expression of Johnston's eyes. Since the sittings were always on Mondays, at the end of a long day's teaching, it happened, incidentally, that the drawing also faithfully reproduced Johnston's jaded, Monday-evening look. It was this tousled, slightly desperate air which caused Greta to christen the portrait 'The Labour Leader'.

Soon after his return from Italy Johnston had written to Frank Rinder 'Now I am on my way to attempt once more the adventure of teaching at the R.C.A. (Only once tried—a day in last October—since November 1926,[2] though before that went

[1]See frontispiece.
[2]Actually November 1927.

twenty-five almost unbroken years.) The class has been kept going by one of my old students who has a real gift for the work. I find that Hope—with *more* than one string left—stands by me faithfully and is my tried and kind companion in all adventures.'

The class had been carried on by Violet Hawkes and Dorothy Bishop. It was Miss Hawkes who had the foresight to photograph his blackboard after the classes, thus preserving an invaluable record of his demonstrations.

Johnston found this return to work a great strain and decided that he must either leave the College earlier or give it up altogether. He offered this choice to the authorities, whose decision was emphatic. 'There need never be any difficulty about your getting away at 3.15,' the registrar wrote. '. . . It is so very much more valuable to have you here for an hour in which your presence can make itself felt and create a movement which others may keep up than that we should suffer your entire absence.'

His presence did indeed make itself felt. A stir of excitement ran through his whole classroom when it became known that Mr Johnston was really coming that day. Some years later, when I was working for MacDonald Gill ('Gill's brother'—afterwards my husband) we were helped on one large mural painting by a student who had been in that class. She told me, then, how much they had loved those lectures and how eagerly they had waited for Johnston to come. I repeated these remarks to my father the next time I was at Ditchling and, according to my diary, 'He said he wished he had known at the time, it would have been encouraging, and then he said he did feel, really, that they enjoyed it, that he was able to give them the feeling that it really was worth doing and a little of his vision, also, the spirit of it, over and above the technical side. He quoted *Man shall not live by bread alone* and spoke of the excitement of the vision. . . .'

This was no doubt what Miss Hawkes had in mind when she wrote 'Our teaching is simply mundane but you teach out of eternity and infinity. We instruct but you inspire.'

When a student, after a course of private lessons, wrote that he had 'illuminated' the work for her and given her a new vision of it, he answered: 'I continue teaching largely for the selfish reason of being taught myself by the experience, but I am glad to be reminded of the better reason and to be encouragingly assured of being helpful—and particularly helpful in the way you mention. Such "illumination" is, in fact, better than writing.'

His lectures were, as Miss Hawkes suggested, far more than a course of instruction in formal penmanship. His discourse roamed far and wide: stars, philosophy, folktales—anything might find a place in them. 'He related his subject,' as Noel Rooke said, 'to everything in heaven and earth' because he saw it as essentially part of a whole. Since writing was an activity of man, the question of man's life on earth and the kind of universe in which he found himself had, for him, an essential connection with the work in hand. Therefore his lectures could embrace almost any subject and must have considerably widened the horizons of those students—and they were numerous—whose educations had been conventionally narrow. At one class he would explain to them his view that 'our reasoning itself is a game, like our chess or our mathematics' or that it was not self-contradictory to say that 'we are predestined to have free will'. At the next, in speaking of the roundness of the letter O, he would describe the experiment with a soap film and a loop of thread—'the prettiest experiment in physics'—which is used to demonstrate that a perfect circle encloses the greatest area that a closed loop can contain.

The art of teaching, which could set him exploring 'eternity and infinity', could also show him at his most human and approachable. I discovered this for myself when I had some lessons with him soon after I left school. I had been shy of encountering an unknown aspect of him, the professional, professorial Edward Johnston, of whom I had dimly heard, but I found him at his sweetest, humorous and gentle. He would laugh at my attempts at letters and describe their faults in such terms that they seemed living creatures, made the more funny and touching by their eccentricities. It was as though he kept the letters of the alphabet as pets, observing their behaviour with a naturalist's devotion,

[264]

but with amusement too. Once, when introducing certain flourished capitals to his students, he observed that '*O*, which never moves a muscle of its face, when it gets into this company does just open its mouth and grin, so to speak.' He hardly moved a muscle of his own face while saying such things, with the result that new students were sometimes afraid to laugh. Those who knew him better could detect the twinkle in his eye and the slight tremor at the corner of his mouth which alone betrayed his amusement.

In this vein he used to ask his students if they knew the difference between a sculptor and a hairdresser and explain that the one makes faces and busts while the other just curls up and dyes, ending by pointing out to them the letters which had curled up and died. He made his maxims memorable by vivid similes: 'Writing between ruled lines is like trying to dance in a room your own height,' he would say, or 'a flourish is no good unless it flourishes, as cracking a whip is no good unless it cracks.' Again, he compared the spacing of letters to the packing of eggs, saying that they should be 'as close as they can be put—tightly fitted without breakages', the essential spaces between the letters being equivalent to the separating wads between the eggs. It was this matter of spacing which led him to ask his students if they knew the song *Is there room for Mary there?* and to explain that Mary's mother had always told her she was in the way, whereupon Mary went and died, asking with her last breath if there would be room for her in heaven. To the delight of the students Johnston added, quite vehemently, that he considered it 'most mean and unchristian of Mary to get her own back on her mother like that'.

Like his conversation, his lectures were always punctuated with these flashes of humour, never more unexpected than when they were drawn from his observations of people, which, though certainly intermittent, could be startlingly shrewd. Thus, when speaking of the importance of a really sharp knife for cutting a quill, he said 'Very often when I ask a student for his knife he laughs. Funny, isn't it, the things we laugh at? What makes him

[265]

laugh? Guilty conscience. He knows what his knife is like.' He made another discovery about the causes of laughter one Monday when he greeted his students with what seemed to him the simplest possible statement of fact: 'I am sorry I did not come last week—I forgot.' To his surprise this evoked a roar of delight. 'It just shows,' he commented, 'that nothing is so funny as the truth.'

This was the lighter side of Johnston's teaching. It had its other aspects: exciting, exhilarating, uplifting, and—on occasion —devastating. As he had told Mrs Rinder: 'I forget other things when trying to clutch one Thing.' The intensity of his concentration upon 'one Thing' often made him oblivious of things that were obvious to anyone else who was present, such as the glances at watches or covert movements towards the door of those with trains to catch. It also made it impossible for him to consider people's feelings when his entire attention was concentrated on their work, and this sometimes demanded a good deal of fortitude on the part of sensitive young students. One of his best students, Irene Bass (afterwards Irene Wellington) recorded that 'No pride was left in you after you had sustained his scrutiny through a magnifying glass, and that slow, positive, remorseless analysis—so unanswerably right. He seemed completely detached, concerned only with Objective Truth, not with whether you could "Take it." He assumed that you could. . . . But the curious thing about his most drastic criticism was that you were never left dispirited but went off feeling braced, thinking: "No, I can't write, but by the Grace of God I will do yet!" '

Johnston was always telling his students things so simple and basic that they had never thought about them before, as when he told them that the first question they should ask themselves before embarking on writing a manuscript was *Why?* The second question was *What?* and the third *How?* Most students had not thought of asking *Why?* It was too fundamental.

One student, unfamiliar with this approach, was deeply disconcerted by his opening remark in her first private lesson with him. She had laid out her best work for him to see and awaited his comments with keen anxiety. He came into the room, picked up one of her manuscripts, looked at it in silence and put it down again, asking, in his detached, impersonal way, '*What* is this?'

It was characteristic of Johnston that he began by asking the question *Why?* where most poeple would have assumed that they knew the answer, without pausing to consider whether they did or not. He would always carry his researches a step further back than other people thought of doing, questioning premises which they took for granted. A certain speaker at a meeting once ended his oration by declaiming 'When I was a child, I spake as a child, I understood as a child, I thought as a child: but when I became a man I put away childish things.' He no doubt resumed his seat with a satisfied sense of having clinched his argument beyond question by enlisting the Bible on his side, but, in the silence that followed, Johnston's measured and resonant voice was heard to ask: 'Was . . . Saint Paul . . . the better . . . for that?'

Johnston was one of those characters round whom stories accumulate irresistibly, some well founded, others apocryphal. One may, perhaps, ascribe to the latter group the story that when he was due to speak at the village hall in Ditchling a search party, setting out three-quarters of an hour after the advertised time of the lecture, found him half way along the road telling a passer-by what he intended to say. This is typical of the stories inspired by him. So, also, is the story that a friend of Hammer-smith days, turning up at Ditchling twenty years later, was warmly received by him but asked to wait a moment while he completed some particularly urgent task. Johnston retired to his workroom and the friend, left alone, waited for an hour and a half, after which he discreetly withdrew. This may very well have happened and, if so, Johnston's version of the story would certainly have been that he had to leave the man for a few minutes and, on his return, found that he had 'apparently dashed off somewhere'. His own tempo was such that, by contrast, the behaviour of other people often appeared to him to be beyond reason hasty and precipitate.

On another occasion a friend, passing the house, saw him standing at the gate, apparently writing a postcard. She asked if his wife were in but, though he seemed to attempt to disengage his thoughts from the matter in hand, he failed to do so and returned no answer. A few days later she met him in the village and he recalled the incident and said 'My wife *was* in. I must apologise for my apparent rudeness but I was putting in the punctuation marks on a card she had asked me to post.'

One maid of ours used to worry him by her excessive liability to shock. Sudden noises or people appearing unexpectedly would cause her to clutch at her heart and assert that 'her stomach had turned right over'. As a result he made a point of walking loudly, coughing and rattling matchboxes whenever he went near the kitchen. On one such occasion, hearing sounds proceeding uninterruptedly from the scullery and determined not to take her unawares, he said, in his most weighty and penetrating tones: '*You hear me . . . Bessie . . . don't you?*' A moment later he came round the corner and found, not Bessie, but the gardener's boy, shoebrush in hand, gazing wide-eyed and open-mouthed.

Johnston had no small-talk and, except with his wife, almost no intimate, personal conversation. He talked in the same way to everyone. It did not matter whether it was the doctor or a shop assistant, a shy lady paying her first call or the plumber unblocking a drain. One of the most familiar early-morning sounds was the distant booming of his resonant voice as he discoursed to the maid who had brought his tea upon the derivation of words or the meaning of faith, while she stood in the open doorway, tray in hand, wondering if the porridge was burning or the newly lighted fire going out. In spite of such practical distractions, however, much of what he said made a deep impression upon the most surprisingly assorted hearers. Everyone he came across he talked to, often at great length, and though sometimes rather puzzled his listeners always seem to have been interested. A nurse who attended him weekly at one time, towards the end of his life, thanked him particularly for his discourse on one occasion: she had enjoyed it so much more than last time, she said: 'Last time it had been about the stars, but this time it was about Hitler.'

Last Working Years, 1928-1935

Johnston was well aware of his tendency to become enthralled by his topic and lose count of time and, in particular, of the danger of his giving students more information in this way than they were ready for or could assimilate. He would sometimes compare himself ruefully to the father in *The Swiss Family Robinson* —a favourite book of his boyhood—who never lost an educational opportunity, and quote, 'Then I told them all I knew about alligators.'

One evening he had been thus inescapably compelled to keep some young visitors standing on the doorstep while he 'told them all he knew' about the planets. It was during this conversation that he made a slip which worried him so much that he afterwards felt obliged to write a long letter of explanation. He had been 'flustered' at the time, he said, by the knowledge that he was keeping them standing in the cold (the word was fantastically inappropriate to the appearance of unruffled deliberation which he invariably presented, but no doubt corresponded to some inner feeling which failed to find expression). He had been about to say that it was interesting to know which planets were which and to be able to tell people this—for his listeners were young enough, he judged, to derive particular satisfaction from this aspect of knowledge—when the thought had crossed his mind 'What do any of us *know?*' and the sentence came out as 'It's rather nice to pretend you know.' Although he immediately corrected himself the words had so shocked him that he felt it necessary to explain again how far they were from his meaning. 'Please be assured,' he wrote, 'that I did not mean that there was any pleasure or satisfaction in shamming knowledge. . . . Some of the most painful occasions in my past have been when through shyness or diffidence I allowed someone to think I knew when I didn't—cheating as it were by default, through a sort of weakness. Since growing older and less shy I have almost too obtrusively and instantly confessed my ignorance of what people were talking about—though still left far behind in the attempt to search out and live the Truth.'

He was perennially fascinated by words and their derivations.

[269]

Last Working Years, 1928-1935

This, too, was an aspect of his devotion to accuracy as well as a result of his work, which involved much study of shades of meaning in an endeavour to make his transcription express the spirit of the text. He undoubtedly loved words for their own sakes, however, and would return again and again to the dictionary where he would browse happily, collecting much interesting information, before arriving at the word he sought. A typical interpolation in a letter to a friend at the Admiralty, is: '(Here I open my dictionary to assure myself that "curiosity" is correct and the first word catching my eye is "futtock",="n. One of ship's middle timbers between floor and top timbers. (perh.=*foot-hook*)" Now that, a commonplace to you, I'd never have thought of—"probably" I guessed, "a thing for hobbling horses with"!' He made many cherished discoveries in this way, the one that pleased him most being the derivation of the word *authentic* from a Greek word meaning *one who does a thing himself*. 'Springs from the central idea of craftsmanship,' he wrote against this in his notebook.

Not only when teaching but in conversation he chose his words with the care of one who loved and valued them and he had, at times, a notable gift for finding the right ones. I remember his describing the kind of firework known as a sparkler, from the moment it is lighted, when 'it says "*spit!*"' and spits out some stars' to its last expiring splutter. I have never seen, heard or smelt an actual sparkler as vividly as I did that verbal one.

He had his views—usually interesting and often unusual ones —on most subjects, even those with which one would not have expected him to concern himself, such as women's fashions. He never dismissed things as nonsense or as impossible, neither superstitions nor frivolity; he considered that to do so was fundamentally unscientific and he was shocked by the number of scientists who made such assertions. He was deeply suspicious of negatives, believing that an attitude of negation or denial was a basically wrong angle from which to approach a problem. 'The moment you deny anything you stand on the edge of a precipice,' he said. The negative, like the minus quantity, was unreal and could only safely be employed as a double negative. 'Not not, never never, impossible impossible,' he used to say; 'three words which apparently can only be safely used when applied to themselves or their own negative implications.' Another word that he distrusted was *ought*. To over-dutiful students, continually asking 'What *ought* I to do?' (and, once, 'How much convention *ought* I to put into this?') he answered by quoting Lethaby's words— words more profound, he came to believe, than Lethaby himself had realized—'My dear Johnston, if you did all the things you *ought* to do you would never have time for the things you *must* do!'

Again, there was the word 'mere'. Nothing, he held, was 'mere' and nothing should be dismissed as 'merely' so-and-so. Everything had a meaning and a reason. Thus with women's fashions, he never regarded them as irrational whims. He saw the leading couturiers not as despots arbitrarily decreeing what women were to wear but as people endowed with a special form of intuition which enabled them to foretell what women *would* wear, to crystallize some feeling in the air of what the time demanded. In an ordinary way he did not notice when his own wife had a new dress, and complained that he found women difficult to recognize because 'they all dressed alike' but now and then something would catch his eye and make a deep impression. Thus it was with a certain photograph of the Duchess of Kent. She seemed to be crossing a street, striding forward with the skirts of her coat swinging out. *There!* he said, *that* was the meaning of fashion. He looked out for other photographs of her after that and was confirmed in his opinion that she was one of the rare people possessing the faculty to raise the design and wearing of clothes to the status of a true art.

This incident was typical in its unexpectedness. It was impossible to foretell what would catch his attention or what would be ignored. It was as though he went about in a sort of dream, immersed in some profound speculation, and then something would break into his private world, flash upon his consciousness with extraordinary vividness and seize his imagination, even as the Duchess of Kent had done, stepping off the kerb.

Last Working Years, 1928-1935

It was the same with music. He was not musical and ordinarily showed no interest in the subject yet occasionally something wholly unexpected would get through to him and make a profound impression. A certain record of the music from the ballet *Sylvia* exercised an almost magical fascination upon him. Wherever he was it seemed to summon him, as a spell might summon a spirit. Once, too, when a gifted guest was playing to himself—extemporizing, as it happened—Johnston appeared, drawn by the sound and said that it was 'like a light in the house'.

Another of the things that he had *seen*, in one of those intense flashes of vision, was the legs of the waitress at Ospedaletti. They had been a revelation. So impressed was he that he asked a man friend if he had ever noticed how remarkably beautiful legs could be. The friend, as it happened, had given some study to this subject and eagerly offered corroborative evidence. Why, only the other day, he had said to himself 'Jove! That's a well-turned limb'. Johnston nodded gravely, noting with interest that his discovery was not unique.

It was this same friend who once recounted to him an incident on a railway journey. He had helped a girl out with her luggage and a man sitting opposite had winked at him and said—rather impertinently, as he thought—'Would you have done that for her grandmother?' Johnston considered this story. 'I suppose he was drunk?' he suggested. 'Oh, no,' the friend explained, 'not in the least. He was simply being facetious.' Again Johnston thought it over in silence and this time his comment was conclusive. 'Oh, George,' he said, with finality, 'he *must* have been drunk!'

He had never in his life been thrown into the company of a mixed lot of boys or men, except perhaps for a short time at the University, and much that was commonplace to more worldly men was unfamiliar to him. Once when he was lunching with a number of colleagues at South Kensington there was a man present whose stories were considered rather doubtful by the others. To Johnston they were unknown, and when, on this occasion, one was related, he rose to his feet, without a word, and walked straight out of the room. The effect was said to have been most impressive.

[272]

Last Working Years, 1928-1935

Round about 1930 Johnston was once again working hard on type designs for Count Kessler. Kessler had reappeared sometime after the war to try to pick up the threads so abruptly broken in 1914. This was not easy as no one remembered exactly what had been done, what left: all was vague, uncertain, half forgotten. The punches for the black-letter type were scattered, some lost, some perhaps never cut, all rusty. Then there was the question of capitals to go with the italic lower case designed by Johnston before the war. Had he got drawings for capitals? Count Kessler asked. If not, would he do them? 'It is a very beautiful fount and it would be a great pity to leave it unfinished.'

Nothing much seems to have been done until 1926 and by that time the italics were forgotten and Kessler was in full cry after his black-letter. His great *Hamlet* with Gordon Craig's engravings was held up for lack of it. In the meantime, Prince, the original punch-cutter, had died. He was a craftsman whom Johnston had held in the very highest esteem, but they were fortunate in finding a worthy successor in G. T. Friend.

It was Friend who described how Kessler used to appear on his lightning visits to England, desperate at the delays, demanding to know why the type was not ready. Friend bore the brunt of the attack, but the answer was always the same: he had not got the drawings. It was up to him to get them, then, Kessler insisted. What could *he* do, in Germany? Friend must keep Johnston up to the mark—that was his job! Now they must catch him at the College—send someone out for a taxi—they must get hold of Johnston instantly, there was no time to lose. They must tell him that the black-letter *had* to be finished—the *Hamlet* was waiting! So they would dash to South Kensington, Kessler fuming with impatience all the way. When at last they arrived and actually caught their man Friend stood by, waiting for the storm to break. But at the sight of Johnston Kessler seemed to melt. Suddenly the fiery impatience vanished. 'My *dear* Johnston,' he said, in tones of the deepest concern, 'you look tired, you haven't been taking care of yourself, you've been *doing too much!*'

The seed of the grass,
The speck of stone
Which the wayfaring ant
Stirs — and hastes on!

Though I should sit
By some tarn in thy hills,
Using its ink
As the spirit wills
To write of Earth's wonders,
Its live, willed things,
Flit would the ages
On soundless wings
Ere unto
My pen drew nigh:
Leviathan told,
And the honey-fly:
And still would remain
My wit to try —
My worn reeds broken,
The dark tarn dry,
All words forgotten —
Thou, Lord, and I.

The Scribe by Walter de la Mare
Part of a framed panel. Black. 1929. Greatly reduced

Last Working Years, 1928-1935

'He liked your father,' Friend explained to me, '—to put it mildly.'

He certainly held the highest opinion of his ability, for when a copy of the magnificent *Hamlet* finally arrived and Johnston wrote congratulating him upon it Kessler answered: 'There is nobody in the world whose appreciation of my printing and books is of more value to me than yours as you undoubtedly are the foremost living expert on the subject.'[1] He was himself well pleased with the work. 'I hope you will be satisfied with the splendid effect of your type,' he had written, when sending the book. 'Everybody here admires it very much indeed.'

Johnston's own view was that the punch-cutters, Prince and Friend, deserved more of the credit than himself. He had only 'traced' the original faces of Schoeffer's type, he said, disguised and blurred as they were by the accidents of printing. This he was enabled to do by his practice in calligraphy, for the type was closely based upon contemporary book hands. The punch-cutters had had what he considered the more exacting task of making '*a necessary adaptation of forms*, in reducing comparatively large drawings to the actual type sizes.'

Kessler next brought his potent enthusiasm to bear upon the idea of a Greek type. This had first been mooted in 1911 when he had taken Johnston to the British Museum to look at Greek lettering and sent him a photograph of the *Doryphoros*, saying 'No script that cannot *stand beside* this, that does not *breathe this spirit* of calm, proud strength and grace is really Greek'. Now, nearly twenty years later, Johnston started his researches upon Greek lettering again and wrote: 'In my two days' preliminary experiments with "pens" (of wood, reed and chalk) and by close examination of the *type* letters, I think I discovered *how* and *with what* sort of pens such Greek letters were written. I am rather thrilled with the hope that this is a true discovery.'

Kessler was enthusiastic. Johnston's drawings for the Greek type were '*Superb—quite in the grand style!*' But a few weeks later, staying at Banyuls-sur-Mer with Maillol, he had forgotten it

[1] A statement which Johnston would have considered absurd.

again. Maillol's enthusiasm for the italic type had so fired him, and inspired them both with so many eager plans, that nothing mattered now except to get the italic capitals completed. This type, said Maillol, harmonized better with his designs than any other he knew. He must have it for his proposed edition of *Ronsard*. Then there was the *Horace*, the *Daphnis and Chloë*—the air of Banyuls-sur-Mer hummed with plans. Maillol returned with Kessler to Weimar to work on his illustrations for the *Horace* and they were joined there by Eric Gill who was doing engravings for Kessler. Weimar was alive with activity and Kessler seemed at the height of his powers.

About this time came a poignant little letter from Friend to Johnston, worried by criticisms from the type-founders and others: 'I am wondering if it is not best to go on without being influenced by everything anyone says. . . . I am entirely with you in whatever you decide.' It is the first hint of trouble, like the first drop of rain.

The problem of the italic capitals was beset with difficulties and fate itself seemed to take a hand against them. They were urgently needed for the Sackville West translation of Rilke's *Duineser Elegien* which Kessler was printing for the Hogarth Press. This was promised for Easter, but in the winter he fell ill with bronchial pneumonia. At the same time there was trouble with the new italic capitals which were printing too heavy or 'squashing'.

Johnston wrote to Friend: 'If you have any doubts in respect of your own part in the matter, be sure that I have none in respect of your work. We are really engaged in an *extraordinarily difficult experiment*. The problem is to make an upper case type now to a lower case made some 17 or 18 years ago—that is difficult enough in itself, but we have a greater difficulty in our modern (at present unavoidable) division and separation of labour.

'1st the designer (myself) guessing at an ideal.

'2nd the punch cutter (yourself) giving it material shape.

'3rd the type-founder (Shanks) reproducing them in quantity.

Last Working Years, 1928-1935

'4th the printer (Cranach Press) applying the types. (Not to mention assistants, photographers, etc.)

'We are all widely scattered between London and Weimar and largely ignorant of each others' work and views.'

In the end, very sadly and to the great disappointment of all concerned, Kessler decided that the new capitals could not be got right in time for the Rilke and it was necessary to make do without them and use old ones.

Towards the end of March 1931, Kessler wrote from Ascona where he was convalescing after his illness. He was still very unhappy about the italic capitals and thought that they would have to be recut. His letter ends 'I am leaving Ascona tomorrow and shall probably be back in Weimar on Monday or Tuesday.' His impatient nature, chafing at the intolerable delays of ill-health, was dragging him back to the work he loved before he was fit to go. The result was a relapse and another long and serious illness which brought the work to a complete stop. In September Johnston wrote to Emery Walker asking for news of him: 'The last I had was from Rothenstein about May or June that he was still very ill.'

There, sadly, the story ends. The italic type was apparently never used except in the Hogarth Press Rilke with the wrong capitals, and in the colophon of another book. The Greek type was never finished. Soon after this the Nazis came to power and Kessler was obliged to fly from Germany at short notice, taking nothing with him. He died in Paris a few years later, in Johnston's words 'a good man who lost not only his fortune but practically all that he valued in life.'

Kessler was not only a connoisseur and patron of the arts, he had also been a diplomatist and had held positions of authority. He was accustomed to command. Something of this aspect of his complex character is revealed by the story of a visit he paid to Eric Gill in the mountains of Wales. Kessler hired a car from the nearest town, drove the long distance to the house and told the driver to wait. It is easy to imagine how the stream of talk flowed on and the hours passed unnoticed while Kessler inspired Gill with enthusiasm for some new project. At last one of the children broke in upon this eager discourse with a message: the driver said he could not wait. Still there was more to say and one idea led to another. A second message had no more effect than the first. At last a boy ran in in some agitation saying 'The driver says he's *going!*' At this even Gill broke off to explain to Kessler —who still seemed unconcerned—that the situation was serious. No other transport was available and urgent engagements awaited him in London. Kessler paused for a moment in what he was saying to remark 'He won't go—I haven't paid him,' and continued his discourse.

Some other work brought Johnston into close touch with Friend at about this time. Early in 1930 Noel Rooke had asked him to design a diploma for the LCC Central School of Arts and Crafts, where his first classes had been held. The idea was that it should be photographically reproduced, but here it came up against Johnston's objection to working for reproduction. He finally suggested, as a compromise, that if they would have the diploma engraved he would write 'a sort of guide' for the engraver who was to 'translate' it from pen-forms to engraving forms.

This sounded all right. The suggestion was accepted and the fee of fifteen guineas agreed upon. As usual Johnston was suffering from that fatal optimism in regard to estimates of time and cost which made him assume that everything would go without a hitch. He was usually wrong in this, but never so disastrously as in the case of the LCC Diploma.

He was asking the engraver, Friend, to do something a good deal more difficult than either of them had at first realized. Friend could have copied the pen-forms or he could have made his own engraving forms, but to copy and yet not copy presented problems; to do it in such a way as to satisfy a critic as stringent as Johnston came near to being an impossibility.

In March 1930, Johnston produced an experimental manuscript and they went to work. Friend engraved plate after plate,

[278]

Last Working Years, 1928-1935

Johnston wrote page after page of notes and drawings. His criticism was exhaustive and relentless, 'as though to a student' he said, explaining that by a student he meant 'one who is applying his intelligence to the elucidation of the Truth and is therefore indifferent to "praise or blame".' This rather optimistic definition was no more applicable to Friend than to most students, but he was determined not to be beaten. 'I want to make a good job of this thing,' he wrote, 'and with you as critic I can accept as much as you like of criticism.'

They did not simply 'want' to make a good job of it, they were obliged to do so by their natures and by being the kind of craftsmen that they were. They went on working at the Diploma until they got it right. They worked at it for five years.

'I'm not sure that our dream is feasible in our lifetime,' Johnston wrote. 'It does seem to want a tradition at its back which neither you nor I possess.' Six months later he wrote 'We can hardly, either of us, expect a remuneration from the LCC at all commensurate with the work and thought spent on it' (this was quite a notable understatement) 'but we can certainly have the craftsman's first satisfaction of *having aimed at well doing* and possibly his second of *"not having done so badly"* and one of his best *rewards* of winning (from a select few, perhaps) some appreciation of these things.'

When at last the work was finished Johnston wrote to Rooke 'Had I known I'd not have touched it under £100 (this is literal).'

In 1931 and 1932 Johnston gave a course of three lectures at the Central School of Arts and Crafts. It was a remarkable achievement on the part of Noel Rooke to persuade him to undertake such a thing, for it was many years since he had lectured except to his own classes and his health was now so uncertain that he was more reluctant than ever to take on anything extra.

The first lecture was in October 1931, soon after I had gone to live in London. I recall a dim impression of the largeness of the hall and then the surprise of seeing him on the platform—in the familiar old herring-bone suit with the bulging pockets. If parents are nervous about their children appearing in public, children are infinitely more nervous about their parents. The sight of him standing there with that lost, isolated look he had in a crowd, intent but mystified as though trying to follow a speech in a foreign language, was not reassuring. He had not been speaking long, however, before even I realized that he really was a lecturer, not just my father, though I fancy I still had a suspicion that it was more by luck than by skill that he dealt with the audience so capably, engaging their attention and evoking their laughter. I remember him reaching up to make his great sweeping chalk lines on the huge blackboard. In his hand he had his home-made chalk-holder, or 'pen', with the beautiful arrow. This arrow was a device he had made for demonstrating to his students that the angle of the nib's edge is constant. It was about eighteen inches long and made of a light whitewood—probably the same holly from which he used to cut out animals for us with a fretsaw. The arrow was fastened across the chalk-holder, at right angles to it, and as he wrote it moved with the 'pen' but remained always at the same angle to the writing line, demonstrating most graphically that he was keeping the edge of the 'nib' at a constant angle.

The lecture was enthusiastically received and afterwards I was standing by my father when an elderly man came up and spoke to him. His face lit up and he grasped the stranger's hand with such warmth and animation that I recognized it as a special occasion. I learned later that this was Harry Cowlishaw, the man who had introduced him to Lethaby. Johnston had not seen him for nearly thirty years and probably had not so much as sent him a Christmas card during that time, but his feelings had not changed. So it was with all his friends; he made no attempt to keep in touch with them and even if they wrote to him he might leave their letters unanswered, yet he retained for them, unfailingly, the same warm, deep affection.

Of this lecture Johnston wrote to Frank Rinder: 'How nice of you to thank me for the blackboard Demonstration. I felt at the time, after the first five minutes, that I was speaking to appreciative friends. Your and Mrs Rinder's "contributions" to that impression were, I'm sure, handsome, and those invisible coins helped to keep an invalid youth *quite* happy on his little platform for an hour and a half. (Note: The lad referred to, now within a few months of sixty, always feels about six when happy and frequently (I am thankful to say) when *un*happy.)

'The next Demonstration may not be as "good" as the first, as it must, being concerned with specific "hands", be less pure science and approach the doubtful field of applied science.'

After a subsequent lecture Greta, who had not been present but had followed it in imagination, wrote to Margaret Alexander, a former student: 'Wasn't it nice to see him write on the blackboard? It looks so easy, as though no mistake in that beautiful, sure sweep were possible. I could see that lecture, the lecturer so unflustered, unpacking the arrow, etc., with marvellous sangfroid. He has had a nice public life lately: two Monday mornings at the Arts and Crafts Exhibition, two lectures with nights away from home and pleasant encounters—not bad for a gentle hermit.'

After one of these lectures Johnston stayed the night with the Rinders at their house in St John's Wood. He wrote beforehand: 'I am not clear that it will be sufficiently interesting to warrant your leaving the Wood. A telephone direction—how to get there from the School by rights-of-way (fairly free of brambles)—will be sufficient to bring me to the shack in the clearing.' In thanking them, afterwards, for their hospitality he said 'such people and such "Things" renew my daily stumbling but daily arising faith.'

In this same year (1932) he became president of the Arts and Crafts Exhibition Society. Margaret Alexander, then secretary, wrote to tell him that he had been elected and Greta answered: 'Your letter announced to the family the great news about the president of the A. and C.S. I gave Him your messages. He *was* so unwilling! Cincinnatus cannot have left his plough with **more** reluctance.'

Last Working Years, 1928-1935

He was indeed reluctant. It was Noel Rooke, once more, who had persuaded him to let his name be put forward, believing he could give the Society something that no one else could—something of its original inspiration. He had finally agreed, but stipulated that he should not be asked to judge manuscripts submitted for exhibition, because 'I'd want to throw out nearly everything, probably, which would be a pity and hard luck on the submitters (who are mostly my children or grandchildren).'

During his presidency he persuaded the Society to try out a scheme whereby exhibitors should supply labels for their work. The aim was 'to help people to see what they are looking at'. These labels were to give, in a few lines 'any interesting data concerning the technical construction or function of the exhibit' or the craftsman's aim in making it. 'Besides the value and interest of Technical and Functional enlightenment,' he wrote, 'is the inestimable value of enlightenment on Intention. I believe that such revelation is possible and also that any revelation of Intention and any light—however small—on the question of Why is of incalculable good.' He took infinite pains over his own labels, spending nearly eight hours over one 130 words in length. In these he specified the materials used, explained the aim of the work and the limitations imposed on it and stated how far he thought it had been successful and what he considered its faults.

He criticized his own work even more severely than that of his students and often specified the faults of a manuscript in the colophon, the scribe's note at the end of the work. On one occasion this criticism was taken almost too seriously by a member of a committee. The manuscript in question was one of Johnston's finest, but he had been dissatisfied with the quality of the materials—the best available—and their effect on the writing. When the committee was asked to pass the account for payment one hard-headed Yorkshireman demanded 'Are you going to pay chap what 'e asks? 'E says 'imself 'e 'asn done it as well as 'e might 'a done!'

When Johnston resigned from the presidency of the Arts and Crafts Exhibition Society his parting message was twofold:

Last Working Years, 1928-1935

'1st. The Society's proper business is Handicrafts—to make things and to make them well—whatever ultimate use is made of their work.

'2nd. That now the solid basis of *Use* has been so largely undermined and undercut by mechanical production the Society must consider giving practical effect to the inimitable and essential value of Handicrafts in pure education and occupation.'

He was never able to come to terms with the idea of craftsmen designing for industry. In vain was the argument put forward that industry was 'here to stay', that we must therefore aim at making it as good as possible and that one way of doing this was by getting real craftsmen—*makers* of things—to design them, rather than relying on the usual 'drawing-board designers'. He could not agree. He knew—and detested—the way that the craftsman's design would be blunted and coarsened in the process of mass production and because he would not compromise or lower his standards he kept aloof from the whole thing.

'The great modern world of money, motors and machines is opposed to us,' he wrote to his assistant at the College, Violet Hawkes. '(Example: My block-letter for the UD, originally intended to be printed from wood types, *may* be still (I don't know) but some of my block-letter designs have been printed by means of a rapidly moving rubber "blanket", which finally rounded off all the square corners.) That world wants quantity and cheapness for all ordinary practical things, that world gets what it wants and pays the penalty of inferior quality and lack of craftsmanship. It admires quality often, as a far off beatitude, and often thinks it possible to combine it with quantity –vainly. You understand, it is our true purpose that we get—our primary intention. That is, for craftsmen, a good work, for business men, finance. . . . The Labour people believe, with the Capitalists, that Mass production, Rationalisation, etc. are the only way. No parties strike for good work (not even the Masters).'

At about the same time his old friend Douglas Cockerell, who had bound so many of his manuscripts, wrote to him on behalf of the Royal Society of Arts asking him to reconsider a previous

[283]

refusal to allow himself to be nominated as a Registered Designer for Industry (an award recently introduced by the Society with the object of raising the standard of industrial design) because 'Your work has had an immense influence for good over a very wide field, even though you have done little with the direct intention of influencing large scale production.'

To this Johnston replied: 'I am really sorry that I feel unable to accept the honour again offered by the Royal Society of Arts. I should be very sorry if the Society thought that I doubted them or meant to take up a "superior" position. I believe in their integrity and their philanthropic activities and I regard the R.D.I. as an honour not to be disdained by anyone—let alone by me— and yet, by me, to be conscientiously (and somewhat reluctantly) refused, because "INDUSTRY" does not appear to be based on good principles or to be aimed at good purpose. In other words I doubt the integrity (and philanthropy) of *typical Industrialism* and regard it as opposed, even actively inimical, to the Arts and Crafts and those who practise them.

'That is no attack on persons or politics (in the sense of Con., Lib., Lab., Ind., Com., etc.—I like *all* the honest ones) but *on a system*, to which the good word "Industry" has become attached.

'With apologies and thanks for your most kind letter, and to all who would try to convert me. My view is rather personal and therefore difficult to express. It is not meant to imply wrong in anyone else. They could hold the honour and support it. I should hold it under a sort of false pretences.'

This letter shows his courtesy and humility in conflict with his principles and also his extreme reluctance to condemn people as individuals, whatever he might feel about a system. He agreed with Charles Lamb—whose words he used to quote with a characteristic little smile of amused affection—that one could not hate a man one *knew*.

His objection on principle to the 'designing' of things by people other than those who actually made them was linked with his antipathy to industry, but separate from it. His objection to designing, divorced from making, was that it was unreal. His objection to industry was primarily that it was concerned with money rather than with the things themselves—thus making of the things produced a means rather than an end. To an artist or craftsman it is, of course, a first essential that the thing made must be an end in itself. This is one of the reasons why art and propaganda can so rarely be successfully mated.

Johnston expressed his views on this subject, very briefly, in a letter to *The Times*, which he wrote in his capacity as President of the Arts and Crafts Exhibition Society. *The Times* had printed a letter from John Milne which stated that the forthcoming Exhibition of British Art and Industry was 'mainly concerned with the application of design to modern processes of machinery, which, however we may regret it, have superseded the craftsman.'

To this Johnston replied: 'Without the craftsman there can be no design in that sense of the word which connotes aesthetic value. In this connection the engineer may be regarded as a craftsman, and the aesthetic value of his work is likely to be in proportion to its fitness for purpose. Unless the design arises out of the actual construction of a thing it is reduced to the level of extraneous ornamentation. Design, in fact, is inherent rather than applied and the "application of design" to mechanical processes suggests an attempt to get the best of both worlds by trying to secure the appearance of craftsmanship without its substance.'

By the early nineteen-thirties Johnston had almost ceased to undertake commissions. One of his last important manuscripts was the 'perpetual calendar' which he devised and made for his wife's birthday in 1932. It consisted of a series of movable cards in a wooden frame and contained, he said, 'the first decent numerals made by me in thirty-five years'. In a label describing this calendar, in an exhibition, he asked that 'cabinet-makers should regard the frame as a *sketch* for a frame', notwithstanding the fact that it had, of course, been made with the same devoted craftsmanship that he brought to everything he did. Indeed this

Last Working Years, 1928-1935

piece of work, with its smoothly sliding panels and its neat little brass fastenings, is particularly evocative of him because it shows his calligraphy so happily combined with his other crafts and displays his characteristic inventiveness.

He is said to have taken this calendar to show to his students and, during the first twenty minutes of his lecture, untied its wrappings with leisurely precision. This process was interrupted by long pauses when his discourse claimed his whole attention and he remained obliviously fingering a knot while he gazed into the distance, supremely unaware that every pair of eyes in the room was riveted to the parcel as his audience waited, in mounting suspense, to discover what it contained.

The writing of a manuscript had always imposed a great nervous strain on Johnston, as well as making heavy demands on his small store of energy. After 1932, with failing sight and his health beginning to deteriorate again, he seems to have found this effort almost beyond him. He continued to keep in touch with his class for the next five years and even as late as 1938 he returned, after a long break, to give three lectures, but by this time he had almost completely given up writing formal manuscripts. Almost his last commission was an extract from Plato which he wrote for Alfred Fairbank in 1934. By this time the effort required to gear himself to the pitch of intensity which his work demanded must have been daunting indeed, yet the manuscript showed no lessening of his power. Indeed he conceded, half reluctantly, that it was, despite its faults, 'in some ways my best piece of work'. With his 'best numerals so far' in 1932, followed by this, he knew himself to be still capable of developing. 'I have not done my best work yet,' he said, 'and I probably never shall.'

It is an old story that by the time wisdom and skill have come to their full maturity the strength to give them utterance has failed. Jotted in his notebook are the words 'Not that thrill and abandon and careless rightness . . .' followed by 'my best work done at the day's end when too tired for more and (perhaps) the same of Life itself.'

[286]

XIV

The Hermit, 1936-1944

Greta's health had been failing for some years and in April 1936 she died.

During the last few days of her life she hardly seemed to recognize her daughters, or even, perhaps, to remember that she had children. Only Edward existed for her then. It was thirty-five years that April since the day he had shown her round the Central School. From that day on he had been the centre of her life and her mind seemed to turn inward to that centre as the surrounding world grew dark.

However much he may have suffered beforehand—when he had been unable to work and had gone about the house looking white and haggard—Edward received her death with a serene fortitude that filled the house with peace, like a benediction.

We had never, I think, fully realized the extent of his devotion to her. He was an undemonstrative man; indeed, in the days of their courtship, Greta's most potent threat had been '*I shall kiss you at the railway station!*' We never saw him kiss her except at meeting or parting. Once in a while she would stand behind his chair and kiss the top of his head and then he would incline his head sideways and rub it against her with a sheepish tenderness, as though he hoped that this might pass unnoticed. Despite this reticence nobody could have mistaken him for a cold man. His eyes and his smile could light up with warmth, and affection be expressed in his amused and gentle laugh, as when he watched the kittens playing.

The Hermit, 1936-1944

On Easter Day, a few days after Greta's funeral, Eric Gill wrote what was probably the last letter he ever addressed to Johnston:

'Most dear Master:

'When you returned from Scotland on or about September 17, 1903, I was so moved, excited, all of a tremble, that I stood in the middle of the street outside what was then the Central School (in Regent Street) so that I might see you through the lighted window of the room where the writing class was. I was so overwhelmingly in love with my girl, and with you. Your marriage was a type of all heavenly fruitions and consummations. I had to look at you from a distance, in secret, before I dared to approach. . . . In my diary, Sept. 17, I wrote only: ''Johnston has returned and is married'' and on Sept. 22 ''to see Mr and Mrs Johnston''. The only other entry, except receipts of money and payments, is Oct. 16 ''to Life class, for first time''. In fact 1903 records nothing but those life shaking events. I hope I shall be forgiven for this delving into memories of those birthdays. I only want you to know, as I think you have not known before, that, as I think, your marriage meant more to me than to anyone else in the whole world except to you and your wife. And so it is impossible for me to say even the perfectly good and truthful things which other friends and lovers might say. Though at a distance and separated by sundering floods and strange mists, your wedded life and mine have run parallel and now they both draw to their earthly close. On this Easter morning you may rejoice more than I, who have not yet suffered. Again I look as it were from the dark street in through a lighted window . . . bearing palms in their hands and crying Hosanna to the son of David. [*sic.*]

'With great love and devotion as always,

'ERIC G.'

It is a fit conclusion and farewell to a friendship so long and so fruitful.

After Gill's death, a few years later, Johnston wrote to his widow thanking her for a collection of his essays[1] and quoted a

[1]*Last Essays* by Eric Gill; Cape.

comment of Rothenstein's on his engraving, that '*he had never seen so swift a line*'. 'Swift is a good word for him,' Johnston added; 'he lived swiftly—deciding swiftly . . . youthfulness of spirit commonly goes together with youthfulness of years. Eric's was less dependant upon actual age, and his best work (such as the engraving on p. 2) has the spirit of Life itself.'

Lila Greig did not long survive her sister, Greta, of whom she had written 'She had an absolutely triumphant life.' It was to Lila, as she lay dying of cancer, that Edward wrote:

'This must be brief, and may be a bit shaky, because I have been in bed for a fortnight—with flu. But the Dr hopes to let me up tomorrow.

'I have long wanted to write to you and to offer comfort if I might.

'Then I thought I would like to send you a prayer—which came to me one day (I like to think from Heaven)—and has been a great comfort to me.

'Of course it was to have been in formal penmanship on vellum or good paper, but comes now to be scribbled on a post-card.

> *O Lord Father of All*
> *bless and love All:*
> *And help All to love Thee:*
> *And help All to love All:*
> *O LORD*
> *Father of All*
> *bless and love All.*   —*for Jesus sake*—

'I say this again and again and think how some day these Reds and Anti-Reds, these Chins. and Japanese, will all love one another—and I shall be no more cross—and still, and ever, He loves and blesses All.'

Alas, he had waited too long; the card was never posted. It is dated September 20, the day on which she died.

To the surviving sister, Anne, thus doubly bereaved, Edward confessed that, with Greta's death, 'half the world' had been lost to him. In a sense this may have come nearer to being literally true than he realized. She had been his liaison officer, the go-between who preserved his contact with 'the world'. Even between him and his own children she had always occupied this position. It was she, also, who kept him in touch with local affairs. He had his own surprising contacts, his long, long talks with the barber, the doctor and the driver of the dilapidated local bus, but of the village and its people he knew almost nothing except what he learnt from her. She, with her intense interest in people, played a leading part in the life of the village, where she was greatly loved. She knew all the genealogies of the local families and who used to work for whom and had married whose cousin. Often she would come back from marketing and burst into a reckless account of the latest news, astonishing us again and again by her inability to learn to be more guarded. 'Who?' Edward would ask, removing his spectacles to fix his eye upon her, 'Who said this? "She?" Who do you mean by "she"?' and then, 'I don't think I *realize* Mrs Smith.' It would take him a long time and much cross-questioning to get the whole story sorted out and he would frequently complain that 'This is such a *garbled* version'. All news had to be accurate and exact, with every statement vouched for, or he would refuse to accept it. He, himself, was almost over-conscientious about not passing on any information which might be inaccurate, misleading or con-fidential. Scandal he barred completely and, when any reached him, made it a rule to reply 'I don't believe it'.

Just as all information brought to him was rigorously scrutin-ized so was all written matter. He would spend hours poring over income tax forms, reading all the notes in small type, dis-covering difficulties unimagined by the ordinary taxpayer and pondering the possible identity of a 'person or persons other than the persons specified'. Particularly was this so with anything he was asked to sign. During the war a petition was brought to the house, a protest against the intention of the local cricket club to buy a motor mower. It stated that, in this hour of their country's peril, the signatories viewed such a project with 'indignation and disgust'. He perused it carefully from beginning to end, giving his full consideration to every sentence, then he handed it back to Bridget remarking thoughtfully, 'I don't think I've felt indignation and disgust since I was about six. It is the sort of thing that babies feel.'

It was Bridget who kept house for him during the eight years by which he survived his wife. This was not an altogether easy task, for he was liable to apply his rigorous standards of perfection to other things besides calligraphy. Once when, thinking to please him, she had made cheese straws, he analysed their failings so minutely that in the end even he was struck by the thought that a cook might find such a reception of her products discouraging. 'You know,' he assured her, 'that if the angel Gabriel had brought me cheese straws, I shouldn't say they were good if they weren't.' She knew it well, as every student in the calligraphy class had known it for years. She not only knew but even sympathized with it, and showed an understanding of the principles involved which, at times, could demand considerable powers of detachment.

As a rule he was oblivious to domestic difficulties and this made it curiously touching and surprising when he showed concern for such things. On one occasion when the maid was away and Bridget was in bed with influenza I had to go and take over the management of the house. I was young and inexperienced in such matters and overwhelmed by all there was to do. My diary gives the following account of my first day there: 'About lunch time I was struggling desperately to light the diningroom fire when Daddy came wandering down in a dressing gown and I realized I had completely forgotten his early tea. I said I was sorry and he answered that it was all right. He said "It makes me realize that 'Life is real, life is earnest,' and 'He who will not work, neither shall he eat,' and other wise sayings of the Prince Consort." He brought me candle-ends to light the fire with and was very sweet. The whole day I was running to and fro without a moment's pause and in the evening, when I was ready to drop, he kept me standing by the door while we discussed the relationship of the density of matter to the distribution of stars in the universe and reduced sixteen million inches to feet, yards and finally miles! He was being so nice that the humour of it struck me more forcibly than the maddeningness.'

His health deteriorated considerably from about the time of his wife's death but he remained nominally attached to the staff of the Royal College of Art and never lost hope of being able to visit his students again until near the end of his life.

James Wardrop, of the Victoria and Albert Museum Library, often used to lunch with him on Mondays, in company with other members of the staffs of the Museum and College. He has described the last time he saw him, on the final day of a summer term, when, after lunch, they stood together for some moments looking out at the quadrangle where the fountain was playing in the sunshine. Then, as he turned to go, Johnston said 'You won't be seeing me for a long time: I'm going away to write my new book, to atone for the sins of 1906.' Wardrop, who had been from boyhood a devoted admirer of *Writing and Illuminating and Lettering*, and said that it had largely influenced his choice of a career, recognized the allusion and answered 'Come, Johnston, I have heard that book described as epoch-making!' 'That just shows you what foolish things people say,' Johnston answered with a smile, 'or, alternatively, how easily epochs are made.'

He was wrestling with his book during all these years (no gentler word could describe this painful procedure). It was, perhaps, inevitable that it should have progressed with almost unimaginable slowness, inevitable, too, that it should have been left unfinished when he died, for he was attempting to achieve perfection, and for that one lifetime is hardly enough. So he went over and over his first chapters and they branched and burgeoned and grew under his hand, each time afresh, as live writing does. They developed immense interpolations and parentheses and finally—as in some biological process—split up into whole clusters of chapters, but still he got no further with the book.

[292]

The Hermit, 1936-1944

In a postcard written to me on St Valentine's Day, 1937, and dated with a rough sketch of two hearts speared by an arrow, he said: 'Bridget had a second relapse but seems getting better. This has been very unsettling and, on the top of my own debilities and shortcomings, led to my doing little (and lunching about 5). Still—like the parrot (It's rather a nice story. Do you know it?) —I think a good deal and keep on making notes. (This is written with my noting pen.) Do planning in sure hope to turn over a new and more effective leaf. On the 6th January, while indexing 2nd section of the Notebook, I lit on *the most hopeful plan* yet for opening chapter I (the problem which has wrestled with me for over three years). And I look forward to trying to carry *this* out fairly soon.'

The postcard is written closely all over, including margins and part of the address side and at the end he says 'This card is clearly destined for the V. and A. Mus. They want some of my MS. yet. (Early 20th centy. example of Aberdeen postcard.)'

In November 1940 he wrote a letter to his daughter Barbara which gives a kind of history of the working out of his book and some idea of the struggle that it was costing him. It begins with an apology for having failed to acknowledge some money she had sent him five weeks before and goes on: 'I am given, I fear, to explaining (chiefly to myself) that this or that can be extenuated, or, at least, explained, by *special circumstances*. And yet I think they were rather special circumstances. . . . Perhaps you know, perhaps not, how long I have puzzled over the question *at what point* in my Book and *how much* (*and how expressed*) should I reveal vital factors in Formal Penmanship. It is a kind of Paradox of Teaching or Learning—To know how to make Things you must make them—("practising" teaches you how to practise—or, rather, how to do practising) but the student cannot make things (we say) until he has learnt how to make them. The solution (of How, then, does he learn?) is found in the theorem (or argument by the Schoolmen, I think) Achilles cannot cross a Room, for before he crosses R he must cross $\frac{R}{2}$ and before he crosses the remaining $\dfrac{R}{2}$ he must cross $\dfrac{R}{2}{2}$ and so on, leaving a fraction always to be crossed. The answer may be found in the fact that Achilles does actually cross it, or, in the Act *itself*, which goes by strides or *jumps* (not stopping to recognise the perpetual decimal left).

'Then the teacher must give vital information in that form, namely partly apprehensible and remainderly jumpable. Now, since 1933 I have stuck over this question and see-sawed over it. In 1934 I decided there must be an "early reference to the three Writing Conditions" and stopped drafting further to write an interpolation. This was to be just a note, but I spent two months that summer over it and produced 17 pp. of typewriting and figs. Naturally I had a reaction (feeling that the s.[1] wd. die of indigestion) and postponed it. And so, year after year since then (and you know what some of the years have been) I have doubted and felt held up. (In '37 and '38 I wrote a 14 p. section for insertion later in the chapter, taking several months). But, having put that section away in my pocket—like your letter and several other letters—I tried to get the *beginning* made, without any reference to it. In the summer of this year I tried short notes and again abandoned them but *somehow got in a good and fairly short par.* . . . Then about the end of this Aug. or beginning of October, again I felt it *must* be done, and it began to work out happily (attached to the good, short par.). When your letter came . . . I was at a kind of constructive crisis and felt it must be gone through with, even breaking my life's rule about acknowledging money. Since then there has been a slow but pretty sure advance (indicated to some extent by the fact that this very morning I decided that the original *chapter I* of about 10 years ago, which split up into three distinct chapters about 7 or 8 years ago, should split into 6 reasonable length chapters and together form *Part One*. Old chaps. II and III will probably follow and become PARTS.'

The letter ends with a diagram of 'typical stroke shapes produced by simple movements of the formal pen' as shown in
[1]the student.

[294]

his book. These strokes are more or less vertical and close together with the white background making clear-cut shapes between them. Under the figure he has scribbled 'This is symbolic of a sort of vision which I had the other day—I think I see the light between the trees at last.'

Another reference to the book in a letter helps to explain why the rate of progress was slow: 'You will understand why this is short when I say that I have this moment composed the following sentence. "He cuts the NIB of the pen to a special shape."—and let us hope it is permanently composed because planning to use that remark appears to have taken twelve weeks.'

Life is hardly long enough for such a rate of progress and in the end he died leaving the book unfinished. It was subsequently edited by Heather Child and published by Lund Humphries in 1971 as *Formal Penmanship*, also by Pentalic Corporation in New York.

Recalling his early years Johnston spoke of the serene writing of his first book—the 'almost irrecoverable serenity of inexperience'—contrasted with the 'not-without-comfort-and-joy travail of my present Book'. The first book had been 'a congenial Task', he said, but the second was 'not a Task but a Quest . . . an absorbing Quest'. The object of the first was 'to hand over a little simple knowledge', of the second 'to tell, if it be possible, some beliefs and hopes'.

In 1939 Johnston was made a Commander of the Order of the British Empire in the New Year's Honours List. The fact that Greta was not there to share it must have robbed this distinction of much of its significance for him, but he welcomed it as the first award of the kind made to a craftsman and hoped that this might mean that craftsmen would in future be regarded as in a class with artists, actors and professional men, as suitable recipients of such recognition. He was also much touched by the comments of local people, 'my neighbours, many of whom I scarcely know' who took it as an honour reflected upon the village because he was '*our* Mr Johnston'.

The Hermit, 1936-1944

When the news was announced he was suddenly surrounded by reporters and cameramen, a strange burst of activity in his secluded life. The thing that pleased him most of all, however, was a column by his old friend *The Londoner* in the *Evening News*. The author, Oswald Barron, was a much-loved friend of Hammersmith days whose writings had always delighted Johnston. Of this one, entitled *The Writing Master*, he wrote to Mrs Barron 'I was so pleased with it that I took it up to bed with me, like a small boy with a Christmas present.'

It was of Barron's death, a year later, that Johnston wrote: 'To me it is as if one of the great landmarks—by which we measure our lives and through which we are made to feel at home in the World—had been taken away. . . . He was one of the *very* few who really understood what in my work I was trying to do. (Many have "admired" it, but he understood my quest and my attempts.) Once in the good old Hammersmith days he said to me "You are my favourite artist" and added something to the effect that my Lettering was straightforward and that there was no nonsense about it—I, of course, and quite truly, said "You are my favourite Critic" . . . We have lost him but his Life is not lost. Such a living personality cannot fade into nothingness, but, to my thinking, will continue on a higher plane with wider opportunities for his special gifts. . . . As Spenser said—"that faire lampe—Shall never be extinguisht nor decay; —For it is heavenly borne and cannot die, Being a parcel of the purest skie." '

In another letter he wrote: 'I still have comfort in sharing Browning's belief that *the best is yet to be*. Sceptically regarded, no doubt, as a fool's paradise, that thought must (even by them) be admitted as the comfort of many comparatively sane persons.'

Such thoughts must often have been in his mind at this time. Once he recorded in his notebook that his work had gone surprisingly easily that day, 'as though my dear Greta were allowed to help me.' At the time of her death there occurs a little interpolation in the notebook: 'This was the last note before Greta left us.' Otherwise she is hardly mentioned in these close-packed pages. At midnight on the first Christmas Day without her, when the gap in the family must have been most keenly felt, he noted only that 'the favourite formula that $2+2=4$' was not a completely satisfying statement because 'all substantial things are unique in substance, place, time or matter . . . therefore we cannot have two similar things in the identical but only in the identical class.' Nearly fifty years before, when his little sister Ada died, he had discovered how great an anodyne mathematical speculations could be.

Shortly after being awarded the CBE he fell very ill with pneumonia and was unable to attend the investiture—'Only just time to counter-order my knee breeches' as he put it. I went down to Ditchling on that occasion hardly knowing what to expect, for the news was not reassuring. I found him propped up in bed with many pillows, a great iron cylinder of oxygen beside him and a fine rubber tube leading from it, attached to his face with adhesive tape and passing into one nostril. All this seemed fearful to me, as the paraphernalia of illness does to the un-initiated. I approached him, masking my apprehension with the forced cheerfulness assumed by those summoned to death-beds. He looked tired and thin and his eyelids drooped so that I was uncertain whether he woke or slept, but when he spoke, though the words came with difficulty and with long pauses between, his voice was exactly as usual. He said: 'The latch of that wretched door has gone wrong again. Unscrew it and bring it to me.'

I looked from him to the door feeling helpless, afraid to ask for fuller instructions because of his difficulty in speaking and because now his eyes were closed again. However, when I had fetched a screwdriver and examined the door I found it quite simple to remove the lock. I did so and took it to him. He raised his lids a little to glance at it. 'Put it there,' he said. 'No, not like that. The other way. . . . Quite right.' He groped on the bed, looking down sideways without moving his head. 'Where are the pliers?' he said sternly. 'They *should* be here.' The nurse hurried forward, exclaiming anxiously 'Nothing's been moved, Mr Johnston. Nothing's been *touched*.'

The Hermit, 1936-1944

The pliers were found and the work proceeded. According to instructions I removed the spring from the lock, tempered it and brought it back to him. He showed me how to hammer it, then passed it back to me, told me to go on like that and closed his eyes. Again I could not tell if he woke or slept. I asked the nurse if she thought I ought to stop hammering. She answered, in her Irish voice, 'Oh no, Miss Johnston, I think Mr Johnston finds it rather soothing.' So, while he lay there kept alive by oxygen, I sat by his side and made the room ring like a smithy.

The nurse endured the conditions surprisingly well. The whole room was full of things arranged in special ways, things that must on no account be moved, and the bed itself was covered with tools and books and a system of branching strings by which he pulled things towards him. On one occasion when I went to Ditchling when he was ill my diary says that 'I went up to see him and found him looking thin with bedclothes pulled over him and tracts of mattress exposed. He was sitting up in bed by the light of two candle-ends stuck in a tin lid, surrounded by old jam jars, books, newspapers, matchboxes, cups, crusts and dust.' This description might give the impression that he was neglected, but in fact, of course, no one was allowed to touch the jam jars —or the dust. Even the bedclothes may well have been arranged according to a system of his own and sternly guarded from interference.

Wherever he was things accumulated round him, to settle gradually under a deepening layer of dust. In the end this simple process achieved such proportions as to drive him out of his workroom altogether. His chronic bronchial condition made him afraid to attempt any clearance himself and he would not allow anyone else to do so. The result was a permanent deadlock. He retreated from his workroom and, as he fell back, the forces of chaos pressed forward after him. His bedroom, which had remained quite orderly as long as Greta shared it, was overwhelmed after her death. Next the diningroom, which took on more and more the function of his study, threatened to become similarly engulfed. It began to seem as though he might gradually take over the whole house, leaving room after room immobilized behind him while, like the Hatter and the March Hare, he moved on to a clean place.

To the end he continued to enjoy playing about with lettering, so long as it was not serious and there was no rush. I say 'playing about' because that is how he would have described it himself—indeed, he often said that he had 'never been serious like other men' but had always played at things. In fact, of course, his 'play', like the intent, concentrated play of children, was a good deal more serious than the average man's work. Thus when he amused himself by writing his friends' initials at the head of letters to them there was no question of just dashing them off; he often did whole sheets of experiments first.

In one such letter, to Sir Sydney Cockerell, beginning 'Dear S.C.C.,' he used for his second page a sheet covered with such trials, ostensibly to save paper—it was wartime—but probably more for the interest it might afford his one-time mentor and critic. He asked that various 'faults' in this letter might be overlooked, '. . . together with the worse fault of trimming the second C's back (because it looked so groggy). "Think rather of the pack-horse on the down" and of the unembarrassed SSS curvetting easily because they know they are only "trials" (and not meant for examples to be admired) of which I seem to have written about 47, all, nearly, having some of that light-hearted freedom which is so much more difficult (to me) to give to that intended to be taken seriously, though Freedom is an essential quality of all good work. Thank heaven I have known the joy of it sometimes, when the heart is warm and the Pen, Surface and Ink and Hand are all doing their best, and then, indeed, nothing can go wrong.'

He wrote these initials about two and a half inches high, using a bamboo cut a quarter of an inch wide, with a large external spring and ordinary writing ink. The rest of the letter was then written semi-formally with an ordinary pen. It was typical of him, however, that his 'ordinary' pen was 'a very fine Relief gold Nib, broken from a fountain pen and soldered by me to the

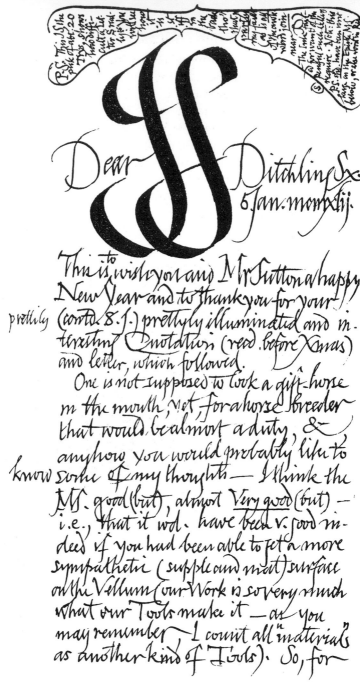

Letter to Irene Wellington (then Mrs Sutton) 1942. Reduced

shank of an ordinary metal nib, fitted with a fixed spring (to increase and even the ink supply) and with a comfortably thickened holder and a cap for the pocket.' This was his favourite pen of any he ever had. His letter to Sir Sydney was delayed for months, he explained, because he had lost it and hoped that if he waited long enough it might be found.

In one of these 'calligraphic letters', as they have been called[1] he explained his reasons for writing them, saying that it pleased him 'to find an excuse for indulging in my old Craft but in a carefree and playful spirit and to find that the old clown can still walk the Tight Rope and go through the Hoops with some *aplomb*, not to say some *éclat*—his own, essential, murmured applause (which is, I trust, part a prayer to One Who "Saw that It was Good") and some scattered but, may I add, *discerning* clapping. And, indeed, if you reflect that "the old clown" referred to is over seventy-two, propped up in Bed, tho' able to get up and sit in a chair for a spell, and writing on a Board against his knees, he may, I think, reasonably say "Not so *Rusty*, Thank God!" '

These large initial letters became quite a feature of this period, so much so that they might almost be described as the final phase of Johnston's work. 'I get a good deal of instructive pleasure from them,' he wrote, 'besides sometimes, apparently, giving a good deal to my friends.' He had always held that obstacles could be made to be helpful if rightly understood and now his increasing blindness yielded him a compensating blessing. He was obliged to write very large or not at all, with the result that he discovered special virtues in large writing and a consequent enthusiasm for it. 'I may say,' he wrote to an old student, 'that I got most profit and understanding and real craftsman's THRILL in formal penmanship after I had begun to write Large and I would recommend writing large more and more to all students (including young children learning).' He was always pointing out that size is an absolute difference and not, as is so often supposed, merely a relative one. Thus 'large writing' was not small writing

[1]See opposite page.

written large, the size was part of its essential nature with a quality of its own.

In these latter years of his life Johnston's financial situation was becoming increasingly difficult. He had never bothered much about money. A small private income and occasional help from his uncle had made it possible to live, and his wants were few. The house was the one extravagance but nothing was spent on it beyond what was essential. Furnishings grew faded and carpets wore into holes; few things were repaired and none replaced. This was partly a matter of temperament but it had its economic basis, too. Now, however, with the advent of war, rising costs overwhelmed his small income, illness brought heavy expenses and he was no longer able to work. In 1943 Bridget wrote to Noel Rooke about the possibility of a Civil List pension, but his subsequent enquiries showed that this would not be available except in a case of near destitution. Rooke, however, did not let the matter rest there. Through him it became known that Edward Johnston was in need of money and, from that moment, the money poured in. Johnston himself was quite astonished by the value set upon him. Not only from societies and other bodies in England but from America, too, there came such sums as to 'justify my thinking that I was in the same class as field lilies and sparrows'. All his life, he had almost given his work away and claimed no copyright in ideas and discoveries and now, when most he needed it, he was freely repaid. It was a rare example of poetic justice.

'Subscribing to me became a fashion,' he wrote to Sir Sydney Cockerell and described how one society to which he belonged had even sent him a circular appealing to him to subscribe to himself. 'I played with the thought that it would be rather a lark to send them a *very large* sum as from a member who wished to remain anonymous,' he commented, with characteristic humour.

By 1944 Johnston was bedridden and had long since ceased to undertake commissions. He had actually been persuaded to write one small manuscript—an inscription in a blotter—as late as 1940, but he had probably made an exceptional effort because it was for the retirement of Frank Pick. Apart from that he had done nothing professionally for about ten years, during which time his health and sight had changed greatly for the worse. Now, however, in the last year of his life, there came a commission of such importance that it could not be disregarded. Winston Churchill, then Prime Minister and the hero of the hour, wanted him to write out some lines from Shakespeare. It was a quotation from Macbeth beginning *Your son, my lord, has paid a soldier's debt*, which he wished to give to Harry Hopkins, President Roosevelt's personal representative, who had lost a son in the war.

Johnston was most anxious to do the work but uncertain whether it would be possible. After much consideration it was finally arranged with Downing Street that he should get one of the best calligraphers to come to Ditchling with a view to doing the work under his supervision if he should not be able to do it himself. He chose Irene Wellington who, as Irene Bass, had been one of his best students at the Royal College. She had at this time been teaching and practising calligraphy for fifteen years or more but she was back at school when she entered Cleves.

She arrived in great elation, thinking this the most wonderful call that could be made upon her. She cannot have supposed that it would be easy, but enthusiasm no doubt masked the more fearful aspects of her situation. There was no time to spare. Johnston had put off his decision as long as possible—and still he had not decided. When Irene arrived, full of eager expectation, he hardly mentioned the work. Knowing time to be short she at once prepared two pieces of vellum, one for herself and one for him, on the chance that he might yet decide to write the manuscript himself. Still he said nothing, decided nothing, gave no instructions, and the precious time slipped by. Irene decided she had better assume that she was to do the work and did a draft for his consideration. She brought this down, very nervously, to the diningroom, which had been converted to a bedroom since he had become an invalid. He put on his spectacles and scrutinized it in silence, saying 'H'm', no doubt, in a way he had, that suggested there was really nothing else that could be said. After due deliberation he remarked that if he were Harry Hopkins he would rather have the typescript of the words that had been sent from Downing Street. No doubt he made plenty of other comments as well, but that was the gist of it; the typescript was neat and unpretentious—he would rather have that.

Next day she wrote the manuscript in earnest and, in the evening, took it to show to him. Once more he scrutinized it in silence and once more gave his opinion. Some time later, when Irene left him, she was wondering why she had ever imagined that she could write and how it had come about that deluded people had actually been paying her to do so, all these years.

Later that evening, as she approached the open door of his room, she heard his resonant tones from within: 'How good that child is being, Bridget,' he said, 'not an attempt to—' but here, horrified to find herself eavesdropping, Irene fled. Even so she slept a little better than she might otherwise have done. It was a sorely needed crumb of comfort.

The next day was the deadline. The manuscript had to be delivered in London that evening, and it was now clear that Johnston would not do the work himself. He had, at last, been explicit about how he wished it to be done. Sharpness of execution and the subtleties of spacing had been 'endlessly and exhaustively considered', but his chief command was that the manuscript should be completely simple—simpler, said Irene, 'than I would have dared to make it.' The words were simple to the point of austerity; they needed no embellishment. They must be left to speak for themselves with their own dignity and forcefulness. The words must be served.

On that last day Irene went early to her room and shut herself in. She took the precious piece of vellum which she had prepared with such infinite pains in the expectation that Johnston himself might use it. As the pen touched the surface she learned the difference between vellum that was merely 'good enough' and that which was as near perfect as scraping could make it. It was a revelation. From that moment she knew that nothing could go wrong. She wrote the words entirely simply as he had told her to do and at once this was revealed as the only and inevitable way for them to be written.

When it was done, she took the manuscript down and showed it to Johnston. This time it had to be right, for it had to be delivered that same day. He took it in silence, put on his spectacles and scrutinized it as before. When he spoke it was in his usual measured tones. 'Well done, Irene,' he said simply. 'That's beautiful.'

This may well have been the only occasion when he ever expressed complete satisfaction with any modern manuscript, his own or anyone else's. Irene found herself unable to answer.

Before she left, that evening, to take the precious document to London, she asked him what she should do with the manuscript she had written first. It had crossed her mind that she would like to present it to Churchill, to keep himself, if he should care to do so. 'You can't do that,' Johnston told her flatly. 'If it's not good enough, it's not good enough for him.' She still looked fondly at it—after all, she had taken great pains with it and it was good according to any ordinary standards. On impulse she said 'I suppose you wouldn't care to keep it yourself?'

'Heaven forbid,' he answered but he looked at the manuscript again and added, with more animation, 'But, look here, I'll tell you what! This skin could really do with more scraping, you know—why not scrape off the writing and use it again?'

It was not until she was safe in the train, on her way back to London, that Irene burst into tears. The strain she could endure, but not the relief. Amazed, she told herself again and again: 'He said "That's beautiful"!'

Characteristically, Johnston had enjoined her to absolute silence in regard to this work. 'I was *bursting* to tell almost anyone,' she confessed, but this was not allowed. It was a purely personal matter between Churchill and Harry Hopkins, Johnston said. He was not going to have it appearing in the papers.

The Hermit, 1936-1944

It was while Irene was staying at Cleves, one day, that she came into the room as Johnston's pencil fell to the floor and heard him exclaim 'Damn!' This was unusually strong language for him. I have more than once heard him say, in reference to something particularly provoking, 'I almost felt inclined to say sort of *dash it!*' However, on this occasion he said 'Damn!', then, seeing Irene, apologised and afterwards explained, in his deliberate way, 'When I say that I always apologise, first to God, secondly to anyone else who happens to be present and thirdly to the Thing itself, for I am aware of the beneficence of the law of gravity and that if a pencil would not roll off a sloping surface it would not stay on a flat one.'

These few words reveal a surprising number of important things about him. To take the least important first, there is his attitude to the *Thing*—the pencil. He had, even more than most craftsmen, a respect for *things* and a feeling that they had a right to their existences and a right to be treated according to their natures and capacities and not blamed for failing through being wrongly used. He hated the modern system of scrapping attendant upon mass production and always wanted to rescue and mend what was thrown away. (I was charmed to find that in *Writing and Illuminating and Lettering* he recommends that ink which is unfit for use should be 'put away'. That is undoubtedly what he would have done with it himself.) He had whole cupboards full of broken saucers, knives without handles, stopped clocks and leaking hot-water bottles. Now and again he would spend two or three days in repairing one of these objects, making it far more interesting and valuable than it had been when new.

Secondly, there is what one might describe as his cosmic vision of life. It was not only when his pencil fell to the floor that he was aware of the law of gravity. He lived with it as he lived with cups of cold tea and the cats and the dictionary, except that whereas these were sometimes absent it never was. Always, I think, beneath the other thoughts, he was aware of his situation as a creature mysteriously engaged in a transient life on a planet in a universe of stars with, beyond it all, the possibility of who could

tell what unguessed at, unimaginable things, or what future for
the individual soul.

This links up with the third point: 'the beneficence of the law
of gravity', the sense of an ordered, intentional and friendly
system and of being part of a pattern designed by a beneficent
creator and resting always in His hands.

'Belief in God and in the ultimate power of Truth informed
all his thoughts and gave them their perspective,' wrote his
daughter, Bridget. 'The idea of Truth dominated him in everything he thought and did.' He held that the three main paths by
which men seek truth are religion, art and science and, in her
words, 'he combined in himself to a quite unusual degree the
attitude of mind of all three.'

He wrote in his notebook that he had been 'Thinking and
saying to Bridget that I felt *we ought to face fundamental Things*.
That (e.g.) my work was better than my students' work—in
spite of my faults (slowness and laziness in particular)—because
of that, chiefly.

'And that is one of the reasons for my wishing to write this
Book (to face fundamental things) and to help others to face
them.'

The jottings in his notebook abundantly illustrate the way in
which he did this, both in regard to his own work and to the
deeper issues of life, all of which he felt to be implicit in it, as
in any other activity. *Laborare est orare* might well have been his
motto—though indeed, the motto of his family, *Assiduitate (By
Perseverance)* was singularly appropriate to his particular gifts.

'I am well aware,' he wrote, 'that I am trying to fit the Truth
into a scheme of my own that I myself may better comprehend
it and that I may better share it with others. Like all private
schemes it is a personal picture of Aspects of the Truth.'

This scheme of Truth, his philosophy, was like a book upon
which he was continuously at work, revising, clarifying, en-
larging and correlating. The notes in his notebook are the
random ideas and discoveries that were always being built into
this construction. It would have been impossible to conceive of

his ever being bored or finding his hermit-like existence dull because this quest underlay all the commonplace happenings of his days. He never ceased from trying to discover the truth about Truth itself, the cosmos and man's position in it.

'Thinking of weight of the earth,' he wrote, 'weight in *tons*, but what are tons in the universe? A ton of earth would weigh more on the sun and less on the moon (so such weight is relative to the attracting body (and relative to the medium, e.g., air at varying pressures) and presumably space-time as well). All things must relate to something, even the Absolute (probably) *Relates* to Everything. (All-ness to All, completeness to All.)'

The fundamental nature of his attitude to his work is illustrated, in particular, by the following notes:

'Three questions every honest and practical man must ask of things, What, How and Why. What is this thing? How is it done? Why should it be done?

'Why should one, why ought one, why must one?

'Why is it good, proper, beautiful, civilized, progressive?

'To man an answer is necessary and he has found one in the idea of God. Things are His will.'

Again he wrote: 'If we think that the Material Creation has purpose or can be fulfilled with purpose, then all material objects —including our bodies—are 'Tools' . . . the flesh is a *sine qua non* for the spirit of man—an opportunity rather than an obstacle.' And again: 'The Earth is our opportunity, a goldmine, a storehouse.'

'The Truth,' he wrote, 'both immanent and transcendental, is also prevailing.'

Of Truth he said, also, 'Its other names are goodness and beauty, the Way and the Life, the Light (of the world), the Word, and many more.

'It is that against which we sin.'

Sydney Cockerell, who, in 1898, first set him on his way, has summed up something of his quality and character thus: 'Johnston has had numberless pupils and followers, but not one of them has attained to his degree of accomplishment. Nor do I think that it is possible to rival him by technical skill without an accompanying range of imagination equivalent to his. Such a quality is exceedingly rare. Artists, poets, dramatists or composers of the highest rank do not occur many times in a century, and Johnston at his best was an artist of the highest rank.

'He was a man apart, a genius, not to be weighed in the same balance with an ordinary mortal. Moreover, he suffered from continual ill health by which he was greatly hampered. I have already referred to his fineness of spirit. Even more than his pre-eminence as a craftsman, it was his clear vision in other directions, his gentle bearing, his unconscious saintliness, his unworldly outlook, his whimsicality, and his whole philosophy of living that endeared him to his pupils and friends and roused their ardent unwavering devotion. By none of them will he ever be forgotten.'

It was to Sydney Cockerell that Johnston addressed what must have been one of the last letters he ever wrote, in August 1944:

'It seems best (at last) just to throw myself on that mercy which you have shown more than once to your *un*-corrigible Friend and Protégé. No earthly counsel would undertake my defence in the most lenient court. My ultimate and only Hope is that—when time is no more—an Ethereal One may find me fumbling for the Heavenly Inquiry Room. . . .

'If, someday, I am helped into heaven (as suggested above) perhaps I shall answer some of your letters and make some hyperphysical response to some of your kind words and deeds. E.g. to that book and that letter from Windsor which were received by me in speechless silence fourhundredandthirtyseven Days ago.'

In conclusion there are some remarks about a copy of the nineteenth impression of *Writing and Illuminating and Lettering* which he was sending to Cockerell with notes of alterations: he had always done this, keeping him up to date with all the small changes and additions that he had made in the course of nearly forty years. (It was to Cockerell that he had confided—though not till after her death—that the initial letters of each paragraph in the preface together spelled out a hidden dedication to his wife.)

[309]

The Hermit, 1936-1944

The letter ends with a single line: 'And now I must try to mark corrections in the book. . . .' There it breaks off.

Perhaps his health took a turn for the worse at that point (the letter had been continued from day to day for a week) or perhaps the prospect of annotating the book seemed too great an effort. And so, somehow, the letter was never sent. Ten years later, when I was going through his papers with a view to writing this book, I came upon it in a drawer. He had found the heavenly inquiry room where 'time is no more' not long after the letter was written, but many years before it reached his friend. 'I am thankful to have been alive to receive it,' Sir Sydney said.

Edward Johnston died on November 26, 1944, and was buried with his wife in Ditchling churchyard, next to the graves of 'Aunty' and Olof and not far from that of David (and, later, Douglas) Pepler. A headstone was carved by Joseph Cribb, Eric Gill's first apprentice, who came with him from Hammersmith to Ditchling in 1907. The serene beauty of the lettering testifies to its origins, not only to the imperishable glory of Rome, but also to that humble class of seven students at the old Central School where Eric Gill learnt his A B C in the opening years of this century.

I will leave it to Johnston himself to say the last words about his life, words spoken not long before the end of his long struggle against illness and blindness and that increasing 'tiredness' that had dogged him all his seventy-two years.

'I still praise God for giving me life. I wouldn't have anything different. I have done good and I have done evil. Some experiences have been excruciating but I wouldn't have had them different. If I were wrecked, on a raft, in the middle of the Atlantic, I would still praise God.

'All I still need is to be redeemed, whatever that may mean.'

Index

Alexander, Margaret, 281
Artificers' Guild, 155
Arts and Crafts Exhibition, 68, 70, 96, 177, 281
Arts and Crafts Exhibition Society, 86, 281–3, 285
Arts and Crafts Movement, 73, 86–7, 113, 154, 159
Artworkers' Guild, 165
Ashendene Press, 144

Barbour, John, 253
Barclays, the, 29, 50, 94
Barrie, J. M., 62
Barron, Oswald, 296
Barron, Mrs Oswald, 296
Beatty, Admiral Earl, 223
Birmingham School of Art, 111, 130
Bishop, Dorothy, 263
Blunt, Judith, 89
Bridges, Robert, 87, 95, 163
Bridges, Mrs Robert, 95
Brown, Professor Frederick, 91
Burne-Jones, Sir Edward, 66, 68, 90
Buxton, Hannah (née Gurney), 24, 26, 29, 33
Buxton, Priscilla, see Johnston
Buxton, Sidney, 36
Buxton, Sir Thomas Fowell, 22–9, 33, 56
Buxtons, the, 50, 81

Cadenhead, James, 67–9, 76, 79, 101
Calligraphers' Society, 170–1, 174

Camberwell School of Art, 101, 111, 121
Cameron, Sir D. Y., 245, 248
Carter, George, 130
Central School of Arts and Crafts, 73, 77, 86, 96–8, 101, 106, 110–11, 113–4, 188, 278–9, 281, 287–8, 310
Chaucer, Geoffrey, 253
Chesterton, G. K., 239, 260
Child, Heather, 295
Chiswick Press, 154
Christie, Laurence, 101, 240
Churchill, Sir Winston, 303, 305
Cicero, 252
Clausen, George, 74, 134
Cobden-Sanderson, T. J., 101–3, 105, 154–5, 159, 165, 259
Cockerell, Douglas, 252, 283
Cockerell, Sir Sydney, 75, 86–7, 89, 90, 96, 101, 148–9, 183, 250, 299, 301–2, 308–10
Confessio Amantis, 252–3
Coomaraswamy, Ananda, 233
Cowlishaw, Harry, 63, 68–70, 72–3, 84–5, 92, 95–6, 280
Cowlishaws, the, 94
Craig, Edward, 235
Craig, Gordon, 190, 235, 273
Cranach Press, 169, 188–9, 277
Cranach Press, *Duineser Elegien*, 276–7
Cranach Press, *Hamlet*, 190, 235, 273
Cribb, Joseph, 310

[311]

Index

Douglas, Adam, 32–3
Douglas, Margaret ('Aunty'), 33, 37–9, 42, 44–6, 48, 51, 55, 56, 60, 71–2, 75, 80, 84–5, 89, 91, 101, 105, 119–21, 123, 144, 148, 156, 158–9, 167, 177–8, 208, 243, 310
Douglas, Mary, see Johnston
Doves Bindery, The, 101, 105
Doves Press, The, 102–3, 105, 132, 154–5, 158, 164, 168, 189, 192, 196
Doves Press, Bible, 105
Doves Press, *Browning*, 164, 168
Doves Press, *Paradise Lost*, 105, 132
Doves Press, *Book Beautiful, The*, 102
Dresden, 185–6
Durham Book, the, 95

Edinburgh University, 55, 61–2, 64, 67–8, 71, 272
Elliott, W. H., 117

Fairbank, Alfred, 176, 286
Farleigh, John, 203
Farrow, 129, 131
Fishmongers' Company, 223
Forest Lodge, Woodford, 56–9
Fox, Caroline, 26
Fox, Nob, 36
Foxes, the, 36n
French, Field-Marshal Earl, 223
Friend, G. T., 273, 275–6, 278–9
Fry, Elizabeth, 24, 26, 28, 170

Gabb, G. B., 106
Gabb, Mrs G. B. (née Wilson), 106
Game, The (Magazine), 197–8, 216, 227–8
Germany, 108, 169, 171, 185–7, 203, 231, 273, 277
Gill, Eric, 73, 100, 101, 105, 127–30, 134, 136, 140, 143–7, 155, 159,

169–70, 182–3, 185, 189, 196–204, 216–7, 220, 225, 230, 232, 276–8, 288–9, 310
Gill, Ethel (Mary), 155, 166, 183, 288
Gill, MacDonald, 128, 136, 198, 263
Gills, the, 158–9, 182, 187, 196, 198, 217, 228, 230, 234
Gill sans (type), 203–4
Gimson, Ernest, 159
Gower, John, 252
Grave Fairytale, 195
Green, Romney, 155, 219–20
Greens, the, 219–20
Greig, Anne, 119, 144, 147, 289
Greig, Greta, see Johnston
Greig, James, 118–9, 132, 144, 242
Greig, Mrs James, 118–9, 144, 147, 161, 198
Greig, Jim, 119, 144, 184
Greig, Lila, 184, 194, 289
Greigs, the, 118, 143
Guild of SS. Joseph and Dominic, 228
Gurney, Hannah, see Buxton
Gurney, John, 23
Gurney, Louisa, 24
Gurney, Priscilla, 24
Gurney, Rachel, 23
Gurneys, the, 23, 24, 29, 50

Haig, Field-Marshal Earl, 223
Hampshire House, 154, 179
Hanburys, the, 23, 24
Hawkes, Violet, 263–4, 283
Hewitt, Graily, 101, 111, 121, 126, 129–32, 135, 140, 143, 145, 172
Hewitt, Mrs Graily, 159
Hoares, the, 94
Hofmannsthal, Hugo von, 190n
Hogarth Press, 276–7
Hogg, John, 137, 146–7, 172
Holden, Sir Charles, 199
Hopkins, Harry, 303–5

Index

Hornby, St John, 144
Housemakers' Society, 170–1

Imprint, The (Magazine), 192–3, 199
Imprint (type), 193
Insel Verlag, 169
International Congress on Art Education, 185

Jackson, Ernest, 192
Jellicoe, Admiral Earl, 223
Johnston, Ada, 36, 41, 46–7, 51, 60, 297
Johnston, Alice (née Douglas: mother of E. J.), 32–3, 35–7, 41–5, 47, 51–3, 55, 60, 120
Johnston, Andrew, M.P., 22–3, 27–31
Johnston, Andrew ('Uncle Johnston'), 29 31, 35, 49–51, 55–9, 61, 63–4, 69, 86, 94, 108, 122, 218–9, 221, 229
Johnston, Andrew ('Tod'), 57, 65, 93–4
Johnston, Andrew Gunnar, 130, 177, 245
Johnston, Barbara (d. of E.J.), 157–9, 162, 164, 166, 168, 177, 179, 193, 207, 209, 221, 237, 239, 293
Johnston, Beatrice, 55, 93–4, 179
Johnston, Bridget (d. of E.J.), 144, 146–8, 154–6, 158–9, 162, 164, 166, 168, 177, 179, 193, 207, 209, 237, 239, 291, 293, 302, 304, 307
Johnston, Charlotte ('Aunt Johnston'), 49, 57–8, 61, 69, 86, 123
Johnston, Edward,
  Teaching, 89, 98–102, 106–10, 150, 210–12, 236, 251, 262–7, 271, 279–80, 286
  Works mentioned:
  Authorship: Carol and Other Rhymes, A, 195; Formal Penmanship, 295;

Manuscript and Inscription Letters, 108, 172, 181; Writing and illuminating and Lettering, 79, 96n, 132, 135–7, 142–3, 145–50, 155, 162, 169–70, 173, 229, 292, 306, 309; Unfinished work on calligraphy (Formal Penmanship), 148, 262, 292-5, 307
Book jacket: Grave Fairytale, 195
Manuscripts: Address to Miss Judith Blunt, 89; Address to John Monteath, 245–6; And does the road wind uphill all the way? 64; A passage perillus makyth a port pleasant, 64; Barbour, 253; Blue Tit, 247; Calligraphic letters, 299–301; Canterbury Tales, 253; Cicero, 252; Collect, 259; Communion Service for Hastings, 106, 111, 126, 132, 150; Confessio Amantis, 252–3; Coronation address to H.M. King Edward VII, 132; Fishmongers' Company Freedom Scrolls, 223; Gloria, 197; Inscription in blotter for Frank Pick, 303; Keighley Roll of Honour, 251–2; Lord's Prayer, The, 88; Magnificat, 49; Night cometh, The, 255; Nut Browne Maide, The, 91, 96; Over the sea our galleys went, 75; Pater Noster, 96; Perpetual Calendar, 285–6; Plato, 286; Prometheus (Shelley), 256–8; Puk-Wudjies, The, 209; Sayings of Artists on Art, 246–8, 255, 259; Stolen Child, The, 88; Sunken Bell, The, 88; Ula and the Rabbit, 209; Valentine, 80
Rubrication: Doves Press, Bible, 105; Doves Press, Browning, 164, 168; Doves Press, Paradise

[313]

Index

Index